The
Greenwood Library
of
American Folktales

The Greenwood Library of American Folktales

VOLUME IV

The Northwest, Cyberspace

Edited by Thomas A. Green

GREENWOOD PRESS
Westport, Connecticut • London

Library of Congress Cataloging-in-Publication Data

The Greenwood Library of American folktales / edited by Thomas A. Green.
    p. cm.
    Includes bibliographical references and index.
    ISBN 0-313-33772-1 (set : alk. paper)—ISBN 0-313-33773-X (vol. 1 : alk. paper)—ISBN 0-313-
33774-8 (vol. 2 : alk. paper)—ISBN 0-313-33775-6 (vol. 3 : alk. paper)—ISBN 0-313-33776-4 (vol.
4 : alk. paper) 1. Tales—United States—History and criticism. 2. Legends—United States—
History and criticism. 3. United States—Folklore. I. Green, Thomas A., 1944–
    GR105.G75 2006
    398.20973—dc22   2006022952

British Library Cataloguing in Publication Data is available.

Library of Congress Catalog Card Number: 2006022952
ISBN: 0-313-33772-1 (set)
        0-313-33773-X (vol. I)
        0-313-33774-8 (vol. II)
        0-313-33775-6 (vol. III)
        0-313-33776-4 (vol. IV)

First published in 2006

Greenwood Press, 88 Post Road West, Westport, CT 06881
An imprint of Greenwood Publishing Group, Inc.
www.greenwood.com

Printed in the United States of America

The paper used in this book complies with the
Permanent Paper Standard issued by the National
Information Standards Organization (Z39.48–1984).

10 9 8 7 6 5 4 3 2 1

Contents

VOLUME IV

Contents

Contents

THE NORTHWEST

Introduction

The Northwest Region, as interpreted by *The Greenwood Encyclopedia of American Folktales*, encompasses the states of Idaho, Oregon, Washington, Alaska, and the Aleutian Islands. The area from roughly northern California up the coast to southern Alaska has commonly been called the Pacific Northwest. This is an area of coasts, mountain ranges, and thick forests, which include rain forests. The eastern fringe areas of the Northwest Region include portions of the Basin and Plateau terrains discussed in Volume III of this series. The focus of this volume will be on the Northwest Coast and the cultures that developed in response to that environment, ecologically and historically.

The Native American cultures of the Northwest Coast attained an extremely high level of cultural complexity due to the abundance and dependability of food resources, and because of the presence of thick jungle-like forests. The people of this region all lived on or very near the coast. The many deep fjords, streams leading to the coast, and offshore islands provided an almost endless coastline where they could build their villages and avail themselves of the ample maritime resources.

Because salmon was such a reliable source of food, Northwest Coast cultures such as the Tlingit were able to develop stable settlements and devote less time to the business of staying alive (see "The Doom of the Katt-a-quins," p. 133, for a vignette of the Tlingit lifestyle.) As a result of this stability, they were afforded the leisure to develop complex social, religious, and technological systems that contrast sharply with their neighbors, the Basin culture of the interior or the Inuit and Yupik (Eskimo) cultures. Moreover, the forests provided a ready supply of timber for the construction of housing, containers, handles and shafts of weapons, and the distinctive Northwestern "totem pole." There was little stone in the area for making tools, so many of their tools were made of hardwood. Thus, it was the skill and knowledge of the people rather than the quality of their tools that enabled them to develop excellence in their art and architecture.

Villages generally were located on the shore, along a large river, or on a lagoon or bay. Just above the high water mark stood the first row of houses. The houses were two to three rows deep depending upon the width of the beach area. The wooden houses of the Northwest Coast tribes were built to last, and a mark of a man's wealth was his house. Among these groups, great effort went into the building of a house and the bigger and more decorated it was, the greater the status it brought its owner. There were all sizes of houses with the smaller ones being about fifteen by twenty feet while a really impressive one might be as large as one hundred feet long by forty feet wide. The average was twenty by forty feet. These plank houses were carefully notched together and assembled without the use of pegs or nails.

Salmon were the mainstay of the cultures in the region. In addition, shell-fish were eaten, and in some of the Northwest Coast groups whaling was carried on. Hunting and gathering—while not nearly as important as fishing—helped to supplement their diet. Deer, bears, and sea mammals were hunted, snared, or in the case of seals, harpooned. There was also a strong feeling that a hunter should purify himself before killing game. Sweat baths, fasts, sexual abstinence, and abstention from water were all used as preparation for hunting and as preparation for war.

As with many other Native American groups, it was believed that an animal or fish allowed itself to be taken. Its spirit, released by death, returned again and again—provided that the proper care was taken and that its spirit was not offended by humans. Both "Legend of Sattik" (p. 140) and "Coyote Creates Taboos" (p. 127) emphasize the same point. The belief carries all the way up the Pacific Coast to Alaska. There was a general belief on the Northwest Coast that salmon lived in houses under the sea. When they were at home, they assumed a human form, ate, and carried on ceremonies just like humans. Assuming fish form, they allowed themselves to be caught. If their bones were returned to the sea, they re-assumed their human form, but would come again. From this belief came religious practices to guarantee the return of their bones to the sea in order to assure the return of the salmon. All other game was treated with respect as well, in both public and private ritual.

The Northwest Coast societies were highly stratified: positions from chief-dom to commoner status were inherited. At the bottom of the social hierarchy were slaves. The principle of status and the accumulation of wealth as a symbol of power is a cultural feature that serves as a unifying feature throughout the Northwest Coast groups. A major means of using wealth symbolically is seen in the trait of giving wealth away extravagantly and publicly, in order to attain status, in a ceremony called a potlatch.

Northwest Coast religions also had a well-developed concept of guardian spirits. Protection by a guardian spirit was necessary to attain success in life. Contact by the guardian might come on its own, but more often the spirit helper was consciously sought. The spirit gave the person to whom it appeared a special talent or the ability to succeed in a certain area of his life. This could be the promise of wealth, success in war, power at gambling, or the curing power of a shaman, for example.

Further north on the coast and into the interior of Alaska and on the Aleutian Islands are the group that Europeans designated as the Eskimo or Aleut. While some Native Alaskans and Aleutians retain the designations, the twentieth century brought about the assertion by the people of their indigenous designations of Inuit—Yupik in the case of the former and Alutiiq for the latter. In the following narratives, the older designations of Eskimo or Aleut are retained following the leads of the original collectors of these narratives because the more familiar designations, though imprecise, tend to be more "reader friendly," and also because the original sources frequently do not provide sufficient information to distinguish the cultural affiliation precisely.

Although the Arctic and sub-Arctic environment shared by the Native Alaskans provides a common environmental baseline, different lifestyles derived from differing specific habitats. The groups living along rivers, for example, tend to be more sedentary, reside in larger groups, and organize into larger kinship units the hunting and gathering bands residing in the Arctic interior. Therefore, it is erroneous to think of the environment as barren. As the Inuit and Yupik north-south range is great, there is variation in topography, landform, climate, vegetation, and fish and game availability. Northern Alaska is tundra stretching from Brooks Range to the Arctic Ocean. The area is swampy and boggy in summer and snow covered in winter. Along the rivers and streams, people hunt great herds of the caribou that inhabit this coastal plain. Hunting in these environments, like coastal whaling, creates community solidarity. These features differ from the maritime dwellers of the coast and riverine fishers.

Neither of the systems mentioned above allowed for tribal consciousness. Groups were organized as bands, a socioeconomic unit with frequently changing membership. An individual was free to move about and associate with any other band. Social organization, particularly in the case of the hunters and gatherers, was built primarily around nuclear families—the mother, father, and children.

This social organization resulted from the harsh environmental factors. The nuclear structure was more supportive to hunting and gathering. The exception to the general rule is found in Southwestern and Southern Alaska. Here we find an extended family organization that arises out of the need for cooperative labor.

Europeans established their presence in the Northwest Region with maritime trades like whaling. The western migration of farm families, which details "How the Lee Family Came to Oregon" (p. 45), began as early as the first half of the nineteenth century. The lure of vast natural resources from the forests attracted everyone from the logging trade to the miners hoping for quick riches (see "The Blue Bucket Mine," p. 47). By the end of the nineteenth century, a cultural mix of European, Asian, and Native cultures existed in the Northwest.

SUGGESTED READINGS

Balilci, Asen. *The Netsilik Eskimo*. Garden City, NY: Natural History Press, 1970.

Chance, Norman A. *The Eskimo of North Alaska*. New York: Holt, Rinehart and Winston, 1966.

Kamenskii, Annatolii. *Tlingit Indians of Alaska*. Translated and with an introduction and supplementary material by Sergei Kan. Fairbanks: University of Alaska Press, 1985.

Oswalt, Wendell H. *Bashful No Longer: An Alaskan Eskimo Ethnohistory 1778–1988*. Norman, OK: University of Oklahoma Press, 1990.

Suttles, Wayne. *Handbook of the North American Indians*. Vol. 7, *Northwest Coast*. Washington, DC: Smithsonian Institution, 1990.

ORIGINS

THE GIVER CREATES THE WORLD

Tradition Bearer: Charlie DePoe

Source: Farrand, Livingston, and Leo J. Frachtenberg. "Shasta and Athapascan Myths from Oregon." *Journal of American Folklore* 28 (1915): 224–28.

Date: 1900

Original Source: Joshua
National Origin: Native American

Historically, the Joshua lived in the Rogue River in southwestern Oregon. They were Athapascan speakers, but relatively little was preserved about their culture. The Giver (the creator figure in this **myth**) is depicted as a benign figure. He is far from omnipotent, failing twice in his attempt to create human beings, for example. The second half of the **myth** is devoted to the development of the human social order. This is a particularly well-crafted narrative for this area of the Western Region. Compare this story to the following "Arrow Young Men: Creation of the World" (p. 11), for example.

In the beginning there was no land. There was nothing but the sky, some fog, and water. The water was still; there were no breakers. A sweat-house stood on the water, and in it there lived two men: The Giver and his companion. The companion had tobacco. He usually stood outside watching, while the Giver remained in the sweat-house.

One day it seemed to the watcher as if daylight were coming. He went inside and told the Giver that he saw something strange coming. Soon there appeared something that looked like land, and on it two trees were growing. The man kept on looking, and was soon able to distinguish that the object that was approaching was white land. Then the ocean began to move, bringing the land nearer. Its eastern portion was dark. The western part kept on moving until it struck the sweathouse, where it stopped. It began to stretch to the north and to the south. The land was white like snow. There was no grass on it. It expanded like the waves of the ocean. Then the fog began to disappear, and the watcher could look far away.

He went into the sweat-house, and asked, "Giver, are you ready?" and he said, "Is the land solid?"

"Not quite," replied the man. Then the Giver took some tobacco and began to smoke. He blew the smoke on the land, and the land became motionless. Only two trees were growing at that time: redwood to the south, and ash to the north. Five times the Giver smoked, while discussing with his companion various means of creating the world and the people. Then night came, and after that daylight appeared again. Four days the Giver worked; and trees began to bud, and fell like drops of water upon the ground. Grass came up, and leaves appeared on the trees. The Giver walked around the piece of land that had stopped near his sweathouse, commanding the ocean to withdraw and to be calm.

Then the Giver made five cakes of mud. Of the first cake he made a stone, and dropped it into the water, telling it to make a noise and to expand, as soon as it struck the bottom. After a long while he heard a faint noise, and knew then that the water was very deep.

He waited some time before dropping the second cake. This time he heard the noise sooner, and knew that the land was coming nearer to the surface. After he had dropped the third cake, the land reached almost to the surface of the water. So he went into the sweathouse and opened a new sack of tobacco.

Soon his companion shouted from the outside, "It looks as if breakers were coming!" The Giver was glad, because he knew now that the land was coming up from the bottom of the ocean. After the sixth wave the water receded, and he scattered tobacco all over sand appeared. More breakers came in, receding farther and farther westward. Thus the land and the world were created. To the west, to the north, and to the south there was tidewater; to the east the land was dry. The new land was soft, and looked like sand. The Giver stepped on it, and said, "I am going to see if the great land has come;" and as he stepped, the land grew hard.

Then he looked at the sand, and saw a man's tracks. They seemed to have come from the north, disappearing in the water on the south. He wondered what that could mean, and was very much worried. He went back to his first piece of land, and told the water to overflow the land he had created out of the five cakes of mud. Some time afterwards he ordered the water to recede, and looked again. This time he saw the tracks coming from the west, and returning to the water on the north side. He was puzzled, and ordered the water to cover up his new land once more. Five times he repeated this process. At last he became discouraged, and said, "This is going to make trouble in the future!" And since then there has always been trouble in the world.

Then he began to wonder how he could make people. First he took some grass, mixed it with mud, and rubbed it in his hands. Then he ordered a house to appear, gave the two mud figures to his companion, and told him to put them into the house. After four days two dogs—a male and a bitch—appeared. They watched the dogs, and twelve days later the bitch gave birth to pups. He then made food for the dogs. All kinds of dogs were born in that litter of pups. They were all howling'.

After a while he went to work again. He took some white sand from the new land, and made two figures in the same way as before. He gave the figures to his companion, and ordered a house for them. Then he warned the dogs not to go to the new house, as it was intended for the new people. After thirteen days the Giver heard a great hissing; and a big snake came out of the house, followed by a female snake and by many small snakes.

He felt bad when he saw this, and went to his companion, telling him that this trouble was due to the tracks that had first appeared in the world. Soon the land became full of snakes, which, not having seen the Giver, wondered how every-thing had come about. The world was inhabited by dogs and snakes only.

One day the Giver wished three baskets to appear, gave them to his companion, and told him to fill them partly with fresh water and partly with salt water. Then he put ten of the biggest snakes into the baskets, crushed them, and threw them into the ocean. Two bad snakes got away from him; and all snake-like animals that live today come from these snakes.

He said to these two snakes, "You two will live and surround the world like a belt, so that it won't break!" Then he crushed five bad dogs in the same way, made a great ditch with his finger, and threw the dogs into the ditch. These dogs became water-monsters. All animals that raise their heads above the water and smell, and then disappear quickly under the water, came from these five dogs.

Pretty soon the Giver began to think again, "How can I make people? I have failed twice!"

Now, for the first time his companion spoke. He said, "Let me smoke to-night, and see if people will not come out (of the smoke)."

For three days he smoked, at the end of which a house appeared with smoke coming out of it. The man told the Giver, "There is a house!" After a while a beautiful woman came out of the house, carrying a water-basket.

Then the Giver was glad, and said, "Now we shall have no more trouble in creating people." The woman did not see him and his companion, as they were watching her. After nine days the woman became sad and wondered who her father and relatives were. She had plenty of food.

One day the Giver said to his companion, "Stay here and take this woman for your wife! You shall have children and be the father of all the people. I am leaving this world. Everything on it shall belong to you."

And the man answered, "It is well; but, perchance, I too may have troubles."

Then the Giver asked him, "How are you going to be troubled?"

So the man said, "Do you make this woman sleep, so that I can go to her without her seeing me." The woman found life in the house very easy. Whenever she wished for anything, it appeared at once. About noon she felt sleepy for the first time. When night came, she prepared her bed and lay down.

As soon as she was sound asleep, the man went in to her. She was not aware of this, but dreamed that a handsome man was with her. This was an entirely new dream to her. At daybreak she woke up and looked into the blanket. No one was there, although she was sure that someone had been with her. She wished to know who had been with her that night. So next evening she prepared her bed again, hoping that the same would happen; but no one came to her. She did the same every night without any one coming near her.

Soon the woman became pregnant. The Giver and his companion were still on the land, watching her; but she could not see them, because they were invisible to her. After a while the child was born. It was a boy.

He grew very fast. The young woman made a cradle for him. After six months the boy could talk. The woman still wanted to know who the father of her child was. So one day she wrapped the child in blankets, and said, "I will neglect the boy and let him cry, and, perchance, his father may come. I will go and look at the country." She started south, carrying the baby on her back. She traveled for ten years, seeing no one and never looking at the child.

After a long time she could hear only a faint sound coming from behind. Nothing remained of the boy but skin and bones. Finally she stopped at SaLōmä, and here for the first time she took the child from her back and looked at it. Its eyes were sunken and hollow; the boy was a mere skeleton. The woman felt bad and began to cry. She took the boy out of the cradle and went to the river to bathe. After she had put on her clothes, she felt of the child's heart. It was still beating! The boy urinated, and was dirty all over. His body was covered with maggots, and he had acquired various diseases.

The woman took him to the water and washed his body. She had no milk with which to feed him: so she sang a medicine-song, and milk came to her. She gave the breast to the child, but it was too weak to suck: hence she had to feed it gradually. As the days went by, the boy grew stronger. After three days his eyes were better. Then they went back to their house, where they found plenty of food. The boy grew soon into a strong and handsome man, and was helping his mother with her work.

One day he asked her, "Mother, where is your husband?" and she replied, "I only dreamed of my husband."

Then she told him all that had happened before he was born; and the boy said, "Oh! Perchance my father may turn up some day."

Then the Giver said to his companion, "The woman is home now." That night the woman longed for her husband. She had been dreaming all the time that he was a handsome man, and that her boy looked just like him. At dusk it seemed to her as if someone were coming. Her heart began to beat. Soon she heard footsteps.

The door opened, and her boy exclaimed, "Oh, my father has come!" She looked and saw the man of her dreams. At first she was ashamed and bashful. The man told her all that had happened before, and claimed her as his wife.

One day the Giver told the man that all the world had been made for him. Then he instructed him how to act at all times and under all conditions. He also admonished him to have more children, and the man had sixteen children. The first one was a boy, then came a girl, then another boy, and so on. Half of his children went to live north of the Rogue River, while the other half settled down south of the river.

The Giver told the man that hereafter he would obtain everything by wishing. Then he straightened out the world, made it flat, and placed the waters. He also created all sorts of animals, and cautioned the man not to cut down more trees or kill more animals than he needed.

And after all this had been done, he bade him farewell and went up to the sky, saying, "You and your wife and your children shall speak different languages. You shall be the progenitors of all the different tribes."

ARROW YOUNG MEN: CREATION OF THE WORLD

Tradition Bearer: Jim Buchanan

Source: Frachtenberg, Leo J. Pages 5–14 in *Coos Texts*. Columbia University Contributions to Anthropology 1. New York: Columbia University Press, 1913.

Date: 1909

Original Source: Coos

National Origin: Native American

The Coos of Oregon shared traits of both the Northwest Coast and Northern California cultures. The people lived in permanent winter villages in houses constructed from cedar planks. Each village operated as an independent unit under the guidance of a headman. During the migration of salmon and eels, the group relocated to seasonal camps upriver. The environment furnished a varied diet of fish, elk, deer, roots, plant greens, nuts, and berries. Everything in the Coos world was believed to have a spirit essence. These spirits could guide and protect the individual; therefore, at puberty, both young men and women made a vision quest to gain a guardian spirit. The following **myth** bears many similarities to the more fully developed "The Giver Creates the World" (p. 7).

Two young men were traveling. They stopped in the middle of their journey, and one of them said, "How would it be if we two should try it? What do you think about it?"

"It would be good if we two should try it," answered the other one.

"We ought to try it with that soot here." They had five pieces (disks) of soot. Now they stopped and dropped one piece into the ocean. The world at that time was without land. Everything was covered with water. Again they dropped one piece (disk). The ocean was rolling over the disk. The next day they dropped another disk. Then they stopped at some small place and dropped another disk into the ocean. They looked at it from above.

Now land began to appear, and they saw it. They were very glad when they saw the land coming up.

The next day they dropped another disk. Land began to stick out (come up). They looked frequently at the waves, which rolled back and forth continually.

"What is your opinion?" said one of the two men. Shall we try it again?"

"With what shall we try it?" asked the other one. The water was still rolling back and forth. "Let us split this mat." They did so, and placed the two pieces over the five disks of soot. Now they went down to examine it. Still the land was not solid enough.

So one of them said, "Let us split this basket in two!" They split it, and put it on the sand beach. The waves were held back now, since the water was able to go down through the basket.

Now the young men went down and examined the land. "This will do," said one of them. "It's good that way."

Now they began to look around the world that they had created. There were no trees.

"Suppose we set up some trees," said one of them.

"It would be very good," answered the other one. Then they stuck into the ground the feathers of an eagle. The feathers began to grow, and developed soon into fir-trees. "All kinds of trees shall grow," said the older man. All the different kinds of trees commenced to grow.

"Suppose we create animals," said one of the young men. "It won't be good if there shouldn't be any animals. The future generations ought to have animals." (Then they created animals.)

Early in the morning they went to look at the world they had created. Suddenly they saw tracks on the ocean beach. "Whose tracks may these be?" asked one of them. They followed the tracks, and soon came upon a person sitting on the top of a snag. "You, indeed, must have made these tracks. Who are you?"

"I am a medicine-man," answered the person whose face was painted all over with red paint.

"You have no right to travel here. This is our world, we have made it. Are you surely a medicine-man?" They seized the stranger and killed him. Then they spilled his blood in all directions, and said to him, "You will be nothing, the last generation shall see you."

Then they turned back. Suddenly one of them became pregnant. The child could not come out. "What will become of us? We ought to have wives." None of them had done anything; nevertheless he became pregnant. The child was all the time trying to come out, but could not do it.

So they sent someone to the north, and told him, "There is a man living there. He is a good man. Bring him here." Someone went to get him. They went out in a canoe. To their surprise, there were no waves.

So they wished that waves would come. "Five times shall the north wind come and bring five breakers." And so it was. They were waiting for the fifth wave. And when this came, they went ashore. (They found the man, and brought him to the pregnant person.) As soon as he saw the pregnant man, he took out the child. It was a girl. From this girl all the people took their origin. She caused the people to multiply, and to inhabit the world.

Now the young men continued their journey. They once more examined the world that they had created, and found it to be good. Everything began to assume its present appearance.

They both had bows. "How would it be if we should shoot towards the sky?" Indeed, they began to shoot. They looked at their arrows as they were shooting them. "You too ought to shoot one arrow," said one of the young men. "Shoot it so that it shall hit the shaft of mine, and it will look as if it were one arrow; but don't shoot too hard!"

He shot and hit it. "Shoot again!" Their arrows became joined, and reached down to the place where they were standing.

"Suppose we climb up now!"

"All right!" They shook the, arrows. "Are they firm? Won't they come apart? Now you try to climb up!" He climbed up.

"This is very good indeed." Then the other man climbed up. They looked down, and saw the beautiful appearance of the world that they had created.

Nobody knows what became of the two young men. Here the story ends.

FABLE OF THE ANIMALS

Tradition Bearer: Unavailable

Source: Powers, Stephen. "North American Indian Legends and Fables." *Folk-Lore Record* 5 (1882): 93–95.

Date: ca. 1882

Original Source: Karok

National Origin: Native American

The Karok historically lived in villages along the banks of the Klamath and Salmon Rivers in Oregon. Their villages consisted of dwellings built from cedar planks and other structures such as the sweat lodge used for health and ceremonies. Like the other indigenous cultures of the area, they fished, hunted, and gathered wild plant foods. The following **myth** of creation explains why Coyote got cunning rather than strength and why in other Karok narratives Coyote serves as **culture hero** for humanity (see, for example, "The Theft of Fire," p. 18).

A great many hundred snows ago, Kareya, sitting on the Sacred Stool, created the world. First he made the fishes in the big water, then the animals on the green land, and last of all, The Man. But the animals were all alike yet in power, and it was not yet ordained which should be for food to others, and which should be food for The Man. Then Kareya bade them all assemble together in a certain place, that The Man might give each his power and his rank. So the animals all met together, a great many hundred snows ago, on an evening when the sun was set, that they might wait overnight for the coming of The Man on the morrow.

Now Kareya commanded The Man to make bows and arrows, as many as there were animals, and to give the longest to the one that should have the most power, and the shortest to the one that should have the least. So he did, and after nine sleeps his work was ended, and the bows and arrows that he made were very many.

Now the animals being gathered together in one place, went to sleep, that they might rise on the morrow and go forth to meet The Man. But the coyote was exceedingly cunning, above all the beasts that were, he was so cunning. So he considered within himself how he might get the longest bow, and so have the greatest power, and have all animals for his meat.

He determined to stay awake all night, while the others slept, and so go forth first in the morning and get the longest bow. This he devised within his cunning mind, and then he laughed to himself and stretched out his snout on his forepaws, and pretended to sleep like the others. But about midnight he began to get sleepy, and he had to walk around camp and scratch his eyes a considerable time to keep them open. But still he grew more sleepy, and he had to skip and jump about like a good one to keep awake. He made so much noise this way that he woke up some of the other animals, and he had to think of another plan.

About the time the morning star came up he was so sleepy that he couldn't keep his eyes open any longer. Then he took two little sticks, and sharpened them at the ends, and propped open his eyelids, whereupon he thought he was safe, and he concluded he would just take a little nap with his eyes open, watching the morning star. But in a few minutes he was sound asleep, and the sharp sticks pierced through his eyelids, and pinned them fast together.

So the morning star mounted up very swiftly, and then there came a peep of daybreak, and the birds began to sing, and the animals began to wake and rise, and stretch themselves, but still the coyote lay fast asleep. At last it was broad daylight, and. then the sun rose, and all the animals went forth to meet The Man.

He gave the longest bow to the cougar, so he had the greatest power of all; and the second longest to the bear; and so on, giving the next to the last to the poor frog. But he still had the shortest one left, and he cried out, "What animal have I missed?"

Then the animals began to look about, and they soon spied the coyote lying fast asleep, with the sharp sticks pinning his eyelids together. Upon that all the animals set up a great laugh, and they jumped on the coyote and danced upon him. Then they led him to The Man—for he could see nothing because of the sticks—and The Man pulled out the sticks, and gave him the shortest bow of all, which would hardly shoot an arrow more than a foot. And all the animals laughed very much.

But The Man took pity on the coyote, because he was now the weakest of all animals, even than the frog, and he prayed to Kareya for him, and Kareya gave him cunning, ten times more than before, so that he was cunning above all the animals of the wood. So the coyote was a friend to The Man and to his children after him, and helped him, and did many things for him, as we shall see hereafter.

In the legendary lore of the Karok, the coyote plays the same conspicuous part that Reynard does in ours, and the sagacious tricks that are accredited him are endless. When one Karok has killed another, he frequently barks like the coyote, in the belief that he will thereby be endued with so much of that animal's cunning that he will be able to elude the punishment due to his crime.

ORIGIN OF FIRE

Tradition Bearer: Unavailable

Source: Powers, Stephen. "North American Indian Legends and Fables." *Folk-Lore Record* 5 (1882): 95–96.

Date: ca. 1882

Original Source: Karok

National Origin: Native American

The following **myth** of their acquisition of fire casts Coyote in the **culture hero** role, and secondarily explains features such as the ground squirrel's distinctive markings and the frog's lack of a tail.

These markings serve as reminders of the bond between humanity and the natural world.

The Karok now had plenty of food, but there was no fire to cook it with. Far away toward the rising sun, somewhere in a land that no Karok had ever seen, Kareya bad made fire and hidden it in a casket, which be gave to two old hags to keep, lest some Karok should steal it. So now the coyote befriended the Karok again, and promised to bring them some fire.

He went out and got together a great company of animals, one of every kind, from the lion down to the frog. These he stationed in a line all along the road from the home of the Karok to the far-distant land where the fire was, the weakest animal nearest home and the strongest near the fire.

Then he took an Indian with him and hid him ender a hill, and went to the cabin of the hags who kept the casket, and rapped on the door.

One of them came out, and he said "Good evening," and they replied "Good evening."

Then he said, "It's a pretty cold night; can you let me sit by your fire?"

And they said "Yes, come in."

So he went in and stretched himself out before the fire, and reached his snout out towards the blaze, and sniffed the heat and felt very snug and comfortable. Finally he stretched his nose out along his fore-paws, and pretended to go to sleep, though he kept the corner of one eye open watching the old hags. But they never slept, day or night, and he spent the whole night watching and thinking to no purpose.

So next morning he went out and told the Indian, whom he had hidden under the hill, that he must make an attack on the hags' cabin, as if he were about to steal some fire, while he (the coyote) was in it.

He then went back and asked the hags to let him in again, which they did, as they did not think a coyote would steal any fire. He stood close by the casket of fire, and when the Indian made a rush on the cabin, and the hags dashed out after him at one door, the coyote seized a brand in his teeth and ran out at the other door. He almost flew over the ground; but the hags saw the sparks flying and gave chase, and gained on him fast. But by the time he was out of breath he reached the lion, who took the brand and ran with it to the next animal, and so on, each animal barely having time to give it to the next before the hags came up.

The next to the last in the line was the ground squirrel. He took the brand and ran so fast with it that his tail got a-fire, and he curled it up over his back, and so burned the black spot we see to this day just behind his fore-shoulders.

Last of all was the frog, but he, poor brute, couldn't run at all, so he opened his mouth wide and the squirrel chucked the fire into it, and he swallowed it down with a gulp. Then he turned and gave a great jump, but the hags were so close in pursuit that one of them seized him by the tail (he was a tad-pole then) and tweaked it off, and that is the reason why frogs have no tails to this day. He swam under water a long distance, as long as he could hold his breath, then came up and spit out the fire into a log of driftwood, and there it has stayed safe ever since, so that when an Indian rubs two pieces of wood together the fire comes forth.

THE THEFT OF FIRE

Tradition Bearer: Klamath Billie

Source: Farrand, Livingston, and Leo J. Frachtenberg. "Shasta and Athapascan Myths from Oregon." *Journal of American Folklore* 28 (1915): 209–10.

Date: 1900

Original Source: Shasta

National Origin: Native American

The primary food sources for the Shasta living along the rivers in southern Oregon were salmon, trout, and shellfish, while those at higher elevations relied more on hunting and trapping wild game for their food. Like other hunters and gatherers in the area, they depended on a variety of plant foods, especially acorns. They constructed permanent winter villages of wood and packed dirt, and, as with other cultures in the area, a sweat lodge was built and used regularly. This particular fire-stealing **myth** is common in the Northwest. It is worth noting that while Coyote does act as **culture hero** in the following narrative, his motive is given as dissatisfaction rather than altruism.

W e shall have to change this rock so that we can have regular fire," said Coyote one day. He was tired of having to pile rocks in order to obtain heat. He was not satisfied. "There is a shaman," he continued, "who has regular fire, and I shall try to obtain some from him." The other people tried to dissuade him from this dangerous undertaking, but he paid no heed to them. He started out, and soon came to the place where the fire was kept. All the fire-keepers had gone on a man-hunt, and only the children were left in charge.

Coyote approached the fire with a stick in his hand. "Who are you? Where have you been?" one of the children asked him suspiciously.

"Oh, visiting relatives around here," Coyote answered.

One child said, "My father warned us that no one but Coyote would come here, and he told us to beware of him."

"Nonsense," said Coyote as he sat down by the fire. His blanket reached to the very fire into which he had pushed his stick, unobserved by the children.

"Don't be afraid of me, children! I am your cousin," he said. His stick began to burn. "Look over there, look!" he exclaimed suddenly; but the children insisted that they had been warned against Coyote, and refused to look.

He laughed at their fears, and reassured them. "Look, children, at Coyote's house!" said he again. This time the children looked, and Coyote dashed out of the house with the burning fire-stick in his hand.

Before entering the fire-house, Coyote had stationed some of his people at different points. Just as he dashed out from the house, the shaman returned, and, suspecting what had happened, he set out in pursuit of the thief. Coyote ran with the fire-stick until he reached Eagle. Eagle ran with it next, and tossed it to Buzzard. The last man to receive the fire was Turtle. He was a slow runner, and was soon in danger of being overtaken, so he hid the fire in his armpit and jumped into the river. The shaman shot him in the back; and Turtle exclaimed, "Ouch! This (arrow) will make a tail afterwards."

When Coyote came home, he inquired after the fire. Buzzard said, "We gave it to the wrong man."

"Why did you give it to Turtle?" Coyote scolded him. He was very angry. Soon Turtle appeared on the opposite bank of the river, and Coyote began to abuse him.

Turtle said, "Keep still, Coyote! I have the fire," whereupon he threw it on the ground, and a great fire started in the mountains. All people came to obtain fire, and there has been fire ever since.

Afterwards Coyote made fire-sticks and instructed his people in the making and use of the fire-drill. He also it was who laid down the law, "Only men shall carry fire-sticks, not women. Let the women pack the wood, and we will carry the fire-sticks!"

COYOTE ARRANGES THE SEASONS OF THE YEAR

Tradition Bearer: Charlie DePoe

Source: Farrand, Livingston, and Leo J. Frachtenberg. "Shasta and Athapascan Myths from Oregon." *Journal of American Folklore* 28 (1915): 228.

Date: 1900

Original Source: Joshua

National Origin: Native American

For cultural background on the Joshua, see the introductory notes to "The Giver Creates the World" (p. 7). The two Suns named in this tale refer to periods that correspond to January, the month of heaviest rainfall in the Northwest. Coyote demonstrates shamanic power in this **myth**. He speaks to the land, causing distances to shorten, and orders the ocean to dry up. He intimidates the Suns, or months, into creating a more orderly climate. Finally, he plays the role of **culture hero** by teaching others how to use medicinal plants and by inventing ritual dance.

After Coyote had come back from across the ocean, he stayed with his wife one year in the Joshua country, and built himself a sweat-house there. He was in the habit of leaving his wife frequently for the purpose of hunting and fishing. A little ways up the river he had a house for drying salmon. One day he went to the drying-house and stayed there a month. Then he went back to his wife, carrying all the dried salmon in a canoe. After his return he went out on the beach at low tide, where he found plenty of eels with red backs. This surprised him, and he concluded that spring must have come. It seemed to him that he must have missed a good many months. He could not understand this; so he decided to go upstream to a prairie and view the country from there.

Arriving at that place, he saw that all the flowers were dry. This convinced him that he had missed all the winter months.

So he went back, and said to his wife, "My wife, everything upstream is dry. It will be midsummer soon." But the woman laughed at him.

Then Coyote told her to throw all the old salmon into the river, as he did not want to mix old salmon with fresh eels. The woman refused to do so, and they quarrelled over it for a long time. She suspected that someone had been playing a trick on her husband: so she decided to hide all the food she could find, and store it away. She did not believe that fall was coming.

Coyote thought that his wife had thrown all the old salmon away, as he had told her to do, and went out to gather fresh eels; but he did not see a single eel. He thought, "Well, the eels will come to-night."

He went back to his wife and told her about his failure. She paid no attention to him, but kept on eating the salmon she had saved up.

At night Coyote went out again. He fished a whole night, but did not catch a single eel. In the morning he was very hungry: so he went down to the beach in the hope of finding something to eat. Again he was disappointed. Nothing had drifted ashore. In the evening he went out fishing again. He was very hungry by this time, and suspected that either the Sun or the Moon had fooled him. For nearly a month he had nothing to eat. He was so weak that he could hardly walk. And all this time his wife was eating the meat she had stored away without his knowledge.

One day Coyote called all the animals and birds together, told them how the Sun had fooled him, and asked them to help him kill the Sun. Coyote was given food, which made him feel stronger. Then they started out in quest of the place where the Sun habitually comes out.

They built a fort there, covered it with tips, and made a small hole through which to watch the Sun. Coyote also made a knife, and was ready to catch the Sun as soon as he should come up, and to kill him. He watched.

Towards daylight the Sun appeared way off. So Coyote told his companions to take a good rest that day, after which they would go to the place whence the Sun had emerged. They started again. Coyote spoke to the land, and the distance shortened. Soon they came to the new place, and made themselves ready. Again the Sun came out, but he was so far that Coyote could hardly see him. Again he told his friends to rest.

In the evening they started out once more. Again Coyote shortened the distance by a mere wish. They came to the new place, but the Sun was still far off. The same thing happened twenty times.

At last they came to a high mountain, which the Sun could hardly make. Then Coyote was glad, and said, "Now we shall surely catch him." So the next night they went to the new place, Coyote shortening the distance as before. Quite a number of his companions were already worn out with hunger and fatigue, and had dropped out. The new place they came to had high mountains on both sides. They made a high wall between these, and felt sure that they should catch the Sun in this place. At night they got ready.

Daylight began to appear, and Coyote warned his friends to beware of any tricks that the Sun might play on them. "He may come out from the ground with his eyes shut," he said, "so that you won't see him until he opens his eyes on top of the mountain, and then he will be out of reach."

At last the Sun appeared at the foot of the slope on the other side of the mountain. He looked very large, and was quite a distance away. So Coyote told his friends to rest that day. He felt sure that they would catch the Sun at night. After sundown they started out, and came to a large body of water.

Coyote held a council with his people, and asked them to look for a place to cross the ocean. Half he sent north, while the other half was to go south. He thought that perhaps the Sun might have his house in the water. Soon they saw lots of reeds. Coyote's friends became discouraged and wanted to go home, but he encouraged them, saying that he had been there before. They were very tired and hungry. So Coyote advised them to eat some roots. These kept them alive; and from that time on people learned the use of roots as medicine.

From the shore they saw a large fog on the other side of the ocean, which disappeared as soon as the Sun came out. Then they were sure that they were near the Sun's lodge. At noon the Sun came up high above them; he was still very far. They did not know how to cross the ocean.

So Coyote called upon the water-people to help him. Ten times he called, but no one came. Then he nearly lost his courage. He and his companions were almost starved to death.

Finally Coyote said to one of his companions, "Strike me over the head twice! Something may happen." His companion refused, fearing he might kill him. Coyote insisted, and told his friends that if he dropped senseless, they should let him lie until someone came, and then they should push him. So Coyote sat down, closed his eyes, and his companion hit him on the side of the head with a stick. A cracking sound was heard. Twice Coyote was hit before he fell to the ground lifeless.

Then the people began to wonder how they should get home without Coyote, he had taken them so far away from home. Night came, and they heard the sound of mice squeaking around them in a circle. At first they did not wake Coyote. Three times the mice went around them before the people thought of waking Coyote. At first they called his name, then they shook him.

At last Coyote stretched himself, and said, "Oh, I am sleepy!"

His friends yelled at him, "Someone has come!" Then Coyote opened his eyes, squeezed his head on all sides, and it got well again.

Soon the Mice began to squeak, and Coyote called to them, "My grandsons, come to me!" Then two Mice appeared. They had no tails; their ears were small, and their hair was very short. Coyote told them that he was their uncle, and that their father was a great friend of his. The Mice listened in silence.

Then Coyote asked them to tell him where the house of the Sun was; but the bigger Mouse said, "If you give us what we want, we will tell you where the Sun's house is located."

"What do you want?" asked Coyote, "dentalia shells?" The Mouse shook her head. Coyote offered them all kinds of valuables, but the Mice did not want them. The night was passing fast, and Coyote was in a hurry: so he took a salmon-net and made two tails of it. To one Mouse he gave the long tail, while the other received a short tail. He also gave them ears, and hair of different colors.

At last he asked them if they were satisfied; and the Mice replied, "Yes." Then Coyote took some fat and rubbed it on their noses, and told them that thereafter they would smell grease, even from a long distance; and this is the reason why all mice today like grease, and why they get into salmon-nets and tear them whenever they are hung up. They do this because their tails were made of salmon-nets.

Then Coyote asked the Mice, "How do you cross the ocean?" and the Mice told him that they had a trail under water. He also inquired about the house of Sun and Moon, and learned that there were one hundred Suns and Moons, and that the Suns and the Moons were the same people. One person would appear as a Sun one day. Upon his return, another man would go out as Moon; then he would come back, go to sleep, and another person would go out as Sun; and so on. Coyote wanted to know if there were any sweat-houses there.

"Only one," the Mice said, "and it is very hot." They also told him that whenever a Sun wanted to enter the sweat-house, he would first thrust his foot in, and then jump out quickly; then he would go in again and jump out. He would do this five times before remaining in the sweat-house for good. "Then," the Mice said, "you can catch him." Coyote also found out that the Moon's country was dry, had no water, and that it was always hot and light there. He also asked the Mice, "Which Sun fooled me last fall?" and the Mice answered, "There were two of them. Their names are Lts__c_ and Can Sun. They are very bad and make all sorts of trouble. The others are good."

Coyote wanted to know how big they were. "Very big," the Mice said, "and very dangerous." Then Coyote told the Mice that he and his companions would rest a whole day, and would make the attack upon the Suns and the Moons the next night.

He asked the Mice to go home and to gnaw through all the bow-strings in the houses of the Suns and Moons. At last he asked them, "Did you say these houses were underwater?"

"No!" replied the Mice, "they are on land."

Coyote suspected the Mice of lying, but decided to take chances. Then he asked, "How far is it from here?"

"A long ways off." The Mice were ready to start at noon. Coyote wanted to know how long the Suns stayed in the sweat-house, and if they had any dogs. "There are no dogs," the Mice said. Then they continued, "None of the Suns urinate very much, excepting the two we mentioned before. These two leave the house often, and urinate for a long time. Whenever they do so, it rains and storms very hard. Watch these two carefully, for they are the ones who played the trick on you." Just before the Mice departed, they agreed to warn Coyote of any lurking danger by squeaking. Then they opened the door and disappeared.

Coyote called his people together and held a council. It was decided to eat the Suns and Moons as soon as they should be killed, for in that country there was no place to bury them. Then he ordered the ocean to become small and dry, and started out with his people.

Soon the light began to grow very bright: they were approaching the home of the Suns and Moons. The sand was exceedingly hot. They came to the sweat-house; and Coyote hid his companions in it, while he himself knelt down inside near the door, where he could catch any one who went in, kill him, and throw him to his friends. Soon he heard the Mice squeaking, and whispered, "My children, I am here!"

The Mice told him that all the Suns and Moons were in the house. So Coyote caused a heavy fog to spread over the place. The Mice said, "The people saw our new tails and furs, and wondered what it meant. They are surprised, and suspect that Coyote has done this and that he is watching them. We have eaten up all the bows and strings in the houses." Coyote was glad.

Then one Mouse went back into the house, while the other remained outside to give warning. Soon everything became quiet. After a little while Coyote heard the slow, heavy footsteps of an approaching Sun, and saw a bright light, accompanied by a faint hissing sound. Then a foot was thrust into the sweat-house and quickly withdrawn. Four times this process was repeated. After the fifth time a Sun put the whole body in, whereupon Coyote killed him, threw him to his people, who ate him up at once. And from that time on the birds and Coyotes have been in the habit of eating dead corpses.

In this manner he killed fifty persons. After the first twenty-five had been killed, Coyote's people became satiated and could not eat any more. So the place began to smell of blood, and the other Suns became suspicious. At last Ltsī ´cā started for the sweat-house. He approached, causing a great noise and wind. Coyote trembled with excitement. Ltsī ´cā urinated for a long time. As he came nearer to the sweat-house, he wondered why it was dark inside. He put his foot in, then withdrew it quickly. Coyote began to waver; he thought that perhaps he had killed enough Suns and Moons. At last Ltsī ´cā came in. Coyote stabbed him, but only scratched his rump. The wounded Sun rushed into the house and gave the alarm. Coyote quickly gathered his people and told them to disperse. Then he produced a heavy fog, so that he could not be seen. The Moons woke up and seized their bows and arrows; but all were gnawed through.

Thus Coyote and his friends escaped. The Mice, too, went home on their trail. They met at their first meeting-place, and Coyote danced the death-dance. Since then people have always been dancing the murder-dance. The wounded Moon had a very bad night; he was very sick.

At noon Coyote looked up to the sky, and said, "Suns, if you ever fool me again, I will come back and kill you all!" The Suns did not answer. Then Coyote settled the length of the year, and divided it into twelve periods, and since then the Suns have never dared to disobey him.

COYOTE FREES THE SALMON

Tradition Bearer: Unavailable

Source: Powers, Stephen. "North American Indian Legends and Fables." *Folk-Lore Record* 5 (1882): 95–96.

Date: ca. 1882

Original Source: Karok

National Origin: Native American

For cultural background on the Karok see "Origin of Fire" (p. 16). In the following **myth**, Kareya, the creator of the world, demonstrates a petty side to his nature that emerges repeatedly in Karok mythology. Coyote, however, uses the wiles of the **trickster-culture hero** to save humans from starvation.

When Kareya made all things that have breath, he first made the fishes in the big water, then the animals, and last of all The Man. But Kareya did not yet let the fishes come up the Klamath, and thus the Karok had not enough food, and were sore a-hungered. There were salmon in the big water, many and very fine to eat, but no Indian could catch them in the big water, and Kareya had made a great fish-dam at the mouth of the Klamath, and closed it fast, and given the key to two old hags to keep, so that the salmon could not go up the river. And the hags kept the key that Kareya had given them, and watched it day and night without sleeping, so that no Indian could come near it.

Then the Karok were sore disturbed in those days for lack of food, and many died, and their children cried to them because they had no meat. But the coyote befriended the Karok, and helped them, and took it on himself to bring the salmon up the Klamath. First, he went to an alder tree and gnawed off a piece of bark, for the bark of the alder tree, after it is taken off, presently turns red, and looks like salmon. He took the piece of elder bark in his teeth and journeyed far down the Klamath, until he came to the mouth of it at the big water. Then he rapped at the door of the cabin where the old hags lived, and when they opened it he said, "Ai-yu-kwoi," for he was very polite. And they did not wonder to hear the coyote speak, for all the animals could speak in those days. They did not suspect the coyote, and so asked him to come into their cabin and sit by the fire. This he did, and after he had warmed himself awhile, he commenced nibbling his piece of alder bark.

One of the hags, seeing this, said to the other, "See, he has some salmon!" So they were deceived and thrown off their guard, and presently one of them rose, took down the key, and went to get some salmon to cook for themselves. Thus the coyote saw where the key was kept, but he was not much better off than before, for it was too high for him to reach it. The hags cooked some salmon for supper and ate it, but they gave the coyote none.

So he stayed in the cabin all night with the hags, pretending to sleep, but he was thinking how to get the key. He could think of no plan at all, but in the morning one of the hags took down the key, and started to get some salmon again, and then the coyote happened to think of a way as quick as a flash. He jumped up and darted under the hag, which threw her down, and caused her to fling the key a long way off. The coyote quickly seized it with his teeth, and ran and opened the fish-dam before the hags could catch him. Thus the salmon were allowed to go up the Klamath, and the Karok had plenty of food.

THE ORIGIN OF THE SEASONS AND OF THE MOUNTAINS

Tradition Bearer: Unavailable

Source: Boas, Franz. "Traditions of the Ts'ets'ā´ut I." *Journal of American Folklore* 9 (1896): 260–61.

Date: 1894–1895

Original Source: Ts'ets'ā´ut

National Origin: Native American

The Ts'ets'ā´ut were a Northwestern Athabascan group. Although they were given this name by their Native American neighbors, the Ts'ets'ā´ut were identified as belonging to the Tinneh stock by folklorist Franz Boas. By the time he was able to make contact with the group, they were reduced to about a dozen members. They had originally been organized as bands of nomadic hunters and gatherers, but their culture had been profoundly influenced by the neighboring, more sedentary Tlingit by the time of Boas field-work. This **myth**, Boas notes, bears many similarities to Tlingit narrative.

In the beginning there were no mountains. The earth was level, and covered with grass and shrubs. There was no rain, no snow, and no wind. The sun was shining all the time. Men and animals were not distinct yet. They were in dire distress. They had little to eat, and nothing to drink.

Once upon a time a man made a bow for his son, who was asleep. When the child awoke it cried for thirst, but his father was unable to give him any water. He offered his son grease to drink, but he refused it. Then the father gave him the bow in order to quiet him, but the boy continued to cry.

Now the father took the bow, and shot the arrow into a small mound of dirt that was next to the fire. When the arrow entered it a spring of water came forth, and the boy drank. From it sprang all the rivers of the world.

But there was no rain and no snow. The animals held a council, and considered how to procure them. They resolved to go to the end of the world, to make a hole through the sky, and to climb up through it. They did so. When they reached the end of the world all the animals tried to tear the sky, but they were unable to do so.

All had tried except two ermines. One of them jumped up, struck the sky, and tore it. The other ran through the hole, and then all the animals helped to enlarge it. They climbed up through it, but when all had passed the hole closed again. They were on a large, beautiful prairie, and walked on. After they had gone some time, they saw a lodge in the far distance. They reached it and entered.

There were many bags in the house. One contained the rain, another one the snow, a third one the fog, and still others the gales and the four winds. The men sat down and debated what to do. Only a woman was in the house. Her name was Goose Woman.

They said to her, "It is dry arid hot on earth. We have nothing to eat, and nothing to drink. Give us what we need, for you are keeping it in your house."

The goose woman replied, "All that you need is in these bags: rain and snow, the winds, the gale, and the fog. If you tear them, it will be winter. The North wind will blow. It will be cold, and the ground will be covered with snow. Then the snow will melt, the West wind will blow, and trees and shrubs will bloom and bear fruit. Then another season of snows and cold will follow."

Now the people tore the bags, and it happened as the woman had predicted. Clouds began to gather, and snow was falling. At the same time the level ground changed its form, and mountains arose.

Then the animals went back. Again the ermine tore the sky, and all went down. Then the animals ran into the woods and separated from man.

THE ORIGIN OF DEATH

Tradition Bearer: Klamath Billie

Source: Farrand, Livingston, and Leo J. Frachtenberg. "Shasta and Athapascan Myths from Oregon." *Journal of American Folklore* 28 (1915): 209.

Date: 1900

Original Source: Shasta

National Origin: Native American

Shasta culture is described in the introductory notes to "The Theft of Fire" (p. 18). Coyote learns compassion only after falling victim to his own "wisdom." This signifies a worldview quite different from the one posited by "Man's Fall" and "Original Sin" of Judaeo-Christian tradition. In this case, Coyote, not human a flaw, is to blame for bringing death into the universe.

Long, long ago Coyote was considered the wisest being to whom all people were wont to go for advice and help in times of distress. Coyote was living with Spider. Each of them had a boy. One day Spider's child died.

So he went to Coyote, saying, "My child died. I should like to have my child come back to life. What do you think of it?"

But Coyote replied, "I don't think it will be right; for, if all dead people should come back, there would be too many spirits in the world, and then there would hardly be room for us living people." Spider went home saying nothing.

After a while Coyote's child died; and he went at once to Spider, addressing him thus: "Friend, you were right a little while ago. My child is dead now, and I am willing to agree that both our boys should come back to life."

But Spider answered, "No, this cannot be done. My child is all spoiled now. It is too late."

Coyote tried to induce Spider to change his mind, but Spider remained inexorable.

THE XUDELE

Tradition Bearer: Unavailable

Source: Boas, Franz. "Traditions of the Ts'ets'ā´ut II." *Journal of American Folklore* 10 (1897): 35–48.

Date: 1894–1895

Original Source: Ts'ets'ā´ut

National Origin: Native American

Folklorist Franz Boas writes the following concerning this **myth**, "I do not know of any Athapaskan **legend** resembling the present in detail, but in the collection of [Algonquin] traditions published by Petitot beings half dog and half man play a very important part. They are described as having the faculty of taking the scent of man in the same manner as the Xudele. Similar tales may be found among all the Eskimo tribes, who call the fabulous inlanders, who are half dog, half men, Adla or Eqigdlit." Ts'ets'ā´ut culture is described in the introductory notes to "The Origin of the Seasons and of the Mountains" (p. 27). The function of the following **legend** may serve not only to explain the nature of martens, but also to warn against the potential dangers of traveling alone in the severe climate of the far Northwest.

The Xudele are cannibals. They are very lean. Their noses are turned up and their eyebrows run upward. Their faces look almost like those of dogs. They wear small axes in their belts, with which they kill men. They take the scent of men like dogs.

One day the Xudele had gone hunting man. They found the tracks of a hunter who was on the mountains. He saw them coming, and tried to escape. When he came near a snow-field that terminated abruptly at a precipice, he cut steps into it and climbed down. Half way down he found a small rock shelter, where he stayed. He resolved to make an attempt to kill his pursuers by a ruse. He built a fire and roasted a porcupine that he had caught. The Xudele saw the smoke and smelled the roasting meat. When they came to the snow-field it had grown dark. They shouted down: "Where are you? Let us have some of your meat!"

The man shouted back: "You must slide down this snow-field, then you will find me. I invite you to take part in my meal!" Then the Xudele began to slide down the snow-field one after the other, and were precipitated into the abyss.

Finally only one of their number was left. He did not dare to slide down, and shouted, "Where are all my friends?"

The man replied, "They are all here."

But the Xudele could not be induced to slide down. He cut steps into the snow, and climbed down as the man had done. Finally he reached the man. When he did not see his friends, he asked what had become of them, and the man told him that they had all perished because they had slid past his shelter.

Now the Xudele, who did not dare to attack the man single-handed, offered to gamble with him, and said they would stake their lives. The man refused. He had employed the time while the Xudele were sliding down the snow-field to make a heavy club, which he had placed near his fire.

While he was talking with the Xudele he watched his opportunity, and slew him with his club. Then he returned to his village and told what had happened. The people were afraid that the friends of the Xudele might come to look for them, and moved to another place.

At another time a man had gone out hunting. It was in summer. He discovered a vast number of Xudele coming right up to him, so that he could not escape. There happened to be a swamp close to the trail, which he was following. He jumped into the mud and lay down, keeping motionless. He looked just like a log. He extended his arms, so that they looked like limbs of a tree. The Xudele came, and one after the other passed him without noticing him.

Finally, one of their number noticed the resemblance of the supposed log to a human figure. He raised his axe, and was about to strike him. But since the man did not wince, he concluded that it was nothing but a log and passed on.

When all had passed, the man jumped up and ran on the nearest way to his village. There he told the chief that the Xudele were coming. He called a council, and they resolved what to do. They killed a number of dogs and cut them up, skin and bone and intestines. Then they pounded flint to dust, mixed it with the meat, and made a soup of it.

When the Xudele came, they invited them to the chief's house and set the soup before them. Before they began eating, a little boy happened to walk past a Xudele, who seized him, tore out his arms and legs, and ate him. The people did not dare to remonstrate.

Now the Xudele began to eat. Soon the effects of the poison—the pounded stone—began to be felt. They acted as though they were drunk, and some of them fell dead. Then the men took up their clubs and killed them one and all.

The Xudele put up traps for catching men on the trails, which they travel on their snowshoes. They cover a stick with moss and snow, which is so arranged that it catches in the snowshoe of the traveler. A few feet in front of this stick is another, sharp-pointed stick, put into the ground point upward. When the snowshoes catch in the first stick, the traveler falls forward on to the pointed stick, which pierces him.

One day a hunter was passing over a trail. He saw a small irregularity of the snow, and discovered that it was the trap of a Xudele. He intended to go on, when he saw the Xudele to whom the trap belonged. As he was unable to make his escape, he tried a stratagem. He struck his nose so that it bled and smeared his chest with blood. Then he lay down on the pointed stick of the trap.

The Xudele approached, and when he saw the man, he smiled and said: "Again my trap has caught something for me." He took the man off the stick, put him into his bag, and, after having reset his trap, turned to go home. The man was very heavy, and he had to put down his load from time to time. Then the man blew the air out of his compressed lips, thus imitating the noise of escaping gases.

The Xudele said," He must have been in my trap for a long time, for the body is decomposing already; the gases are escaping." When he arrived at home he threw the body down near the fireplace.

The man glanced around furtively, and, saw stores of dried human flesh in the house. There was a black woman in the house, and three children were playing near the fire.

The Xudele went to fetch his knife in order to skin and carve the man, and he sent his wife for water. The man saw an axe lying near the fire, and when the Xudele turned his back he jumped up, seized it, and split the head of his captor.

The Xudele cried: "Sxinadle, asidle," and died. (It is said that the Xudele always utter this cry, which is unintelligible to the humans, at the time of their death.) When the children saw their father dying they ran out of the house, assumed the shape of martens, and ran up a tree. The man threw the body of the Xudele into the fire.

Then he went out of the hut to kill the woman, whom he met carrying a basket of water. He split her stomach with his axe. Then two minks jumped out of her and ran into the water. She died and he burnt her body. When he returned to his country he told what he had seen. Therefore we know that the martens and minks descend from the Xudele.

ORIGIN OF THE ADLET AND THE WHITEMAN

Tradition Bearer: Unavailable

Source: Rink, H., and Franz Boas. "Eskimo Tales and Songs." *Journal of American Folklore 2* (1889): 125.

Date: 1889

Original Source: Eskimo

National Origin: Native American

It is erroneous to think of the Eskimo habitat as barren land. As their north-south range is great, there is variation in topography, landform, climate, vegetation, and fish and game availability. The arctic is a desert in truest sense of the world. The cold reduces the amount of moisture in the air so that some areas receive as little as four inches of precipitation a year, making it a difficult task to obtain fresh water. Summers are short and defined by the temperature being above freezing. When streams begin to flow, water travel becomes possible; however, walking becomes virtually impossible over the swampy tundra because of the melting surfaces. At the onset of winter and freezing temperatures, the people begin to settle down. Nuclear families are often organized into bands. Determinates for band leadership may include family allegiance, personality traits, or physical strength. An episode in the following **myth** of the origin of the Adlet and the Whiteman recalls a central figure in Eskimo **myth**, the female sea spirit with various names: Takanakapsaluk, Nuliajuk, and Sedna, for example. In myths she is a terrifying presence living in a house at the bottom of the sea. In these myths the shamans often travel on spirit journeys to confront her and her entourage of monsters in times of famine or danger in order to win her help for the people. For example, they ask her to provide seals and other sea mammals, which were believed to grow from the severed parts of her own body. Compare the following narrative to "The Xudele" (p. 29).

Saviqong (i.e., the knifeman), an old man, lived alone with his daughter. Her name was Niviarsiang (i.e., the girl), but as she did not want to take a husband she was also called Uinigumissuitung (i.e., she who did not want to take a husband).

She refused all her suitors, but at last a dog, spotted white and red, whose name was Ijiqang (i.e., the powerful eye), won her affection and she married him. They had ten children, five of whom were Adlet and five dogs.

The legs of the Adlet were like those of dogs, and hairy all over, the soles excepted, while the upper part of their bodies was human. When the children grew up they became very voracious, and as the dog Ijiqang did not go hunting at all, but let his father-in-law provide for the whole family, Saviqong found great difficulty in feeding them. Moreover, the children were very clamorous and noisy; so at last their grandfather, being tired of their manifold demands and the trouble they gave him, put the whole family into his boat and carried them to a small island. He told Ijiqang to come every day and fetch meat.

Niviarsiang hung a pair of boots on his neck and he swam across the narrow channel separating the island from the mainland. But Saviqong, instead of giving him meat, filled the boots with heavy stones, which drowned Ijiqang when he attempted to return to the island.

Niviarsiang thought of revenging the death of her husband. She sent the young dogs to her father's hut and let them gnaw off his feet and hands. In return, Saviqong, when his daughter happened to be in his boat, threw her overboard, and cut off her fingers when she clung to the gunwale. As they fell into the sea they were transformed into seals and whales. At last he allowed her to climb again into the boat.

As she feared that her father might think of killing or maiming her children, she ordered the Adlet to go inland, where they became the ancestors of a numerous people. She made a boat for the young dogs, setting up two sticks for masts in the sole of one of her boots, and sent the puppies across the ocean. She sang: "Angnaijaja. When you will have arrived on the other side, you will make many little things. Angnaija."

THE ORIGIN OF THE NARWHAL

Tradition Bearer: Unavailable

Source: Kroeber, A. L. "Tales of the Smith Sound Eskimo." *Journal of American Folklore* 12 (1899): 169–70.

Date: 1897–1898

Original Source: Eskimo

National Origin: Native American

The Arctic can be a land of meager resources. The neglect and even abandonment of those who are not able to contribute to community survival was a matter of course in the traditional culture. The cannibalistic Adlet appear in this tale (see "Origin of the Adlet and the Whiteman," p. 32 as one of the trials the siblings must endure in their quest for community. This tale is widely distributed not only among the Eskimo, but also among Athabascans and the Bella Bella of the Northwest Coast.

There was a blind boy (or young man) who lived with his mother and sister. They went to a place where there was no one and lived alone. One day, when they were in their tent, a bear came up to it.

Though the boy was blind he had a bow, and the woman aimed it at the bear for him. The arrow struck the bear and killed it. The mother, however, deceived her son and told him he had missed it. She cut it up and then cooked it. The young man now smelled the bear-meat, and asked his mother whether it was not bear he was smelling. She, however, told him he was mistaken. Then she and her daughter ate it, but she would give him nothing. His sister, however, put half her food in her dress secretly, to give him later.

When her mother asked her why she was eating so much (noticing that she seemed to eat an unusual quantity), the girl answered that she was hungry. Later, when her mother was away, she gave the meat to her brother. In this way he discovered that his mother had deceived him. Then he wished for another chance to kill something, when he might not be thus deceived by his mother.

One day, when he was out of doors, a large loon came down to him and told him to sit on its head. The loon then flew with him toward its nest, and finally brought him to it, on a large cliff. After they had reached this, it began to fly again, and took him to a pond].

The loon then dived with him, in order to make him recover his eyesight. It would dive and ask him whether he was smothering; when he answered that he was, it took him above the surface to regain his breath. Thus they dived, until the blind boy could see again. His eyesight was now very strong; he could see as far as the loon, and could even see where his mother was, and what she was doing. Then he returned. When he came back, his mother was afraid, and tried to excuse herself, and treated him with much consideration.

One day he went narwhal-hunting, using his mother to hold the line. "Spear a small narwhal," his mother said, for she feared a large one would drag her into the water by the line fastened around her. He speared a small one, and she pulled it ashore. Then they ate its blubber.

The next time two appeared together, a small white whale and a large narwhal. "Spear the small one again," she told him. But he speared the large one, and when it began to pull, he let go the line, so that his mother was dragged along, and forced to run, and pulled into the water.

"My knife," she cried, in order to cut the rope. She kept calling for her knife, but he did not throw it to her, and she was drawn away and drowned. She became a narwhal herself, her hair, which she wore twisted to a point, becoming the tusk.

After this, the man who had recovered his sight, and his sister, went away. Finally they came to a house. The brother was thirsty, and wanted water. He asked his sister for some, telling her to go to the house for it. She went up to it, but was at first afraid to go in.

"Come in, come in!" cried the people inside, who were murderous Adlet. When she entered, they seized her and ate her. She had stayed away a long time, and finally her brother went to look for her.

He entered the house, but could not find her. An old man there, after having eaten of her, tried to say he did not have her, and did not know where she was. The brother, however, kept stabbing the inmates of the house with a tusk he had, trying to make them confess, but vainly, and finally killed them.

Then her brother put her bones together and went away, carrying them on his back. Then the flesh grew on the bones again, and soon she spoke, "Let me get up!"

But he said to her," Don't get up!"

At last she got up, however. Then they saw a great many people, and soon reached them. By this time his sister had quite recovered; she ate, and went into a house. She married there, and soon had a child. Her brother also married.

THE WOMAN WHO MARRIED A DOG

Tradition Bearer: Unavailable

Source: Kroeber, A. L. "Tales of the Smith Sound Eskimo." *Journal of American Folklore* 12 (1899): 168–69.

Date: 1897–1898

Original Source: Eskimo

National Origin: Native American

This Eskimo **myth** differs from the well-known father-daughter type (see "The Origin of the Adlet and the Whiteman," for example), in that the girl character's father does not die. The father's insistence on his daughter's marrying in this and other narratives is due to the fact that the Eskimo subsistence in their harsh environment was based largely on the hunt, and an extra hunter in the band made starvation less likely. The fear caused by attempting to cope with their severe environment also fostered beliefs not only in the beings cited in this **myth**, but mermen, giant worms, ten-legged polar bears, and other monsters. Folklorist A. L. Kroeber notes that he could not determine what nakassungnaitut were.

Near the head the bay on Inglefield Gulf lived a man and his daughter. The girl, however, refused to marry any one. Finally, when she refused suitor after suitor, her father grew angry and threatened to make her marry a dog. She warned him that if he said this often she might take him at his word.

Indeed, one of the dogs just then broke his line and came into the house. She soon married him. When she grew pregnant, her father and the other people drove her away, and the dog carried her across the water to an island, named Qemiunaarving, off the mouth of the bay.

The dog used to bring her food from her father, floating it over by means of a skin of a ground-seal, which was prepared like an ordinary seal-skin float. One day, the father, desiring to kill him, filled the skin with stones and tied it to him, hoping thus to drown him. But the dog was so strong that he kept on swimming in spite of the stones (which would have drawn down any other being), and finally, although he almost sank, reached the island in safety.

The woman gave birth to a great many children, both persons and dogs. When they were somewhat older, she one day ordered them to kill their father, the dog, which they did, devouring him. Then she called her children in pairs, a male and a female together. "You two be qablunat (Europeans), and go away from here, and dress in clean clothes, and do not inspire fear."

"You two be nakassungnaitut, and be savage, and also go away," she said to the next two.

"You two be wolves," she went on to another pair, "do not pursue people nor frighten dogs, and go away.

"And you two be tornit [giants]" she said, "and go away from here; but you shall have no dogs, and shall fear them, but you shall not make people afraid.

"And you be inugaudligat [dwarves]," she added to the last pair. Thus she sent them all away. The qablunat sailed away in the sole of a boot. And then she went back to live with her father.

RECOVERING THE SUN

Tradition Bearer: Unavailable

Source: Boas, Franz. "Notes on the Eskimo of Port Clarence, Alaska." *Journal of American Folklore* 7 (1894): 205–6.

Date: ca. 1894

Original Source: Eskimo

National Origin: Native American

Many Eskimo live in an environment where the land is mostly tundra and remains permanently frozen except for a few inches of surface, which thaw during the brief summers. Also characteristic of the northernmost areas are the nights of deep winter when twilight occurs at noon. A **myth** such as the following gives voice to the anxiety that this lack of light can generate. In the course of the search for the sun, the party in the **myth** covers a territory filled with monsters and approaches the edge of a world that Eskimo tradition maintained was flat and balanced on wooden pillars. The party succeeds because of a **motif** that has appeared in other Eskimo narratives: a young woman defies a parent.

Once upon a time the people were assembled in a singing house. While they were dancing the sun disappeared, and nobody knew what had become of it. The people were unable to go hunting, and soon all their provisions were exhausted. Then they told the women to mend their clothing carefully, and to make as many boots as possible. These they put into bags and set out in search of the sun. It was dark all the time. They followed the seacoast, and went so long that they wore out their boots. Then they took new ones from their traveling-bags.

After many days they came to a country that swarmed with seals, walrus, and deer. There they found a people whose language they did not understand. After some time, however, they learned to converse with them. They asked these people if they had seen the sun.

The latter replied that they would come to five places. At the fifth place there lived a woman who had both the sun and the moon in her house. Then they went on. It was very cold, and they ran as fast as they could in order to keep warm. When their provisions began to run short, they reached another country that swarmed with game.

They found a people whose language they did not understand, but after some time they were able to converse with each other. There they obtained the same information as before, and went on.

It was very cold, and they ran as fast as they could, in order to keep warm. When their provisions began to run short, they reached a third country that swarmed with game.

They met a people whose language they did not understand. After some time they were able to converse, and upon their inquiries they were told that at the second place that they would reach there lived a woman named Itudlu'gpiaq, who had both sun and moon, but that it was very doubtful if they would be able to obtain it.

Then they went on. It was very cold, and they ran as fast as they could, in order to keep warm. When their provisions began to run low, they reached a country that swarmed with game. There they found dwarfs, who tried to escape when they saw the strong men coming. They caught them, however, and learned that at the next place they would find the house of Itudlu'qpiaq, who had both sun and moon.

They went on. On their way they found ice and driftwood obstructing their way, but they kicked it aside. At that time the people were very strong and able to lift heavy stones. After they had gone a long time they saw a singing house. When they came near, they went very slowly, because they were afraid.

At last one of the men tied his jacket around his waist and tied his pants around his knees. Then he crept cautiously through the entrance and put his head through the door in the bottom of the floor. He saw a young woman, Itudlu'gpiaq, sitting in the middle of the rear of the house. Her father was sitting in the middle of the right-hand side of the house, her mother in the middle of the left-hand side. In each of the rear corners a ball was hanging from the roof. At the right-hand side was a large ball, and at the left-hand side a smaller one.

Then he whispered: "Itudlu'gpiaq, we came to ask you for some light."

Then her mother said: "Give them the small ball."

The man, however, refused and asked for the large ball. Then Itudlu'qpiaq took it down and gave it a kick. It fell right into the entrance hole. The people took it and ran outside. Then they tore the ball to pieces and the daylight came out of it. It was not warm at once, but it grew warmer day after day. If they had taken the small ball it would have been light, but it would have remained cold.

BROTHER AND SISTER

Tradition Bearer: Unavailable

Source: Boas, Franz. "Traditions of the Ts'ets'ā´ut I." *Journal of American Folklore* 9 (1896): 257–68.

Date: 1894–1895

Original Source: Ts'ets'ā´ut

National Origin: Native American

Franz Boas notes that the following **myth** is related to two Tlingit traditions: the origin of earthquakes (a narrative that contains the **motif** of an incestuous brother and sister) and the story of Raven, the Northwest Coast **trickster/culture hero**. During the course of the tale, the brother's power increases from human to superhuman. His final transformation is into Raven. In this incarnation he took on the ability to control forces of nature.

Once upon a time there were four brothers and a sister whose parents had died. One day they went up Tcu'nax River until they reached its headwaters, which are called xaga. There they stayed hunting the mountain goat. The eldest of the brothers had fallen in love with his sister, who returned his affection. Then the other brothers grew ashamed.

They tied the two together with cedar-withes, so that the man's head was between the feet of the woman, while her head was between the man's feet, and thus left them. The eldest brother, however, was so strong that he tore apart his bonds, and liberated himself and his sister. He found a cave, which they used as a dwelling-place. After some time his sister gave birth to a boy.

One day, when she left the house, she saw many mountain goats grazing on the hill opposite. She ran back into the cave, and called her brother, "Come and look at the mountain goats."

He went out and looked at them. On this, they fell dead and rolled down the mountain towards the cave. He had attained supernatural powers. His gaze killed whomever and whatever he looked at. Then he said to his wife: "Go and gather stones, with which to skin the goats."

She went down to the river, and gathered many thin pebbles. When she had brought them to the cave, her husband was not satisfied with them. He himself went to the river, and found many new stone knives and axes. These he carried to the cave, and he and his wife began to skin the goats. But they did not cut open their bellies and strip off the skin, as it is the custom to do; they cut the feet, and skinned them as we do martens. In this manner he skinned one buck, a she goat, and a kid, and father, mother, and son put on their skins.

Then the father said, "Now I will go down the river and build houses for our use." He started, and after he had gone some distance he made a natural bridge across the river, and many caves in the sides of the mountains.

Then he said to his wife: "Now I will make the sea. The ocean shall be in the west, the land shall be in the east." Thus the sea was created.

And he continued: "I will make a hole, so that the water of the sea may run down through it and come back again. Then there will be ebb-tide and flood-tide."

But his wife asked him, "Do not make the hole here, for men are living nearby, and the hole might swallow them. Make it far away in mid-ocean."

Henceforth they lived under the bridge. One day many Ts'ets'__ut went up the river to see what had become of the brother and sister who had been left. Among the travelers were the brothers of the couple. When they approached the headwaters of the river, they saw the natural bridge, and the caves, which they had not seen before. The kid was frolicking under the bridge, and every one of its steps made a deep impression in the rock. It was scared when it saw the people and jumped back into the cave in which it was living. The people saw a glaring light coming forth from the cave. Then the mother came out, to see what had frightened the kid. She saw the people sitting on their knees, and wondering at the marvelous changes that had taken place on the river.

She went back and told her husband what she had seen. He said: "If among these people are our brothers who bound us. Let us kill them!" His wife did not reply.

Then he stepped out of the cave, and when he looked at the people they all died. One woman only had hidden herself. She was saved. The natural bridge where these events took place is called Tseneniaga.

Then the husband and his wife separated. She went up the river. When she arrived at its source, she made a rock resembling her in shape. It may be seen up to this day. It looks like a woman carrying a babe on her back. She went on to the headwaters of Nass River, where she continues to live on the bank of a lake up to this day.

The man went down the river, and wherever he camped he made rocks of curious shape as marks of his presence. Now his name was Qa, the raven. The

Tlingit call him YeL. Among others he made two rocks, which look like men with arms. One of these has fallen over, while the other one is still standing. Its name is SdgL (the same in Tlingit). He wandered all through the world. Finally he traveled westward.

At that time the sea was always high. In the middle of the world he discovered a rock in the sea. He built a house under the rock, made a hole through the earth, and a lid that fitted it. He put a man in charge of the hole; he opened the lid twice a day and twice a day closed it. When the hole is open, the water rushes down through it into the depth, and it is ebb; when the lid is put on, the water rises again, and it is flood.

Ta'eL, a Tlingit chief, when hunting sea otters, was taken out to the rock by the tide. The current was so strong that there was no possibility of escape. When he was drawn towards the rock, he saw a few small trees growing on it. He managed to throw his canoe-line over one of the trees and thus succeeded in escaping from the whirlpool. After some time he heard a noise that was produced by the closing of the hole. Then the water began to rise, and he paddled away as fast as he could. Before the ebb began, he pulled his canoe on to a rock, and when the flood set in again continued his homeward journey. Finally he reached his home in safety.

THE SAD WOMAN

Tradition Bearer: Mrs. C. A. Anderson

Source: Golder, F. A. "Aleutian Stories." *Journal of American Folklore* 18 (1905): 215

Date: 1905

Original Source: Aleutian

National Origin: Native American

The Aleutians call themselves Unangan, which means "the people." Their native habitat was the Aleutian Islands, which trail off to the southwest from Alaska. Related to the Eskimo, they subsisted on hunting sea mammals and fishing. Atka and Attu are two of the furthest west and most isolated islands in the Aleutian Chain.

Many, many years ago the people of Atka and Attu were continually at war with each other, frequently surprising each other with fatal results. At this particular time, the Atka warriors gathered a large fleet of bidarkas [Aleutian kayaks], and one dark night fell on the Attu inhabitants, of whom but three escaped, two boys and a woman. The boys were soon discovered in the cave where they were hid and killed, but the woman was not found. After the victors had departed, the woman came out, and was painfully surprised to know that she was the only human being on the island.

For seven years she lived in this solitary state, and during all this time neither smiled nor laughed. She lived mostly on sea-lions and sea-otters, which she killed with clubs while they were on the rocks. In the eighth year her sadness came to an end in the following manner. She had as companions a young duck and sea-gull whom she had befriended; one day, as she was fishing along the beach, these two birds began to fight, which so amused her that she laughed out.

Not long after, some suitable driftwood came ashore, and she set about building a new home. While busily engaged with her stone hatchet in trimming a log, she thought she heard a noise behind her, and on looking around saw a man. This so frightened her that she cut off one of her fingers. A little later some more Atka people came over and settled in Attu, and they are the ancestors of the present inhabitants of that island.

THE FIRST SHIP SEEN BY THE CLATSOP

Tradition Bearer: Charles Cultee

Source: Boas, Franz. Pages 277–78 in *Chinook Texts*. Smithsonian Institution Bureau of American Ethnology Bulletin 20. Washington, DC: U.S. Government Printing Office, 1894.

Date: 1890–1891

Original Source: Chinook

National Origin: Native American

This **legend** comes from the Clatsop, the people that historically inhabited the northwestern tip of modern Oregon. When encountered by the Lewis and Clark Expedition in 1805, the Clatsop were reported to number about four hundred persons in villages along the Columbia River.

They subsisted on fishing and hunting. By the time Franz Boas recorded the following narrative, only two Clatsop speakers survived.

The son of an old woman had died. She wailed for him a whole year and then she stopped. Now one day she went to Seaside. There she used to stop, and she returned. She returned walking along the beach. She nearly reached Clatsop; now she saw something. She thought it was a whale. When she came near it she saw two spruce trees standing upright on it.

She thought, "Behold! It is no whale. It is a monster." She reached the thing that lay there. Now she saw that its outer side was all covered with copper. Ropes were tied to those spruce trees and it was full of iron.

Then a bear came out of it. He stood on the thing that lay there. He looked just like a bear, but his face was that of a human being. Then she went home. Now she thought of her son, and cried, saying, "Oh, my son is dead and the thing about which we heard in tales is on shore." When she nearly reached the town she continued to cry.

The people said, "Oh, a person comes crying. Perhaps somebody struck her." The people made themselves ready. They took their arrows.

An old man said, "Listen!" Then the people listened.

Now she said all the time, "Oh, my son is dead, and the thing about which we heard in tales is on shore."

The people said, "What may it be?" They went running to meet her. They said, "What is it?" "Ah, something lies there and it is thus. There are two bears on it, or maybe they are people."

Then the people ran. They reached the thing that lay there. Now the people, or what else they might be, held two copper kettles in their hands. Now the first one reached there. Another one arrived. Now the person's took their hands to their mouths and gave the people their kettles. They had lids. The men pointed inland and asked for water.

Then two people ran inland. They hid themselves behind a log. They returned again and ran to the beach. One man climbed up and entered the thing. He went down into the ship. He looked about in the interior of the ship; it was full of boxes. He found brass buttons in strings half a fathom long. He went out again to call his relatives, but they had already set fire to the ship.

He jumped down. Those two persons had also gone down. It burnt just like fat. Then the Clatsop gathered the iron, the copper, and the brass. Then all the people learned about it. The two persons were taken to the chief of the Clatsop.

Then the chief of the one town said, "I want to keep one of the men with me." The people almost began to fight. Now one of them was taken to one town. Then the chief was satisfied. Now the Quenaiult, the Chehalis, the Cascades, the Cowlitz, and the Klickatat learned about it and they all went to Clatsop. The Quenaiult, the Chehalis, and the Willapa went. The people of all the towns went there. The Cascades, the Cowlitz, and the Klickatat came down the river. All those of the upper part of the river came down to Clatsop. Strips of copper two fingers wide and going around the arm were exchanged for one slave each. A piece of iron as long as one-half the forearm was exchanged for one slave. A piece of brass two fingers wide was exchanged for one slave. A nail was sold for a good curried deerskin. Several nails were given for long dentalia. The people bought this and the Clatsop became rich. Then iron and brass were seen for the first time. Now they kept these two persons. One was kept by each chief; one was at the Clatsop town at the cape.

HOW THE LEE FAMILY CAME TO OREGON

Tradition Bearer: Jane Lee Smith

Source: Wrenn, Sarah B. "Interview of Jane Lee Smith." American Life Histories: Manuscripts from the Federal Writers' Project, 1936–1940. Manuscript Division, Library of Congress. 12 October 2005. http://memory.loc.gov/ammem/wpaintro/wpahome.html.

Date: 1939

Original Source: Oregon

National Origin: Anglo American

The westward migration of the Lees is revealed in part through **legends** recounted to tradition bearer Jane Lee Smith and in part through personal experience narratives. The following combination of the two **genres** is typical of the ways in which **family sagas** are preserved in oral tradition.

My father and mother crossed the plains in 1847, with the usual experiences attending that long trip. Something unusual that happened was the thunder storm they encountered shortly after crossing the Platte river. Father and mother were walking, it seemed, when this terrible thunderstorm came up. Suddenly there was a tremendous flash of lightning, followed by a roar of thunder. Father and mother were both thrown on to their knees. In the wagon in front of theirs two little children were in the rear of the wagon box; they had been leaning out and playing with the horns of the oxen trudging along behind. One of the children was found to be stunned, but not otherwise hurt; the other one was killed.

Among father's oxen was an old animal they called Brindy—for Brindle I guess. Once on the plains Brindy was found to have an arrow in his flank. It was supposed an Indian had shot it, but nobody knew just when it happened. Anyway, after that, Brindy had it in for redskins. Every time one came near, Brindy would snort like all get out, so they always knew when Indians were lurking around. We had Brindy for many years. After I was born and big enough to go berrying we children were down in the pasture, picking strawberries. Brindy and the other cattle—father had quite a bunch of Durham cattle by then—were not far away quietly munching grass, when all at once we heard Brindy snorting. Woughf! Woughf! he went, and there those cattle were, all lined up for battle, with old Brindy out in front, pawing the ground and snorting like mad. We couldn't imagine what was the matter, and then we saw two squaws, creeping through the brush and out of sight as fast as they could go. Old Brindy wasn't going to let any "Injuns" have the strawberries of his folks.

What did we wear in those days? I guess we wore just about all there was to be found to wear, kitchen stove an' everything. It was worse 'n the hats the women wear now. Hoops and petticoats, an' corset covers an' corsets—great big heavy stiff things—I don' know how we managed so many clothes.

There was a fleshy lady living down on the Luckiamute that got caught in a hole in the river on her pony. The Luckiamute was always a mighty treacherous stream. Every time there was a freshet the current would change, so one never knew just where to ford the stream. This lady was with a party and they were all horseback. She was on a little pony, and she was kinda big and fat. The pony stepped in a hole, and with her weight on it, it couldn't get out. The lady had hoops on, and when the men went to help her, her hoops caught on the curved under horn of the side saddle. They tried to get the hoops out and in doing so twisted them, and there she was. The pony couldn't budge and they couldn't get her off, and the pony couldn't get out of the hole as long as she was on its back, she was so heavy. Finally they gave a big tug at the hoops and got 'em loose, an' then they managed to lift her up and hold her till the pony struggled out, an' then they dropped her in the saddle and she rode the pony on across—an' was she "red in the face."

THE BLUE BUCKET MINE

Tradition Bearer: William Harry Hembree

Source: Sherbert, Andrew C. "Interview of William Harry Hembree." *American Life Histories: Manuscripts from the Federal Writers' Project, 1936–1940.* Manuscript Division, Library of Congress. 12 October 2005. http://memory.loc.gov/ammem/wpaintro/wpahome.html.

Date: 1938

Original Source: Oregon

National Origin: European American

The very skillful narrator includes a number of validating devices designed to encourage acceptance of his story, such as his experience in the mining profession, his long residence in the area, and his use of the names of participants in the events. The following narrative would be best classified as a **personal legend** that concludes with a **personal experience narrative**. Such hybrid **genres** are common in oral tradition.

I was born in Monmouth, Polk County, Oregon, October 7, 1864, and was christened William Harry Hembree. My father's name was Houston Hembree. He was named for the illustrious Sam Houston and was born in Texas, though his family later moved to Missouri. My mother's name was Amanda Bowman and she was born in Iowa, coming to Oregon in 1848.

My father left Missouri for Oregon in one of the first emigrant trains of the great migration of the 1840's arriving in the Willamette Valley sometime in 1843. The train that my father came to Oregon with is said to have been the first "wheels" ever to make the entire journey from the east to the Dalles Mountains.

The wagon train of which my father and his kinfolks were members was more fortunate than the parties which followed the old Oregon Trail in the years immediately after. The Indians did not trouble the earlier emigrants, were friendly in fact, according to accounts given me by my father. It was not until the later emigrants came through that the Indians began to attack travelers— in 1844, 1845, and thereafter. Father's train arrived at The Dalles with exactly the same number of members as it had when it left Missouri.

In between other activities, even as a young man I was interested in gold mining. I have prospected in the past 50 years in almost every section of Oregon where gold had been, or appeared that it might be, found. I have panned every river and creek in the state where I thought there was a remote possibility of making worthwhile findings. In recent years I have operated small mines with more or less success. I am at present beginning the operation of a mine in Clackamas County, near the Marion County line. The sample essay looks good, and in spite of many former disappointments in similar enterprises, I have every hope that this one will turn out prosperously. However, if it doesn't, I shall promptly find another likely-looking hole-in-the-ground, and with a true prospector's unquenchable optimism, my hopes will doubtless rise again.

Perhaps the most widely publicized Oregon gold mine, if there ever was such a mine, is the famous "Blue Bucket." I have been erroneously credited with knowing a great deal about this mysterious, lost mine. As a matter of fact, in common with many other persons, I have been tremendously interested in the historic Blue Bucket; have gathered a considerable amount of data concerning it; and have journeyed to the region where it was supposed to have been located. I might even go so far as to say that I am satisfied in my own mind that I have been to within a few furlongs of the actual spot where it was. However, until the elusive Blue Bucket is actually and indisputably rediscovered, one man's story is as good as another's. Here's mine:

The Blue Bucket mine got its name from the fact that a wagon train, which is supposed to have stumbled onto the rich gold deposit, was made up of a string of wagons, the bodies of which were painted blue. In those days wagons had no hub nuts to hold a wheel in place on the axle. Wheels were held on the axle by what was called a linchpin, which was merely a pin, or bolt, that slipped through a hole in the axle outside the hub of the wheel. Between the hub and pin was a washer, which rubbed on the hub. To prevent wear, it was necessary to constantly daub the axle, at the point of friction, with tar, which the immigrants carried in buckets that hung on a hook at the rear of the wagon. The tar buckets of this particular wagon train were also painted blue.

The train made a "dry camp" (no water in sight) one night on a meadow in a valley between two ridges of hills. Needing water for their horses, members of the train set out on foot, each in a different direction, to attempt to locate a small creek or pond nearby. Each carried one of the blue tar buckets, in which to carry water if any were found. One member came upon a wet, cozy spot, where it appeared water was near the surface of the ground. He dug down, using the bucket as a spade, and upon raising the bucket found it filled with wet dirt containing nuggets of gold. And that was how the Blue Bucket mine was discovered.

I was privileged once to see a diary said to have been kept by a man whose name, I believe, was Warren. The man was a member of the Blue Bucket train. In the diary he kept a day by day log of the train's progress. By a series of calculations, based upon the mileages and directions given in the diary, I was able to reach a position that must have been in the vicinity of the fabulous mine.

To further convince me that I actually did find the mine's exact location, in my search I one day stumbled onto a weathered portion of a wagon box, with unmistakable traces of blue paint still visible on its bleached boards. That the wagon box was of the wagon-train era was evidenced by the foot that it was built like a scow, or flat boat, and was caulked with rags, fragments of which were still intact. Emigrant wagons were constructed in such manner to permit them to ford streams handily without damaging their contents.

Well, there's my story of the Blue Bucket mine. Many think the mine never existed. I think it did, however, I realize that my story would carry far more conviction were I able to exhibit a few buckets of gold taken from it—regardless the color of the buckets.

Heroes, Heroines, Tricksters, and Fools

THE CHILDREN OF THE DOG

Tradition Bearer: Unavailable

Source: Boas, Franz. "Traditions of the Ts'ets'ā´ut II." *Journal of American Folklore* 10 (1897): 37–39.

Date: 1894–1895

Original Source: Ts'ets'ā´ut

National Origin: Native American

Just as other regions of the United States have their narratives of shape-shifting witch wives, the Native American Northwest has this very widely spread tale of the husband and his offspring who shape-shift between human and animal forms. This **tale type** in which the wife is deceived into marrying a dog differs from others in this region where the union between a human wife and dog husband were voluntary. In the former case, the spouses are victims. In the voluntary unions, the human partner in particular is conceived of as a marginal, though often powerful, violator of cultural norms.

Once upon a time there was a woman who went every night hunting porcupines. During the daytime she hunted marmots. While out on the mountains she built a shelter of branches. One night, when she had gone to sleep, a young man entered her hut. He looked just like her lover, and she thought he had followed her.

In the morning she boiled some of the porcupine meat and both partook of it, and in the evening the young man went out to hunt porcupines. As soon as he had left the hut, he put on his blanket and appeared in his true shape. He was one of the dogs of the village. He crawled into the dens of the porcupines and caught a great number. Then he took off his blanket and reappeared in the shape of a man.

For three nights he stayed with the woman. During the daytime he went hunting marmots, and he never went out without bringing back a vast amount of game. Then he ate of the food that the woman had cooked and they went to bed. In the third night he arose about midnight. He had assumed his true shape, and ate the meat and gnawed the bones of the marmots and of the porcupines.

The woman awoke by the noise and saw a large dog eating their provisions. She turned to the man, intending to awake him, but there was nobody to be seen. Then she took a club and killed the dog.

Early in the morning she made a bundle of the remaining dried meat and returned to her village. She did not tell any one of what had happened. But soon she felt that she was with child, and when this came to be known nobody knew who had been her lover. After two months she was about to be confined. The women of the village assembled to assist her, but what was their terror when she gave birth first to two male dogs, then to a female dog! They all fled, even her mother. Only her brother's sister remained with her. The women told the people what had happened, and all the inhabitants of the village resolved to desert her. They packed their belongings and left the place. Only the young woman and her pups remained.

They grew up rapidly. Every day their mother went gathering food for them. As soon as she left the hut, the pups took off their skins, and played about in the shape of children. They had nice, light skins. When they saw their mother approaching, they put on their skins, resumed the shape of dogs, and lay in the ashes of the fireplace.

One day their mother did not go very far. She heard voices of children near her hut. They seemed to be playing and singing. Cautiously she approached the hut, walking noiselessly over the snow; but the children had seen her coming, and put on their blankets before she was able to come near.

On the following day she went up the mountains, and there she pushed her staff into the ground and hung her blanket of marmot skins over it. Again she approached the hut cautiously. When she came near, she saw two boys and one girl playing around. The latter went to look from time to time, and returned on seeing the staff that was covered with the blanket.

She said to her brothers: "Mother is still out gathering wood."

Then the mother jumped into the hut. On one side of the fireplace were two dog-skins; on the other there was one. She took the first two, and threw them into the fire. Before she was able to take the last, the girl had run into the house, put it on, and was transformed into a dog. Then the boys sat down in a corner of the house, crying for their skins. Their mother gave them blankets made of marmot skins. She made garments and snow-shoes, bows and arrows, and the boys began hunting squirrels. When they came to be larger they hunted larger animals, and the bitch accompanied them. She was a very good hunter. They had such a vast supply of game that they did not know what to do with it. Their house was quite filled with supplies.

The people, however, who had left the woman were unsuccessful in hunting, and were almost starving. They returned to their old hunting-ground, and were surprised to find the woman still alive, and to see the two young men.

One day the two hunters went out to hunt mountain goats. Their dog accompanied them. Then a goat attacked the dog, gored it, and threw it down the side of the mountain.

Later on the two young men married women of the tribe.

Once upon a time they went hunting, accompanied by seven men. They hunted mountain goats near the sources of Tcunaq River. They killed a whole herd. Only one kid escaped by climbing a high, precipitous rock. There it stood, crying pitifully. The men of the party wanted to return, but the two brothers were so eager to kill the poor kid that they began the dangerous ascent of the steep rock. They had no pity. Then the rock began to grow and carried them up so high that there was no possibility of return. They succeeded in reaching a cleft. There they sat close together warming each other, but after three days one of the brothers died.

On the following day the men of the tribe went to the cliff and shouted to the brothers, but there was no reply. The other one had died also. When they turned away to rejoin their tribe, on looking at the rock they saw blood flowing down from the place where the brothers had died, and also from the retreat of the kid. The blood may be seen on the rock up to this day.

QAUAXSAQSSUQ

Tradition Bearer: Unavailable

Source: Kroeber, A. L. "Tales of the Smith Sound Eskimo." *Journal of American Folklore* 12 (1899): 178.

Date: 1897–1898

Original Source: Eskimo

National Origin: Native American

Although certain elements of the following **legend** may sound fantastic (the killing of three large bears with only a knife, for example), most of the following is consistent with the shaman in Eskimo culture. Often the shaman is a misfit or an outsider personality, with a physical or mental aberration that sets him or her off from the rest of the group. An additional accuracy is that Eskimos did traditionally use assassination as a way of punishing crime or controlling deviance.

Qauaxsaqssuq was a boy that was maltreated by all. In the day-time his mother hid him in the beds, but at night she had to take him out. Then he slept either in the doorway or on the roof, over the lamp-hole, in order to get at least a little warmth. He was generally lifted and carried by the nostrils, the crooked fingers being inserted in them. He always remained small, but his feet grew very large.

He was a great angakoq (shaman), and was very strong. Finally he grew tired of the bad treatment he received, and showed his strength, after which, though he never killed any one, he was much dreaded and feared.

Once he was indoors, lying on the bed without any boots on, when a man arrived inquiring for him. "Qauaxsaqssuq has gone into the house over there, and is inside," he was told.

Then the man called to Qauaxsaqssuq from outdoors, "Qauaxsaqssuq! Three large bears have come over from the land, and are now on the ice. Come out!"

"Yes," said Qauaxsaqssuq, and hastened to dress and put on his boots. Then he came out and saw the three bears. Holding only a knife in his hand, he ran after them. He had no dogs to harry the bears and bring them to bay, but he soon caught up with them. He first seized the old one and twisted off its head, so that it was immediately dead. Then he took the cubs and knocked their heads together, and twisted their necks until they were dead. Then he took them up, the old one on one side, the cubs on the other, and carried them home. He brought the three bears to the assembled people, who proceeded to cut them up, put them in pots, cook them, and eat them.

Qauaxsaqssuq was immensely strong, and what was heavy for others was very light for him. In spite of his small size, he could easily lift the largest rocks. He had enemies, who, however, were afraid to do anything against him openly. So once, when he went away to Qavanganiq, where he had a kayak, they secretly cut a hole in the skin-covering of his kayak. When Qauaxsaqssuq got into his boat, and out into the water, the boat began to fill with water, and thus it was that Qauaxsaqssuq drowned.

THE GIANT WOMEN

Variant A

Tradition Bearer: Jim Buchanan

Source: Frachtenberg, Leo J. Pages 72–78 in *Coos Texts*. Columbia University Contributions to Anthropology 1. New York: Columbia University Press, 1913.

Date: 1909

Original Source: Coos

National Origin: Native American

On the Northwest Coast, the Native American equivalent of the "boogeyman" is the Cannibal Giantess. The foreboding, jungle-like forests in the region have encouraged the development of narratives of the Sasquatch, the Cannibal Giantess, and other traditional monsters. The following supernatural **legends** of the Giantess are told in the archaic style. Variants B and C have been modified from the original English translations to bring them closer to contemporary usage.

The Giantess was all the time enslaving people. Whenever she saw a man, she would thus say to him: "Come here, my husband!" The people got tired of it when they heard about it. Whenever a man died, she would carry away the things that were put in his grave. Such was the custom of the Giantess. Whenever children played, she would go there amongst them. She would play a while, and would then pick out the children that had valuables around their necks. When she was about ready to go home, she would take hold of a boy and put him into a basket.

With this as her pack, she would run. He (the boy) could not get out. With him she went back, and brought him home there. She had there a hole as a door. In the mornings they two usually slept, in the evenings they would sit up. Such was the custom of the Giantesses.

One younger brother remained. He was dreaming continually. He was dreaming thus: "You shall pull the door, which is a bunch of hard wood. The hard wood is amongst brick-weed. If you arrive there and pull the door, it will come open."

In the evenings they catch clams. They bring them home and eat them. Thus one will say to a boy: "What a surprisingly fat clam, poor boy!" She will give it to him. The clam is full of sand; still she will give it to him. The child will not eat it.

She will take it to him. "Come close here, you poor boy!" Thus a Giantess will say to him. He will dodge. "Let me feel of you!"

In his dream he saw his younger sister. Something was hanging from her ear. She had put her heart there. His sister was twisted to one side as he looked at her.

Thus the sister said: "My heart is caused to be there, that's the thing you are looking at. They two go to bed with their heads resting against each other. In the daytime they two sleep. They two warm themselves. At the edge of the fire they two warm themselves." Thus the sister said, "They two always talk thus: '(Come) close here, let me feel of you!' Thus the Giant women talk.'" Thus the child girl spoke to him.

Now, indeed, the child (boy) said to his father, "Let me go there!" Indeed, he went there.

He arrived there, and saw the bunch of hard wood. It was amongst brick-weeds. When he saw it, he looked around in all directions. He was thinking thus: "My dream was just like this. I saw it thus." Indeed, he pulled the bunch of hard wood. He pulled it in all ways. He pulled it once. Indeed, it was a door. He looked down, and saw his younger brother.

"This is I, O elder brother! Nothing has happened to me as yet." Thus he informed his elder brother.

He looked at him from above. "What is the Giantess doing?"

Thus said the younger brother. "There are two of them, indeed."

"What are they two doing?"

"They two are sleeping. My sister's heart is hanging from her ear." Thus he said to his elder brother.

"You must take care of yourself," said his elder brother. "I am going home. There is no way to go down. I will inform my father, and will bring several ladders." Thus the younger brother was talking.

Again he shut the door there. "We will arrive in two days." Thus he said.

He went home again. Thus he was relating: "I saw my younger brother. I opened the door." Thus he said when he returned.

The father said, "Indeed, it is so." They gathered pitch. Everybody was gathering that thing. Two days they were gathering that pitch.

Thus the father said: "Now we will go there." They took along a ladder. Indeed, they arrived there. Indeed, he again opened the door. He saw his child below. "Father, I am still well." Thus spoke his child. "What are they two doing?"

"They are sleeping, indeed." Thus his child made it known to him. He put down the ladder, and went down on it. The children were brought up.

Indeed, they two were asleep with their heads resting against each other. They quickly gathered the clothes, the money, and the bows. They quickly put pitch below. Clear around they put the pitch. Their two dresses were full of pitch. They did not know it. They were sound asleep. Their hair was tied together. They two did not know it. Now they finished.

Now the people lighted the pitch everywhere. Their house was full of pitch. It began to blaze everywhere. So then the people went out. The door was shut again, and was made heavy by means of big stones. The people were standing there at the top of the door. The inside part of their entire house began to burn. Their two dresses began to burn. One Giantess jumped up when it began to burn. "Why do you hold me back?"

"You, indeed, are fighting with me. Let me free!" As they were pulling each other, they came apart. One jumped towards the door. She jumped upwards. She bumped against the door as she jumped.

Now the other one jumped upwards. "Why does it not come open as I go out?" Five times she jumped up. Still she could not go out. Both jumped up five times. The inside part burned entirely. They were watching the door. At the sixth time her heart went out. Her heart was beaten to pieces. Also the heart of the other one was beaten to pieces. Thus they said to them: "You shall be nothing. The last generation shall see you. You shall do nothing to people."

The men took the children home. One child's heart was hanging on her ear. The boy was the only one who was all right.

Thus the father was talking: "Suppose the thing that is hanging on the ear were cut off?" Indeed, it was cut off.

No sooner was it cut off, than the child died. "It would have been good if it had not been cut off." Thus they were saying.

Now here it ends. Thus they tell the story about the Giant women.

Variant B

She was all the time stealing people. Whenever she found a person, she would take him home. No one knew whither she carried them. This became the topic of their conversation.

One morning many young men from the village came together. One of them said, "Suppose, we go there! You shall hide there at such a distance, while I will do the same." No one knew how many men they were. They went there; and, indeed, they were hidden everywhere, one by one.

One came there. Indeed, he saw the Giantess going down into the water. The young man held a knife. The young man wore a buckskin shirt.

The Giantess smiled as she was coming. "Halloo, my husband! Come! We two will go home." Thus she said to the young man.

"Not so." Thus answered the young man. "Bring your money!"

"Not so, my husband! Only then shall you have it, when we get home." Thus spoke the Giantess.

"I, too, am a bad man. Do you see this knife?" Thus spoke the young man. He took off his shirt. He spread the shirt out on the ground. "This you shall fill with your money."

Indeed, the Giantess went and brought the money. She put it there in the shirt. "Come now, my husband! We two will go home. Only then shall you, indeed, have my money." Thus the Giantess spoke.

Five times she went for her money. "Now come, my husband!" The young man examined it and tried the weight.

As he lifted the shirt, it was full. "This ought to be the right weight." Thus the young man was thinking.

"Come now, my husband! We two will go home." Thus she said to him.

"Go again, bring your money!" Indeed, she went.

The young man ran away. He carried the money and ran. He already saw the Giantess come. The young man was out of breath, and jumped to one side. Now another man ran from there and carried the money.

The Giantess came in a hurry. "Come, my husband!" The young man ran, and then jumped aside.

Now another person ran from there. He carried the money.

"Come, my husband!" Thus said the Giantess. Thus they ended it. The last one ran with it.

She, too, the Giantess, ran. She almost overtook him. "Come, my husband!"

The Giantess came to a village. "Which one is my husband?" Thus spoke the Giantess. She was beaten. Many persons were clubbing her. They hit her with a knife. But nothing happened to the Giantess. They were hitting her with sticks. "What shall we do if we don't kill her?" Thus they were thinking.

Now, the Giantess began to pull them to and fro. She pulled them in the direction of her home. She dragged them all. Indeed, she dragged all the people towards her.

There lived one old woman. She had a granddaughter. Thus she said to her: "Where is she taking them?" Thus she asked her granddaughter.

"She is already far away." Thus spoke her granddaughter.

"Take me there, granddaughter. I know where her vulnerable spot is. Only give me a knife, granddaughter. We two will go there." Indeed, they two went there, she and her granddaughter.

"Come here, O elder sister! You shall help me." Thus spoke the Giantess.

"Is that you, indeed, O cousin?"

Thus that old woman spoke: "Where is her foot?" Thus that old woman spoke. "You put my hand there." The old woman was blind. Indeed, they put it there to her foot. The old woman seized the knife. She felt for her foot, and began to cut her leg. The Giantess fell. The dear old lady killed the Giantess.

Her body was spread out. It was entirely made up of bones. The bones were hard when they examined them. This was the reason why they could not kill her. No matter how long they would shoot arrows at her, they would strike there against her bones. They also hit her with a knife, and likewise they could not kill her. However, that dear old lady killed her. That old woman knew her.

Then they all went to get her money, and they divided among themselves the money of the Giantess. They were not going to do anything, when they should possess the clothes of the Giantess.

Thus the story is being told. Now there it ends.

Variant C

People were living on a small place. Some old woman had five children and two little grandsons. One morning they went away severally. The grandsons remained alone. In the evenings she taught the grandsons to dance. Indeed, the two children were dancing. Thus that old woman was teaching them a dance. Every evening she taught them a dance. One evening the two children were dancing. The fire was burning, the house was full of pitch. The house was continually burning.

One evening the door just opened slowly. "Come, grandsons, come here behind my back! You two lie down!" There the old woman covered them with blankets.

"Come in, my sisters!" Thus spoke the old lady.

Indeed, they entered. Their faces were painted in different ways. Thus these two entered. They two entered with a dance. They two danced with their faces turned away from the fire. Thus the old woman spoke: "You dance well, my sisters." She put more wood on the fire. "You two dance somewhat closer to the fire." Thus spoke the old woman.

Thus said one Giantess: "Not there, a little faster." The dear old lady heard as the Giantess spoke. Their two dresses were caused to melt. Made of pitch were the dresses of the two Giant Women.

"You two dance still closer to the fire." Thus spoke the old woman. The old woman was splitting pitch-wood. Their two dresses began to melt.

She lighted them with split pitch-wood. She applied it blazing to the dresses. Thus she did to both (of them). Their two dresses were burning. They burned for a long time, and the two Giant Women did not know it. Then they two examined themselves.

They flew outside. The old woman was looking at them as they were running about in the woods. They two went back to the place whence they came. That old woman looked on as they two disappeared.

The next day she examined her grandsons. To her surprise, both were dead when she lifted their two blankets.

The children of that old woman came back. "The Giant Women scared us." Thus the old woman related. "They killed all my grandsons when I covered them with blankets."

Now they searched there in the direction where these had gone. Indeed, they went there. Indeed, they found their house. One Giantess lay dead at a little distance from the door, while the other one had fallen at the very door. They lay dead. One man entered inside. Their money was seen as it was hanging. It was gathered up and taken home. Their house was set afire. They became rich when they came into possession of the money the Giant Women.

Thus the story of the Giant Women is being told. Here it ends.

THE GIRLS WHO MARRIED STARS

Tradition Bearer: Unavailable

Source: Boas, Franz. "Traditions of the Ts'ets'āʹut II." *Journal of American Folklore* 10 (1897): 39–42.

Date: 1894–1895

Original Source: Ts'ets'āʹut

National Origin: Native American

Tale of women who marry star husbands are found literally across Native North America, as are other transports to and transformations of the heavens (in this collection, see for example, the Wichita "The Two Boys Who Slew the Monsters and Became Stars," Vol. III, p. 212). The first segment of the following tale falls into the narrative category that folklorist Stith Thompson has labeled "Star Husband Type I: The Wish to Marry a Star." The girls' subsequent desertion of their wished-for husbands, their rejection of other suitors, and their death, suggests that the tale carries a subtext concerning being content with one's lot in life.

There were two sisters who were playing in front of their house. They made a small hut and lay down in it to sleep. During the night they awoke, and saw the stars in the sky.

One of the sisters said: "Do you see that white star? I will have him for my husband. You take that red star." They joked and laughed on this proposition, and finally went to sleep again. While they were sleeping two men entered their hut. One of them wore a white blanket, the other wore a red blanket. The latter married the elder sister, while the former took the younger for his wife. They removed them from the house into the sky. They were the two stars of whom the girls had been speaking.

When the sisters awoke and saw the strange men by their sides, they did not know where they were. On the following morning their mother called them to come to breakfast. When she did not receive an answer, she grew angry and went to call the girls. Then she saw that they had disappeared. During the night a boy had heard how the girls had been talking about the stars, and thus the people were led to suppose that the stars had abducted the girls. The stars go out every night with bow and arrows hunting caribou. Then they look through the holes in the sky and see what is going on on earth.

The two stars who had married the girls also went out every night, and brought home many caribou. The young women skinned and carved them. They made gloves, shoes, and dresses from the skins. They cut long thongs from the skins of others, cutting spirally around their bodies. They hid the clothing and the thongs carefully from their husbands.

There was no water, no cloud, and no rain in the sky, and they were always suffering thirst. They had nothing to eat but meat. Therefore they longed to return to their own country. When they had prepared a sufficient number of thongs and of cloths they made ready to escape.

One day, when their husbands had started on a long hunting expedition, they went to the hole in the sky. They tied stones to one end of a thong and let it down towards the earth. When one thong was paid out they tied a new one to the end of the first, and thus they continued from morning to night. The one woman brought the cloths and the thongs from their hiding-place, while the other let them down.

Finally, after four days, they felt the rope striking the ground. They could not see the earth because it was hidden by smoke. They shook the thong and it fell a little farther, but finally it seemed to have reached the ground. At least they felt that it was held by something. Now they tied two pairs of sticks together, one being on each side of the rope. They put on four suits of clothing, four pairs of shoes, and four pairs of gloves. The elder sister stepped on one pair of sticks and they began to glide down, the sticks acting as a brake. The rope swung to and fro, and the sister who had remained behind gradually lost sight of her. Finally the young woman reached the end of the rope and found herself on the top of a tall tree. Her clothing and her gloves were almost worn through by friction. Then she shook the rope, and upon this signal her sister began to slide down in the same manner.

She came down very much quicker, because her sister was holding the end of the rope. Looking upward, she beheld a small dot in the air. It was coming nearer and increased in size. Soon she recognized her sister, who finally reached the top of the tree. There they were on the top of a tall spruce-tree, and there was no way of getting down. They broke off some branches, and made a bed in the tree. The elder sister, before starting, had tied an additional piece of thong around her waist, thinking that she might use it in case the long rope should not have reached the ground. She untied it and fastened it on to the long rope, but still it was not long enough.

After a while, the young women saw a number of men passing the foot of the tree. They were armed with bows and arrows, and were on snowshoes. They recognized the wolf, the bear, and many other animals. They called to them, asking them to help them down, but they passed by without paying attention to their entreaties.

The next morning they saw another man approaching the tree. They recognized the fisher. They called him, and he at once climbed the tree. The young women asked him to carry them down, but he demanded that they should first marry him.

The elder one said "I will do so, but first carry me down." The fisher finally agreed and carried her down. When they arrived at the foot of the tree, she demanded from him that he should first carry down her youngest sister. Reluctantly he was compelled to do so. Then he demanded from the youngest sister that she should marry him.

She said: "I will do so, but carry me down first." He took her down. When he insisted upon his former demand, the elder sister said: "We are almost starved; first bring us some food." He went away and soon returned, carrying a bear that he had killed. During his absence the young women had lighted a fire. He wanted to roast the bear meat, but they said they wished to eat it boiled. Then the fisher made a basket of bark, and placed stones into the fire, which he intended to use to boil water in the basket. Meanwhile the young women had hidden a few pieces of meat under their blankets, and now they pretended to go to fetch water in which to boil the meat. As soon as they were out of sight they ran away down the mountains. After a while the eldest sister flung a piece of meat at a tree, asking it to whistle. They went on, and again she threw a piece of meat at a tree, asking it to talk. In this manner she continued to give meat to all the trees.

When the young women did not return, the fisher followed them to the brook, where they had gone to fetch water. He discovered their tracks, and saw that they had escaped. He pursued them. Soon he came to the tree, which they had asked to whistle. It did so when the fisher went past. Then he thought they were on the tree, climbed it, and searched for them. When he did not find them, he continued his pursuit. He came to the second tree, which spoke when he went past. Again he thought the young women might be on the tree. He climbed up, but did not find them. Thus he lost so much time that they made good their escape.

Towards evening they reached a deep canon. They walked along its edge, and soon they were discovered by the grizzly bear that was residing here. He wanted to marry them, and they did not dare to refuse.

But they said: "First go and bring us something to eat. We are almost starving." While the bear was away hunting, the girls built a platform over the steep precipice of the canon. It overhung the abyss, and was held in place by two ropes, which were tied to a tree that grew near the edges of the canon. Its outer edge was supported by two slanting poles, which leaned against a ledge a short distance down the precipice. When the bear came back, he found them apparently asleep on this platform.

He did not bring any meat; he had only roots and berries. The young women said that they could not eat that kind of food, and demanded that he should go hunting again. It had grown dark, however, and the bear proposed to go out on the following morning. They lay down on the platform, and the young women induced the bear to lie near the edge, while they lay down near the tree to which the platform was tied. They kept away from the bear, promising to marry him after he should have obtained food for them. Early in the morning, when the grizzly bear was fast asleep, they arose without disturbing him, cut the ties with which the platform was fastened to the tree, and it tipped over, casting the bear into the abyss.

The young women traveled on, and for a whole month they did not fall in with a soul. Then, one day, they discovered tracks of snowshoes, and soon they found the hut of a woman who had given birth to a child. They entered, and recognized one of their friends. They stayed with her for a short time, and when the young mother was ready to return to the village, they sent her on in order to inform their relatives of their return. She went to the mother of the two lost girls, and told her that they were waiting in the woods, but she would not believe the news. The young mother returned to her friends and told them that their mother would not believe that they had come back.

Then they gave her as a token a skin hat that was decorated with stars. She took it to the village and showed it to the mother of the two young women. Then she began to think that there might be some truth in the report, and went out to look. There she saw and recognized her daughters. At that time all the men were out hunting. The women on hearing of the return of the two lost girls went out to see them, and they told of their adventures. Then they climbed two trees, tied their skin belts to the branches, and hanged themselves.

HUNTING EXPLOITS OF THE GOD K'MUKAMTCH

Tradition Bearer: Unavailable

Source: Gatschet, Albert S. "Oregonian Folklore." *Journal of American Folklore* 4 (1891): 140–41.

Date: 1891

Original Source: Modoc

National Origin: Native American

The Modocs were hunters and gatherers that inhabited southern Oregon. They lived in small bands and housed themselves in wickiups, dwellings shaped like an inverted bowl. As is apparent from the following narrative, the creator figure of their myths, K'mukamtch, exhibited the common flaws and impulsive nature of the **trickster** at his most inept.

After creating the world, K'mukamtch took a stroll on the surface of the earth, and perceived five lynxes sitting on trees. Being dressed in an old rabbit-fur robe pierced with holes, he tore it to pieces and threw it away, exclaiming: "If I kill the five lynxes around me, I shall have a better fur-cover than that one."

He picked up stones, but when he threw one, he missed his aim and one of the lynxes climbed down the tree and ran away. Sorrowfully he said, "I won't get a good mantle this time!"

Then he threw a stone at another lynx, and, missing it, the animal likewise jumped down and disappeared. "Now my fur-robe will become rather small!"

The three remaining lynxes sat on their trees and scoffed at the unsuccessful deity. This tickled him. He threw another stone and missed again; another and another, all with the same result, and when the last one of the beasts had scampered off, K'mukamtch ejaculated, "Now the skin will not even cover my back!" And while singing, he went to pick up the pieces of his old fur-cover, which he had torn up, pinned them together with wood-splinters, put it around his body, and continued his way.

Having gone to a short distance, he found an antelope suffering from the toothache, and stretched out on a clearing in the woods. He spread his pieced-up mantle over the animal, and began to kick at it to make it bloodshot. He looked around for a stone-knife to skin it with, but after having released it of his hold the antelope ran away behind his back.

He turned around, saw it running, and said: "My antelope looks exactly like this one!" The animal then ran past him, and when he saw his own mantle lying on the back of the antelope he cried. "Stop! Stop! The Indians will laugh at you when they see that you are wrapped in that miserable old rabbit-skin of mine."

THE FIVE GRIZZLY BEARS

Tradition Bearer: Jim Buchanan

Source: Frachtenberg, Leo J. Pages 92–105 in *Coos Texts*. Columbia University Contributions to Anthropology 1. New York: Columbia University Press, 1913.

Date: 1909

Original Source: Coos

National Origin: Native American

In spite of the superior strength of the Grizzly Bears and the youngest Grizzly brother's power of supernatural sight, human cleverness triumphs. The death of the youngest Grizzly is very much like the death of the Cannibal Giantess in the Coos tale "The Giant Women" (p. 55). The final declaration by the old woman that foretells the nature of all descendants of the Grizzly Brothers gives this narrative the quality of **myth**.

They lived there together. They were five brothers. No man ever could pass by there. Whenever they saw any one pass there, they killed him right away. Even if two persons passed by, still they would kill them.

A little farther away many people were living. Everywhere they were talking about it. People were afraid of the brothers. They had killed too many people. So thus said the chief of the people who lived farther away: "How would it be if we should arrange some games?" Thus spoke their chief. "They may or may not come here to take part in the games."

Now, verily they said, "It will surely be good when people will play. Different people will play here." So, indeed, they prepared the ground for the games. A stone wall was put up high. On top of it a crosspiece was placed. "If we bring up anyone here, and if the head goes over this cross-piece, then at the same time we shall hit the head." Over there people were going to play. And also here at the stone wall, close to the ocean, people were going to play. The wall was put up in the ocean. Then their chief thought. "This is a good plan."

Then, verily, different people came to play there. Then they tried it. "Please, you try it!" Thus one was thinking. A rope was placed around his head. One person was standing below. He was going to watch the players. Now, indeed, he ran from above. His neck was fastened with a rope. So he came to the man who was standing below. Thus he said: "I was almost out of breath as I was running from above."

Thus he said: "You shall run up again."

Then he fixed the rope. "Here on this side make a knot." Indeed, he had it so. Indeed, he ran upwards. Someone was pulling him from above; nevertheless it seemed as if he was running up by himself. Lucky money was going to be their stake. Whenever the lucky money was rolled down, he the player would then run down. He would desire to overtake it, to take hold of it. Their stake would fall into the ocean, and someone would go and get it.

Now, the five brothers (the Grizzly Bears) heard about it. On this side one man was living. Thus the elder brother said, "How would it be if I should go there? I should see the people play." Thus he was thinking. Indeed, he went there.

Indeed, he came there to the man who lived there. He asked him, "What are they doing?"

Thus he spoke. "People are playing. It will be good, indeed, if you get there. You must go there quickly." Thus he spoke: "Money is their stake. They play for it. No one can overtake it and seize it. If one takes hold of it, it belongs to him. So their chief said. "Now, indeed, he saw it when he arrived there. Suddenly Black Bear ran up. Thus he was thinking. "Won't I be able to run up?" Thus he was thinking: "Like some old woman that one is running up there."

Now Raccoon ran up. He saw, as they fixed him, as they put a rope around his neck.

Thus one said to Raccoon, "When you are pulled from above, then you shall turn the knot around your cheek, and you shall run up." Now, surely it was thus. It seemed as if he was really running, but he was pulled up from above. Now the lucky stake was let down. The person who arrived there looked at it. He ran down at the same time that the stake was let down. The lucky money fell into the water. One man stood there. He watched it whenever it fell into the water. He always went to get it.

Grizzly Bear looked on as people were thus playing. High up different people were playing. Thus someone said to Grizzly Bear, "It's your turn now. You will see people playing up above. Different people are playing there. You will see them." Indeed, so he told him, "I will put a rope around your neck."

Thus answered Grizzly Bear. "Not so, I will climb up without a rope."

"Certainly, climb up."

He ran. He went a little way up and slid down again. Grizzly Bear looked up. Thus he said: "All right! Put a rope around my neck." Now, indeed, he placed a rope around his neck. He made a knot on the back. Indeed, he was drawn up from above. He arrived there at the cross-piece. They struck his neck. It seems he did not look out, and was killed. He was rolled aside from where the people were playing.

The next day another Grizzly Bear came. "What may be the reason why he does not come back?" Thus he said to his younger brother. "I, too, will go there."

Indeed, he went, and he came to the man who was living there. Thus Grizzly Bear spoke: "Have you seen my elder brother?"

"Here are the remnants of his meal, behold, look at them!"

Grizzly Bear believed it. "Where did he go?"

"There where people are playing. Different people are playing there. They are playing with lucky money. You shall go there. Your elder brother may be there among them." Thus he spoke to him.

Indeed, he went, and he arrived there. Indeed, to his surprise, he saw the people play. Thus he was thinking. "Won't I be able to run up?" Thus he was thinking. "Like an old woman that one there is running up."

"Do you want to play? Your elder brother may be high up. They are playing there. He may be there among them. Different people are playing there." Thus one said to him. Raccoon ran up. The stake was let down, and he followed it. The stake fell into the water. Someone went after it, and brought up the lucky stake. Grizzly Bear looked at it.

"Now, it's your turn, Grizzly Bear." Thus one said to him. Indeed, he now ran up. He did not care. He only wanted to climb up. Indeed, one put the rope around his neck. Grizzly Bear said nothing. The knot was tied on the back. He came very near getting on top. He was out of breath. His head came to the cross-piece. His neck was struck, and he was killed. He was rolled aside.

"What may be the reason why he does not come back? I will follow him." Thus another Grizzly Bear said.

Indeed, he went, and came to the man who lived there. "Have you seen my elder brothers? Did they two pass by here?"

"Surely, they two ate here. Look, here are the remnants of their meal!"

"Where did they two go?" "There where they play. Different people play there. Your two brothers are among them."

Indeed, he went there; and, to his surprise, be saw the people play. Black Bear ran up. Thus Grizzly Bear thought. "Won't I be able to run up? Like an old woman, that one there is running up."

Indeed, he came there. Thus Grizzly Bear said: "Where are my brothers?" He was gradually getting mad.

Raccoon ran down from above. "People are playing above, there your two brothers may be playing. Do you want to climb up?"

It did not seem as if he cared very much. He just wanted to climb up quickly. Indeed, someone put the rope around his neck, and tied the knot on the back. Indeed, he was drawn up from above. He ran at the same time, while someone drew him up from above. His head came to the cross-piece. His head was hit, and he was killed. Thus they the Grizzly Bears were all killed. Thus they were coaxed.

The youngest brother was dreaming all the time. This was his dream: "Your brothers were simply killed." He was afraid if he should go there. Now he got ready, put his belt on, and then went. He came to the man who was living there.

Thus Grizzly Bear spoke: "Have you seen my brothers?"

"They used to eat here whenever they came here. Look! These are the remnants of their food; they all left their remnants here."

Indeed, he saw it. "People play there, perhaps they too play there. You will see them there if you get there." Indeed, he came there. He came there to the man who was watching, and to the people who were playing. Raccoon ran down.

He looked on. "Won't I be able to run down?"

Indeed, he came there and looked on for a long time. People were playing there. Then he spoke thus: "Where are my brothers?" Thus someone informed him. "Different people play above, they are there among them."

Thus someone said: "Do you want to climb up?"

"Indeed, I want to climb up there."

"Come, you shall certainly climb up." Indeed, he came there. Someone put a rope around his neck.

He took hold of the rope and took it off his neck. "I will run up without a rope." He ran. He climbed up quickly. When he had come halfway, he was out of breath. He could not hold on. Again he slid down from there. They looked at him from above. He heard as the people played above.

Thus someone said to him: "How will you climb up?" He was watched all the time. He became very much agitated.

He said thus: "All right! Put the rope around my neck." One tied a knot on his back. He did not want it that way.

"If I do it that way, then you will surely play."

He did not believe it. So Raccoon ran down. He looked at him, and, indeed, he had a knot on his back. Now Raccoon pretty nearly got on top. He began to slacken up a little bit, and turned the knot around. At the same time someone drew him up from above. "Do you see it?"

"Certainly, I see it." Thus spoke Grizzly Bear. Indeed, thus he spoke. "Put the rope around my neck." Indeed, a man made the knot on the back. Indeed, he ran up, while someone pulled him up from above. His head came near the cross-piece. He was looking out. His head was hit. He dodged as he was struck. Just the rope was hit. The rope came apart and rolled down below. It fell into the water when it rolled down.

"Indeed, my dream was true. My elder brothers were killed."

He swam out into the ocean. He ran away and swam far out. They could not follow him. He was seen as he swam. Thus he was thinking: "In which direction shall I go?" He began to swim towards the ocean. "Where shall I get ashore?" Thus he was thinking.

He was cold as he was swimming ashore. Indeed, he came ashore at the mouth of the river. One old woman was living there. Thus he thought: "I will go there." He came ashore crawling. He could not stand up. Now, indeed, he came to the old woman that lived there.

She recognized him when he got there. "Is that you, indeed, who arrived, grandson?" That old woman frightened him. "Don't you do anything, grandson." Thus spoke the old woman. "You are merely cold. You shall warm yourself here." She was going to kindle a fire. "You will get warm." Indeed, she kindled a big fire.

Grizzly Bear fell asleep right away, as soon as he got warm. Thus she said to him: "You sleep, and let me get some wood." She put big quantities of wood on the fire. At the same time she kindled it on the top. "Now you sleep, let me look for wood." Thus spoke the old woman.

Indeed, she took a small basket and began rapidly to look for pitch. She rapidly filled the small basket. She came back to her house, and put the pitch into a bowl. With red-hot gravel-stones she boiled the pitch.

The man who slept scented it. "What is this scent?" Thus spoke Grizzly Bear.

"It's only the wood which I caused to burn so very hard." Thus spoke that old woman. Grizzly Bear again fell sound asleep. He slept with his mouth wide open. The pitch was boiling. The old woman took the pot and poured the pitch into his mouth. Red-hot gravel she put into his mouth. Then old woman ran away into a corner and looked on from there.

Grizzly Bear got up and began to jump around. He was looking for that old woman; and when he saw her, he seized her. He bit and chewed her between his teeth. She came out from there, from his mouth. The woman was sitting between his teeth. She again came out from there.

Thus Grizzly Bear was thinking: "Thus I will kill the old woman." That old woman knew who he was, and Grizzly Bear knew the old woman. Grizzly Bear again seized that old woman. He was thinking thus: "I will now swallow her entirely." Indeed, he swallowed her entirely.

That old woman came out through the anus-hole. The old woman cut out his heart. Thus she got even with him. Then she came out through the anus-hole. That old woman looked on as he died. Now she had killed him. The old woman was thinking, "What shall I do with him?" Thus she thought.

Everyone came to know it when they had killed all the Bears. Everybody came to know it. Thus spoke the old woman: "You shall be nothing. The last generation shall see you." Thus spoke that old woman. "The last generation shall eat your meat. You shall be nothing. You will always be an article of food. Whenever you see someone, you will run away. Whenever you scent them the people, you will run far away." All this that dear old woman was saying.

Now here it ends. Thus people tell the story.

THE GIRL WHO MARRIED HER BROTHER

Tradition Bearer: Klamath Billie

Source: Farrand, Livingston, and Leo J. Frachtenberg. "Shasta and Athapascan Myths from Oregon." *Journal of American Folklore* 28 (1915): 212–14.

Date: 1900

Original Source: Shasta

National Origin: Native American

The following narrative suggests the various ways a family can be shattered through "meanness" as well as through incest. There are suggestions in the narrative that Anediwi'dowit is not simply a social problem to her family, but that she poses a supernatural threat as well. The intimidation of her mother and siblings and the fact that she has a single vulnerable spot on her body provide evidence that she has at least has power; she may even be a shaman.

A mother and her ten children were living together. The oldest was a girl, called Anediwi'dowit She was mean; and her mother had to hide from her the youngest child, a boy, called O'manuts.

Anediwi'dowit was wont to ask her mother, "Where is that child you bore some time ago?" to which her mother would reply, "Oh, I lost him long ago."

Every morning Anediwi'dowit saw her mother go down to the spring. She followed her, and noticed that the water was disturbed, as if someone had been swimming there.

One day Anediwi'dowit found a long hair in the water. She measured it with the hair of her other brothers, and found it to be too long. So she decided to learn whose hair it was. Every night she camped at the spring, until one morning she saw a strange man come down to bathe. Then she knew who had been disturbing the water, and to whom the hair belonged. It was O'manuts.

She fell in love with him, and decided to marry him. She went home and asked her mother to prepare some food for her, as she was going away. Her mother gave her food, and Anediwi'dowit asked, "Who wants to accompany me?"

The oldest brother said, "I."

"No," replied the girl, "not you." In a similar manner she refused to go with any of her other brothers. Finally she ran to the side of the house, put her hand there, and said, "This is the one I want to take along."

Then O'manuts came out from where he had been hidden all these years, and said, "All right! I'll go with you."

They traveled all day. When night came, Anediwi'dowit said, "Let us stop here!" So they stopped there, and the girl began to prepare the bed. O'manuts suspected what she wanted of him, but he said nothing. He only wished she might fall sound asleep, so as to be able to run away from her. When she was sound asleep, he put a log in his place and left her, returning to the house.

He ran home, and shouted, "Let all get ready to come with me!" They did so, and before departing cautioned everything in the house not to tell Anediwi'dowit where they had gone. But they omitted to tell Ashes.

Early in the morning Anediwi'dowit woke up and began to speak to the log, thinking it to be her husband; but soon she found out the deception, jumped up in anger, and cried, "I'll kill you!"

In the mean time O'manuts and his family had entered a basket and were drawn up to the sky. Anediwi'dowit came home, and inquired of everything in the house as to the whereabouts of her mother and brothers. No one would tell. Finally she asked Ashes, and was told that they had gone up to the sky.

She looked up, and saw her family halfway up the sky. She began to weep, and called for them repeatedly to come down. But O'manuts had told them not to look back, no matter how often she might call. Soon, however, the mother looked back, and the basket began to fall. Anediwi'dowit was glad when she saw the basket coming down. She made a big fire, intending to kill her family as soon as the basket should fall into it. The basket came down; but, when O'manuts hit the ground, he flew right up and floated away. Anediwi'dowit thought she had killed them all, and was very glad.

After a while O'manuts came down on the ocean beach, where two Sea-Gull girls found him. At first the girls were afraid of him; but he assured them, saying, "Don't be afraid of me! Touch me, wash me, and you will find that I am all right!" The girls did as directed, and O'manuts married them. After a while his wives became pregnant and gave birth to a boy and girl.

As soon as the children grew up, O'manuts gave them a bow and arrow, and taught them how to shoot, saying, "When you grow up, I want you to go to my sister over yonder, and watch her secretly." The children grew up and went to their aunt's house, who scared them so, that they ran back in a hurry.

Then O'manuts said to his children, "Let us all go and kill my sister! She is mean. She killed my family." The children promised to help him.

So they all went, and O'manuts began to fight with his sister; but he could not kill her, because the only vulnerable spot, her heart, was in the sole of her foot.

In vain O'manuts shot arrow after arrow at her. He could not kill her. His arrows were all gone, and he was almost exhausted, when Meadow-Lark came to his help. She told him to look at Anediwi'dowit's heel. He did so, and saw something bright and shining. On Meadow-Lark's advice he directed an arrow at that spot, and thus succeeded in killing the terrible Anediwi'dowit.

COYOTE AND THE OLD WOMAN

Tradition Bearer: Charlie DePoe

Source: Farrand, Livingston, and Leo J. Frachtenberg. "Shasta and Athapascan Myths from Oregon." *Journal of American Folklore* 28 (1915): 233–38.

Date: 1900

Original Source: Joshua

National Origin: Native American

Coyote assumes his typical role of **trickster** and transformer of the environment in this **myth**. As usual, he is ruled by his impulses and his desires, rather than by intellect or ethics. This is his characteristic behavior in the Native American cultures of this area of the Northwest region.

In the old days different people were living in the world. The Joshuas were the Coyote people. At that time there lived at Dime five boys and their grandmother. The grandmother instructed the boys how to make spears and bows and arrows, and how to put poison on the arrows, just as their father, who was a seal-hunter, used to do. The boys made a canoe out of a red-wood log that had drifted ashore during a big storm, and the old woman gave each of them a basket-hat to wear, in case the canoe should upset. They also had different kinds of spears, and a skin rope which the old woman had shown them how to make. At that time Coyote lived at Joshua. He had never been to Dime, but had heard that various kinds of food could be obtained there.

One fine day, when the ocean was very smooth, the oldest boy said to his grandmother, "This is a good day for hunting. Give us much food, as we may not be back today." The old woman placed much food in the canoe; and the boys went away, leaving her alone. At the same time Coyote decided to visit Dime. He put on his best clothes and went up the beach. Pretty soon he arrived there.

He looked into the sweat-house: no one was inside. Then he walked up to the house, where he found the old woman working alone. She had only an apron on, and Coyote wished he could get possession of her. He thought, "I will go in and talk to her." So he opened the door; but the old woman shouted, "Wait until I put on a dress!" "Oh, never mind! Stay just as you are!" he replied. Then Coyote entered the house, and asked her where her grandsons were. She told him that they had gone out hunting, and asked him if he wanted any food; but Coyote replied that he would rather wait until the boys got back with fresh food. After a while he told the old woman that he was going into the sweat-house to sleep, and asked her to wake him up as soon as her grandchildren got back. He cautioned her not to wake him by poking him with a stick from the outside, but to come into the sweat-house. He reasoned that, once he had her inside, he would be able to take possession of her.

So he went into the sweat-house, sat down, and wished a storm to come up on the ocean. Soon a heavy gale began to blow. The woman called Coyote to come and help her, but he never moved. She begged him to go up on the mountain and look for her grandchildren: he paid no attention. She poked him with a stick: still he did not move. The gale was growing worse. At last the old woman entered the sweat-house, seized Coyote, and began to shake him.

Then he opened his eyes and asked her what the trouble was. She told him to come out and watch for her grandsons; but Coyote said, "Go out first! I shall follow immediately." At first the old woman refused, because her back was bare, and she had to stoop in order to pass through the small opening of the sweat-house; but Coyote insisted, and they quarreled over it. At last the old woman gave in; but as she stooped to leave the sweat-house, she exposed her private parts, and Coyote had intercourse with her and killed her. Then he dragged her body back into the sweat-house.

In the mean time the boys were far out on the ocean. As soon as the storm broke out, they thought of Coyote, and said, "It must be Coyote who is the cause of this storm. Let us go back! He may be hurting our grandmother." So they began to paddle homewards, and approached the shore. They saw smoke coming from the house. They perceived Coyote, but did not see their grandmother anywhere. The breakers were still very high, and the boys did not know how to make the shore. Suddenly a great wave caught the canoe and carried it clear to the shore. The canoe was full of seals.

Coyote was waiting for the boys on the beach, and, when asked if he had seen their grandmother, he replied, "Yes, she is in the house. She has treated me well. I knew your father. He used to teach me how to eat seal-meat with my head covered with blankets, so that no one should see me. Now I will show it to you here in the canoe."

The boys said, "Show us!" So Coyote entered the canoe, covered his head with a blanket and told the boys not to lift it unless he told them to do so. Coyote had just started to eat, when the youngest boy exclaimed, "Let us better go and see if our grandmother is in the house! You know Coyote is always lying. Let us hurry!"

So they ran to the house, but found no one there. Then they entered the sweat-house, where they found the old woman dead in a corner. They ran back to the canoe, and heard Coyote laughing to himself and boasting of the trick he had played on the old woman.

The boys were very angry, and decided to take revenge on Coyote. He was still in the canoe eating seal-meat. They fastened a rope to the bottom of the canoe, and by means of their magic power they sent it clear out to sea. Afterwards they revived their grandmother.

After a while Coyote called, "Grandsons, lift the blanket!" There was no answer. He called again. Everything was quiet. Then he threw off the blanket, and found himself alone out in the ocean. He did not know how he got there. He looked into the canoe, and saw an old basket, an old hat, a mussel-digger, and a hat made of cougar-skin.

At that time different monsters were living in the ocean. The boys called on all these monsters to go and devour Coyote. While the canoe was drifting, Sea Monster came out from the water, and, perceiving Coyote, he asked him, "What seems to be the trouble with you?" Coyote said, "I have no paddle and cannot get ashore." Then Sea Monster told him, "I am going to call a man who will take you ashore." And Coyote answered, "All right! Bring him here!" Soon he heard a hissing sound; and Sea Monster appeared, telling him that a man was coming to save him. Coyote thought that Sea Monster was lying, so he asked him to come close to the canoe. Sea Monster was afraid, but Coyote promised not to hurt him. Then Sea Monster stepped into the canoe; but as soon as he did so, Coyote seized the mussel-digger and thrust it into his tail. Since then Sea Monster has had a crooked neck and a long tail.

After a while a seal came along, and Coyote asked him to come nearer. Seal at that time had a head like a dog. Seal approached, and Coyote asked him if he had come to save him. Seal replied, "Yes!" Coyote asked him to come closer. Seal did so, and Coyote put the old hat on his head and told him to dive. Soon Seal came up again, with a hat on his back; and Coyote laughed at him, saying, "Hereafter you shall live in the water. You shall come out on rocks. You shan't kill people any longer. People will kill you when you are asleep, and will eat your meat."

Pretty soon Killer-Whale came along, spouting water like cataracts, from his big, open mouth. Coyote asked him to come close, but not to hurt the canoe. Killer-Whale approached, and was asked again to open his mouth wider. He did so, and Coyote threw the cougar hat down his throat, and told him to go to the bottom of the ocean and not to come back until he called him. After a while Coyote called him, and Whale appeared. His mouth and his teeth were very small. Then Coyote told Killer-Whale to leave that region forever. " Hereafter," Coyote said to him, "you may use your dorsal fin as a weapon." Since that time Killer-Whale has been using his dorsal fin as a weapon.

Not long afterwards Coyote saw a large Whale coming from the west. The Whale looked as large as a mountain, his mouth was wide open, and he had huge teeth. Coyote was afraid he might swallow the canoe or else break it with his tail, so he stood up and shouted to Whale to come to the edge of the canoe. When this was done, he threw the basket into Whale's mouth, and ordered him to dive, and to stay under the water until he called him. Whale came up again, and his jaws were just as they appear today. Then Coyote told Whale, "You will eat fish hereafter, and not people. You will come ashore to die." Whale started to leave; but Coyote thought it would be better if he jumped into his mouth, as he might be taken ashore by him. So he called Whale back and told him to shut his eyes and to open his mouth; whereupon he jumped into Whale's throat, and the boys pulled the canoe back to their landing-place.

The Whale took Coyote all over the ocean. It was warm inside, and Coyote had nothing with which to make an air-hole in the body of the Whale. At last he scratched his head and wished for a knife or any other weapon. Soon a spear-point came out of his ear, with which he began to cut the Whale's entrails. The Whale became sick, and Coyote advised him to go ashore; but he did not know which way to go. He stayed five years inside the Whale. During that time he had lost his hair and skin. He was eating nothing but grease. He had succeeded in cutting through the Whale within a few inches of the skin, so that the light shone through it, but the water could not come in.

At the end of five years Coyote heard breakers and knew that he had come ashore. In the morning, when he saw daylight coming, he thought, "Maybe someone will find me here." Pretty soon he heard people talking in a strange language.

People had approached, had looked at the Whale, and said, "This Whale is not from our side of the ocean. Let him go back!" So when the high tide came, Coyote wished the Whale to go back. The Whale went out to sea again. After another year he came ashore on the south side of the Umpqua River. At that place there lived a chief who had five daughters, one of whom was adolescent, and who therefore did not sleep in the house. When the Whale came ashore, Coyote peeped through a small hole in the Whale's skin, and recognized the country. So he opened the Whale and came out. He was in a dreadful condition. He was bald, his ears were gone, his skin was rotting—he was a mere skeleton. He could hardly walk, and had to crawl on his hands and knees. His eyes were full of grease, and he could hardly see.

Soon the adolescent girl came upon the Whale, walked around him five times, and found Coyote's tracks. She followed them until she found Coyote resting under a log.

Coyote asked her, "Where am I?"

The girl answered, "At my village." She had on a short dress, and Coyote thought he would have intercourse with her.

So he asked her, "Who is your father?"

And the girl answered, "The chief of the Indians on the southern bank of the Umpqua River."

"Why do you go around at night?" Coyote asked again. Then the girl told him, and Coyote began to laugh.

Then the girl said, "How did you get into the Whale?" So Coyote told her the whole story. Then Coyote put his hands on each part of her body, asking her to name them. He began with her head, then went down to her chest, touched her arms and breasts, came down to her leg, went up the other to her shoulder, and down again over her navel to the private parts. As soon as he put his hand there, the girl became unable to move.

Then Coyote asked her, "How many brothers have you?"

"Five," answered the girl. "How many sisters?"

"Three," she replied.

"Which of them do you sleep with?"

"I sleep between my second and my eldest sister."

"What time does your mother get up?" Coyote kept on asking.

"Sometimes early, and sometimes late," answered the girl.

"What time do you get up?"

"Oh, sometimes early, and sometimes late." Coyote also found out many other things from her; such as how she acted when in the house, where she kept her beads, and so on. After he got through questioning her, he told her to sit down close by him and to shut her eyes, whereupon he pulled off her skin and put it on himself. He made himself look just like the girl. Then he took her body, turned it into a steel-head salmon, and sent her into the ocean, telling her to live in the north.

Then Coyote entered the house, disguised as a girl. The mother was awake, while the other three girls were still asleep. "Why do you come in so late?" asked the mother. "Oh, a whale has come ashore," Coyote answered. The mother was very glad. Then Coyote lay down with the girls, making them sound asleep; but their mother began to wonder at their sound sleep, for they had never acted like that before. So she looked closely, and perceived Coyote's leg, as it was sticking out from the blanket. Then she seized a sharp rock and cut it off.

Coyote shot up through the smoke-hole, after having had intercourse with the three girls. He went back to the land of the Joshuas.

The people were very angry at Coyote, and pursued him; but a heavy fog came up, so that he could not be tracked. After a while the three girls became pregnant, and could not get up. They were ashamed, and told their mother that they knew not how it had happened. They had slept all the time, and only remembered that their sister had come in to sleep with them.

Then the old woman made her daughters lie down on flat boards, and stepped on their abdomens. Soon five Coyotes were born. The old woman told her daughters to wash, and to gather roots for medicine. She dried the little Coyotes in smoke, pulverized them, and threw the dust to the north, saying, "You stay in the north and do not come here! There are enough Coyotes in the south."

THE DEATH OF THE GRIZZLY BEARS

Tradition Bearer: Klamath Billie

Source: Farrand, Livingston, and Leo J. Frachtenberg. "Shasta and Athapascan Myths from Oregon." *Journal of American Folklore* 28 (1915): 214–216.

Date: 1900

Original Source: Shasta
National Origin: Native American

Tales of the enmity between humans and grizzly bears is common in the Northwest region, as is the **motif** of an orphan and his or her grandparents. That the orphan is teamed with Coyote to defeat the entire Grizzly clan underscores the true power of seemingly helpless in **myths** and other types of tales. Moreover, Coyote's wish to befriend the boy attests to the affinity between humans and this **trickster** figure that is an enduring **motif** in Native American folklore. Compare the following **myth** to "The Five Grizzly Bears" (p. 66), another tale in which the youngest brother shows the greatest intelligence.

One winter Coyote, his wife, and ten Grizzly Brothers were living together. Louse was Coyote's wife. Not far from their lodge there lived a poor orphan and his grandmother. The boy was in the habit of visiting Coyote's house and its inmates.

One day the boy came to the house and looked in. The oldest Grizzly saw him, and said, "Halloo, boy! I knew your father and mother well. Your father was a good hunter. He knew how to obtain food. Your mother knew how to dig camas. But now you are alone and poor." The boy began to cry and went home.

When his grandmother saw his tears, she said, "I told you not to go to that house. The Grizzlies are mean, and always scoff at you. It was they who killed your people."

In the evening the boy sharpened his flint knife and went to the house of his enemies, hiding himself behind a bush. He knew where the chief was sleeping. As soon as they were all asleep, he took out his knife, cut off the chief's foot, and ran home.

In the middle of the night Grizzly woke up, and began to groan, "Oh, someone has cut off my foot!"

Coyote was the first to wake up, and he shouted at the other Grizzlies, "Wake up! What is the matter with you people? Don't you hear what the chief says?"

He had seen the boy cut off the chief's foot. He had followed him outside, where he picked up the bones, which the boy had thrown away, and threw them into the fire. He had also put the moccasin of the cut-off leg into the fire, so that it became burnt and black. He did all this because he wanted to befriend the boy, and shield him from the anger of the ten brothers.

As soon as the Grizzlies were awake, Coyote said to the chief, "I warned you that your foot would slip off that rest some day and burn, and now it has happened." The chief thought it might have been so, but his brothers were doubtful.

In the morning Louse said to Coyote," I thought I saw someone go out last night." Coyote said, "No one went out. I was awake all night." His wife was certain of it, but he kept on telling her that she was mistaken.

After a while, one of the Grizzly Brothers recollected that on the previous day they had mocked the orphan boy, and expressed his belief that it was the boy who cut off the chief's foot.

Thereupon Coyote said, "I'll go to the boy and ask him." The others agreed, and Coyote started out. He found the boy eating bear-meat. He warned him to keep quiet, and not to say anything when questioned about the happenings of last night. The boy promised to obey; and Coyote returned home, telling the chief, "The poor boy is crying. He is not feeling well. I am sure he did not cut off your leg."

But the youngest Grizzly kept on saying, "No, I think he did it." Finally Coyote was sent again to bring the boy before the chief. Upon arriving at the orphan's house, Coyote said to him, "I have come after you. Be careful, now! If the chief asks you, 'Shall I crush you with my hands?' say, 'No;' if he says, 'Shall I swallow you?' answer, 'Yes.'"

When the boy was brought into the house, the chief asked him, "Did you cut off my foot?"

The boy answered, "Yes."

"Why did you do it?" the chief asked again. "Was it because I mocked you?" "Yes," replied the boy. Then Grizzly said, "What shall I do with you? Shall I pulverize you in my hands?"

"No!" said the boy. "Shall I swallow you?"

"Yes," answered the boy. Thereupon Grizzly opened his mouth, and the boy jumped into it. Once inside, he took out his knife and cut his enemy's heart. The Grizzly chief died.

His other brothers wanted to dig a grave in which to bury him; but Coyote intervened, saying, "Don't do that! Someone will open the grave, thinking it a cache of food. Better make a corral fence, put him there, and cover him with brush. The people will recognize it easily as a grave." So the Grizzlies made a fence and buried their brother. As soon as they disappeared, the boy came out from the chief's body and went home.

In the evening Coyote said to the Grizzly Bears, "I am going to see the old woman and find out how she is getting on." He came to the house, and found the boy and told him all he had done for him. At night he went back to his own house, and told the Grizzly Brothers that he was going to stay with the old woman. That was merely a pretence, for in reality he wanted to help the boy carry the bear-meat.

During the night the youngest Grizzly had a dream, in which he saw Coyote help the boy carry the meat of his dead brother. He woke up, and said to his brothers, "Let one of you go and see whether the dream is true!"

One Grizzly went there, and saw Coyote in the act of carrying away the last piece. He gave chase; but Coyote and the boy reached in safety the house, the door of which, upon the boy's wish, turned into stone, thus defying all attempts of Grizzly to break in. The enraged Grizzly walked all around the house, saying, "Boy, how can I get inside?" The boy, in the mean time, was heating rocks; and when they were red-hot, he said to Grizzly, "I'll tell you how to enter, but you must come in hind-feet first." Grizzly consented, and the boy opened the door a little bit. As soon as the Bear's body was halfway in, the boy wished the door to close tight. The door closed, and Grizzly was caught fast, whereupon the boy killed him by means of heated rocks. In the same manner all the other Grizzlies were killed with the exception of the youngest one, who became the progenitor of all Grizzly Bears that are alive now.

COYOTE AND RACCOON

Tradition Bearer: Klamath Billie

Source: Farrand, Livingston and Leo J. Frachtenberg. "Shasta and Athapascan Myths from Oregon." *Journal of American Folklore* 28 (1915): 220–21.

Date: 1900

Original Source: Shasta

National Origin: Native American

The **myth** below features Coyote in his usual persona of **trickster** and inadvertent transformer of the universe. Driven by jealousy, revenge, and greed, he causes the creation of the Pleiades. The **motif** of Ashes as informer appears also in "The Girl Who Married Her Brother" (p. 71).

Coyote and Tcinake, the Raccoon, were living together. Each had five children. One day Coyote said, "A feast is taking place not far from here. Let us go there!" to which Coon replied, "All right!" They went to the fair and had a good time. Coyote fell in love with two girls; but they preferred Coon, and paid little attention to Coyote. Towards evening Coyote said to Coon, "I am going away for a little while. I'll be back soon. Do you watch those two girls!" While Coyote was gone, the two girls invited Coon to go with them, telling him that they did not care for Coyote. Coyote returned and looked for his friend. In vain he called his name repeatedly: he could not find him.

At last Coon appeared; and Coyote asked him, "Where have you been? Where are the girls?" Coon told him that the girls were in the woods, whereupon Coyote accused him of having taken them. He was very angry.

After a while they started home. On their way they saw a squirrel running into a tree-hole. Coyote asked Coon to put his hand into one end of the hole, so as to scare the squirrel and drive it to the other side of the opening, where he (Coyote) was waiting for it. Coon reached into the hole with his hand, and Coyote seized and began to pull it. Coon shouted, "Hold on! This is my arm."

"No," said Coyote, "this is the squirrel." And he kept on pulling until the arm came off, and Coon died.

Then Coyote went home, carrying Coon's body. Upon his arrival home, he distributed the meat among his children; but the youngest boy, angry because he was not given an equal share, ran over to Coon's children, and said, "My father has killed your father. He did not bring home all the meat. Tomorrow he is going for more."

Whereupon Coon's children said, "All right! Tomorrow we shall kill your brothers, but we will spare you. We shall take you with us." The next day, while Coyote was away, they killed his four children and left them on the floor. Then they ran away, enjoining everything in the house not to tell Coyote where they had gone. They forgot, however, to caution Ashes.

Coyote came home, and tried to wake his children; but they were dead. He asked everything in the house to tell him where the murderers of his boys had gone. No one knew. Finally he asked Ashes. The Ashes flew skyward, and Coyote followed their flight with his eyes. Before they were halfway up the sky, Coyote saw Coon's children, and his own boy trailing behind them. He wept, and called to them to come back; but they would not listen to him. Then he tried to catch them. He could not overtake them.

The children remained on the sky as stars. They are the Pleiades. The five big stars are Coon's children. The smaller star behind them, the red star, is Coyote's boy.

COYOTE'S AMOROUS ADVENTURES

Tradition Bearer: Klamath Billie

Source: Farrand, Livingston, and Leo J. Frachtenberg. "Shasta and Athapascan Myths from Oregon." *Journal of American Folklore* 28 (1915): 209.

Date: 1900

Original Source: Shasta

National Origin: Native American

Typical not only of the Shasta's version of Coyote, but of Native American **tricksters** in general, is an apparently restless wandering. His shape-shifting and final taunts to victims of his deceptions also are typical.

Once Coyote perceived two girls walking along the road; and he said to himself, "I should like to have these girls. I wonder how I can get them!" A small creek ran parallel to the road. "I will go into the creek and turn into a salmon," said Coyote. He did so, and pretty soon the girls came to the creek.

Upon seeing the salmon darting to and fro, one girl exclaimed, "Oh, here is a salmon! Let us catch it!" So the girls sat down on opposite banks of the river, and the salmon swam back and forth, entering their bodies.

The elder girl said to her sister, "Do you feel anything queer?" and her sister answered, "Yes, I feel fine."

Thereupon Coyote came out of the creek in his true form, and laughed at the girls, saying, "You thought it was a salmon, but I fooled you." The girls were angry, and cursed him.

He kept on going downstream. Coyote went on for some time, until he heard a girl singing. It sounded to him as if she were singing, "I wish Coyote would come here!" He kept on running in that direction, until he came to a place where he saw Duck-Girl. She was making a basket and singing a love-song.

Coyote said to her, "I'd like to stay with you."

The girl consented; so he said, "I will first get wood for the fire, and then I will sleep with you." They lived together for a long time. After a while Duck-Girl became pregnant.

One day Coyote said to her, "I am going to get more wood." While he was gone, the girl entered the basket, which started to roll down the river-bank. Coyote came home, and, seeing the basket roll down the bank, ran after it. He could not catch it; and the basket rolled into the water, and began to float downstream.

Coyote ran down to the river and extended his penis, in order to intercept the basket; but when the basket came, it just floated past him and could not be stopped. After a while children's heads began to stick out from the basket, which kept floating downstream until it reached the ocean. Coyote tried several times to catch the basket, but his attempts were unsuccessful.

COYOTE AND PITCH

Tradition Bearer: Klamath Billie

Source: Farrand, Livingston, and Leo J. Frachtenberg. "Shasta and Athapascan Myths from Oregon." *Journal of American Folklore* 28 (1915): 218.

Date: 1900

Original Source: Shasta

National Origin: Native American

The tale of "Coyote and Pitch" bears obvious similarities to the "tar baby" tales that in the United States are most closely associated with African American traditions. As far as can be determined, the following narrative was not adapted from African American sources, and variants of the **trickster** tale exist in the repertoires of other Native American Northwest coast cultures. Unlike the African American tar baby, Pitch moves and speaks under his own power. Coyote, of course, exhibits the same aggression and arrogance as his African American counterparts Rabbit and Anansi.

One day Coyote heard that Pitch, the bad man, was coming. He went out to meet him, and said, "I can whip you, no matter who you are."

Pitch answered, "I can't fight with my hands." Thereupon Coyote struck him with his fist; but the fist stuck fast.

Then Coyote said, "If I strike you with my left hand, I'll kill you."

"Go ahead, do it!" answered Pitch. Coyote hit him, and his left hand stuck fast. "I'll kick you," said Coyote; and Pitch replied, "All right, kick!"

Coyote kicked, and his foot stuck fast. "If I kick you with my left foot," threatened Coyote, "I'll surely kill you."

"Do it!" mocked Pitch. Coyote kicked again, and his left foot stuck fast. "I will lash you with my tail!" shouted Coyote, whereupon his tail stuck fast. Then Coyote became angry, and threatened to kill Pitch with his ear; but his ear, too, stuck fast. Finally Coyote hit him with his head. The same thing happened. His head stuck fast.

Now Coyote was stuck to Pitch, and could not pry himself loose. After a while his friend Spider came there, and saw Coyote's predicament. "How can I help you?" inquired he.

"Cut my hand away, but do not cut it," said Coyote.

"It will be easier to burn it away," suggested Spider.

"No!" said Coyote, "scrape it away!" Spider did so, and after a while Coyote became free.

COYOTE AND BEAVER

Tradition Bearer: Charlie DePoe

Source: Farrand, Livingston, and Leo J. Frachtenberg. "Shasta and Athapascan Myths from Oregon." *Journal of American Folklore* 28 (1915): 238–40.

Date: 1900

Original Source: Joshua

National Origin: Native American

The **trickster**'s characteristic gluttony and audacity once again get Coyote in trouble. He, in fact, exposes his guilt in his first confrontation with Beaver and, in the second, proposes his own means of execution. Only the supernatural power that is usually **trickster**'s "escape clause" allows him to survive. The collectors' supplementary notes to the tale observe that this is one of the rare Northern Athabascan narratives also found among a Southern branch of the culture, the Apaches.

Ten miles up the Rogue River, Beaver and his five children were living together. Not far from them Coyote was living. One morning Coyote said to his wife in the sweat-house, "I am going away today."

His wife said, "You better stay here!" But Coyote answered, "I am going, anyway." Mista'ne was Coyote's friend. Before departing, Coyote told him to watch for him at a certain rock, as he might not be back for a long time. "If you see a bone or anything dead," he said to Mista'ne, "know it will be my body. Bite it, and I will come to life again."

Then Coyote departed, no one knew where. He approached Beaver's house from the north side. Beaver was hunting every day. He ate all kinds of wood and called it salmon. Only one kind, the mītāltsis-wood, he did not eat. His children were fat and strong.

When Coyote came to the river, he shouted for Beaver to take him across. Nobody answered! He shouted three times. At last Beaver's children came, and began to swim around him. Coyote decided to kill them: so he jumped into the river, and began to swim too. He swam across and came to Beaver's house. Old Beaver was not home. Coyote entered, and said to the children, "Children, don't be afraid of me! I am your uncle." Then he went outside, put rocks into a basket, and heated them. Then he took some wild-cabbage, ground up a piece of mitu'ltsis-wood, put it into a pot, and gave this to the children, saying, "Here is fresh salmon your father left for you. It tastes good!" Then he pretended to eat this food. Beaver's children ate it and died. Then Coyote took the dead bodies outside, placed them on heated rocks, and covered them with sand. First he put one body into the ground, then hot rocks, then another body, and so on. Then he went into the river to swim. He was afraid of the old Beaver, and did not dare to cook the meat in the house. After he was through swimming, he took Beaver's children off the fire, and placed them in a cool place. Then he went swimming again. When he came out of the water, he began to eat. The meat tasted fine, so he ate half of it. Then he bathed again. By sundown he had eaten all the meat. Then he hid the bones of the children under a small basket, and went into the river again; but he had eaten so much, that he felt sick. So he tied a log around his body in order to keep himself afloat. Towards night he came back to his wife. She questioned him about his trip, and he told her that he had not been on any mischief. He had just called on his cousin, who gave him plenty of food. In the mean time Beaver had come home and found his children's bones. He felt very sorry. He saw Coyote's tracks, suspected him at once, and wished he would come back, so that he could take his revenge.

After five days Coyote decided to go to Beaver to find out how he was taking his loss, and whether he suspected him. He took along his knife, a bow, and six arrows. From a distance he could see Beaver sitting on the bank of the river, and sharpening his knife. He was crying, and his hair was white with mucus [as a sign of mourning]. Coyote came nearer. Beaver never looked up. Coyote watched him from a distance, and thought," I guess everything is safe. I will ask him to take me across." He waited for Beaver to raise his head, so as to attract his attention.

He wondered in what language to address him. He did not want to be recognized. He decided to use the California language. So he called out in that language, "My friend, come after me in a canoe!" Beaver never looked up, but kept on working. Five times Coyote called him.

Then he spoke in Joshua: "I did not kill your children, if that be the reason why you won't bring your canoe." Suddenly Beaver disappeared; and Coyote stood there with his bow half drawn, and waiting for Beaver to come up again. Beaver began to swim around in a circle, and Coyote got dizzy from turning his head so often. At last Beaver darted up from behind, seized Coyote, and dragged him down into deep water. Coyote was drowned. Then Beaver tied a heavy rock around him and sunk him.

Coyote stayed in the water ten years, when the rope with which he was fastened to the rock began to rot, and broke. In the mean time Beaver married again, and had two children. He was still afraid that Coyote might re-appear: therefore he warned the children not to eat any mitu'ltsis-wood.

All this time Mista'ne had been staying in the sweat-house. One day a storm broke out. The water rose, and different things drifted ashore. Among them he saw a small bone, so he went into the water and brought it ashore. After having squeezed the water out of his hair, he took the bone and bit it. Then Coyote came to life again. He said to Mista'ne, "I have been asleep. Why did you wake me?"

Then Coyote went home; and his wife asked him, "Where have you been?" Coyote said, "I have been way east visiting my relatives."

After a while Coyote decided to take revenge on Beaver. He dressed up like a California Indian, put many things into the canoe, and went to Beaver's house. Upon his arrival there, he shouted in the language of the California Indians, "Friend, I have come with beautiful presents for you! I heard that you have been sick."

Beaver came out of the house, and said, "It is well." He offered Coyote some salmon; and after Coyote finished eating, he said to Beaver, "Let us gather wood! Let us see who is the stronger! Perchance I can help you when Coyote comes to trouble you again."

Beaver consented: so they made a great fire and heated rocks. Coyote remembered the taste of beaver-meat, and wanted to eat some more. He gathered plenty of grass, and proposed a test of strength with Beaver. They were to bury and cook each other, and the one who got cooked first was to admit himself beaten. Then Coyote dug a deep hole and buried Beaver. He covered him with leaves and grass, and began to cook him.

Pretty soon Beaver shouted, "Uncover me! I am half cooked. I shall die." Coyote took him out, but Beaver was not cooked at all. He had escaped certain death by digging himself deeper into the ground.

It was Coyote's turn now to be buried. He was scared, and said, "Let us put it off for another time! I am in a hurry now."

But Beaver said, "No! We have agreed to that test, and we will finish it now!" So they heated stones, and Beaver began to bury Coyote.

Before he was all covered up, Coyote said to Beaver, "I'll shout when it gets too hot." Beaver told him he would walk around the hole, and be on hand whenever Coyote called. After a while Coyote shouted, "Open! It is hot!"

But Beaver said, "Why, I haven't even covered you yet." Then he kept on throwing dirt and grass on the hole. Pretty soon no sound could be heard. Beaver called out to Coyote, "Are you alive?" No answer came. Then Beaver opened the hole and looked in. The meat was all gone: nothing but the bones was left. So he tied a rock around him and threw him into the river.

Coyote stayed in the water twenty years. At the expiration of that time the rope broke, and Coyote was brought back to life by his friend Mista'ne.

He went home, and again his wife asked him, "Where have you been all this time?"

"Oh, I have been travelling all over the world," Coyote answered.

THE GREAT SNOWFALL

Tradition Bearer: Unavailable

Source: Boas, Franz. "Traditions of the Ts'ets'ā´ut II." *Journal of American Folklore* 10 (1897): 35–37.

Date: 1894–1895

Original Source: Ts'ets'ā´ut

National Origin: Native American

As Franz Boas writes in his notes to the following narrative, "[The grizzly bears] were men. It is not quite clear if they were men of a grizzly bear clan, or if the story happened at the time when all animals were still men." If they were anthropomorphic bears, then the tale would be classified as a **myth**. Given the details of the story, however, the more likely interpretation is that they were human members of the grizzly bear clan, making the following an example of a **legend**. See "The Five Grizzly Bears" (pp. 66) and "The Death of the Grizzly Bears" (p. 79) for narratives that are clearly mythic, rather than legendary.)

Once upon a time a number of families of the wolf clan and of the eagle clan lived in a village at Portland Channel. Nearby there was a village of grizzly bear men. They attacked the village, and killed everybody with the exception of one boy and one girl of each of the two clans.

They were crying all the time when they saw their relatives killed. Then one of the grizzly bear men went to their hut, and threatened to kill them if they should not stop crying. But one of the boys took his bow and arrow and shot the man in the chest, thus killing him. After this had happened, they dug a deep ditch in their hut, and buried all their relatives who had been killed.

They left the place of these misfortunes and went down the mountains. After some time they reached a house, in which they found an old, old man who had been left by his friends to die alone. He said to them: "Stay here until I die, my grandchildren, and bury me when I am dead."

They stayed, and he asked them why they had left their country. When they had told him, he asked them to return, because salmon were nowhere as plentiful as in the river on which their house had stood. He also warned them, saying: "The sky is full of feathers. Take good care to provide your-self with plenty of meat, and build a strong house." He was a great shaman, and was able to foresee the future.

After two days he died. The young people buried him. Then they started to return to their home in obedience to what the shaman had told them. They followed a river, and when they were near its source they saw an immense herd of mountain goats coming down towards them. They did not stop to shoot them, but ran right up to them and dispatched them, cutting their throats with their knives. Then they went back to the camp in which they had left the girls, taking along only a kid that they had killed. They threw some of its meat and tallow into the fire, as a sacrifice to the dead shaman who had directed them to return home.

On the following day they moved their camp to a hill that was located in the midst of three lakes. There they built a strong hut as directed by the shaman. The two girls went out to fetch the meat of the mountain goats. While they were drying it, the boys strengthened the poles of the house, joined them with stout thongs, and thus prepared for a heavy snowfall. They put the meat into the house.

On the following day the snow began to fall. They lived on the meat of the mountain goats, but they sacrificed as much to the dead shaman as they ate. It continued to snow for two months. They could not go out to gather wood for their fire, but they had to burn the bones and the tallow of the goats. The smoke kept a hole open in the roof of their hut; and, when looking up, they could see no more than a very small speck of light. But after two months they saw the blue sky through this hole. The sun was shining again. Then they dug a hole towards the surface of the snow and came out. Nothing but snow was to be seen. The rocks of the mountains and the trees were all covered. Gradually the snow began to melt a little, and the tops of the trees reappeared.

One day they saw a bear near the top of a tree. When they approached, it crawled back to its lair at the foot of the tree. Now they started on their way to their old home. After a long and difficult march, they reached it just at the time when the candlefish were coming. They caught a plentiful supply and were well provided with provisions.

In summer there were salmon in the river. They caught them and dried and split them. They married and had many children. They were the only people who were saved from the heavy snow, and from them descended the present generations of people. They multiplied very rapidly, for they married very young, as dogs do. At the end of the first summer, only a small part of the snow had melted. A few rocks appeared in the mountains, but in the fall new snow began to fall. In the spring of the following year it began to melt again. The trees were gradually freed from snow, but some of it has always remained on the mountains, where it forms the glaciers.

The two couples who had been saved from the snow grew to be very old. Their hair was white, and they were bent with old age. One day the young men climbed the mountains to hunt mountain goat. One of the old men accompanied them, but he was left behind, as he could not walk as fast as the young men did. When he had reached a meadow high up the side of the mountain he heard a voice from the interior of the rocks saying: "Here is the man who killed all our friends." When he looked up he saw a number of mountain goats above. He did not know how to reach them, since his legs were weak. He took two sticks and tied one to each of his legs in order to steady and to strengthen them. Thus he was enabled to climb. He reached the mountain goats and cut their necks. He killed thirty. Among these was a kid. He took out its tallow and put it on his head; he cut off its head and took it under his arm to carry it home. He had stayed away so long that his friends had given him up for lost. He told them of his adventure. He roasted the kid's head and ate it. On the following morning he was dead.

THE FIGHT BETWEEN THE COYOTE PEOPLE AND THE BAT PEOPLE

Tradition Bearer: Klamath Billie

Source: Farrand, Livingston, and Leo J. Frachtenberg. "Shasta and Athapascan Myths from Oregon." *Journal of American Folklore* 28 (1915): 222.

Date: 1900

Original Source: Shasta

National Origin: Native American

The reason for the fight between the Coyotes and the Bats is Coyote precipitation of a battle under the guise of predicting it. The **trickster**, of course, survives. His concluding promise may be sincere, but it will never be kept. He is, after all, Coyote, and pacifism is against his nature.

One day Coyote said, "I hear there is going to be a big fight between the Coyote people and the Bat people. Let us go there!" He went, taking along many people. The fight began, and many were killed on both sides; but the Bat people were stronger, and Coyote's side was beaten. He lost most of his relatives.

Finally one old man said to Coyote, "I'll tell you how you can kill the Bat people. Let them go back into the house tonight, and do not molest them! In the morning we shall return. Let every man arm himself with a stout stick. Thus we shall kill them." Coyote agreed, and went home with those of his people who had not been killed.

In the morning he returned to Bat's house; and the old man told him, "Station your people by the door, and, as the Bats come out, hit them with the clubs!" Coyote did so, and all. The Bats were killed except one, who escaped. Coyote was very glad, and gave much money to the man who showed him how to overpower the Bat people.

One of Coyote's people, an old man, did not take part in the fight. When Coyote came home, that man scolded him, saying, "Now you see how many people were killed on account of you!"

Coyote felt sorry, and replied, "All right! I won't do it again."

COYOTE AND THE STUMP-MAN

Tradition Bearer: Klamath Billie

Source: Farrand, Livingston, and Leo J. Frachtenberg. "Shasta and Athapascan Myths from Oregon." *Journal of American Folklore* 28 (1915): 216–18.

Date: 1900

Original Source: Shasta

National Origin: Native American

Coyote plays his role of **culture hero** in the following **myth** by ridding the land of a monster. The monster is a carnivorous, ambulatory stump; therefore, like Coyote, he exists between categories. Unlike Coyote (in this **myth** at least), however, his motives are overtly destructive. The **motif** of a rope to climb to the heavens is a recurrent one in the tales of the Northwest Region.

Coyote was traveling all over the country. He came to a house in which there lived an old woman, and asked her, "Where have all the people gone?" The woman replied, "They went long ago over yonder hill, and have never returned. I am anxious about them."

Coyote decided to follow them and find out what kept them there. The old woman warned him that he might be killed, but he disregarded her warning and started out. He soon found a trail, which he followed until he reached its end. While looking around for another trail, he saw a stump. He seized his bow and shot at it. To his surprise, the stump kept on dodging the arrows, so that he missed it repeatedly.

This convinced him that the stump was a person, and responsible for the disappearance of the people. He kept on shooting until all his arrows were gone, whereupon the stump assumed the form of a person, and began to pursue him.

Coyote ran until he came to a big lake. In danger of being seized, he asked himself, "Do I die now?" An answer was given him, "No! Just jump into the water!" Coyote did so, but in turning around he stuck his nose out.

The Stump-Man saw it, and said, "He is mine now! He cannot get away from me. I will rest a while." Coyote heard everything, and kept still. After a while Stump-Man got ready to pull him out; but, upon Coyote's wish, the lake became full of fir-cones; so that whenever Stump-Man stuck his spear into the water, he pulled out nothing but fir-cones. After many useless attempts, Stump-Man gave it up and went to sleep. Pretty soon he began to spin around, rising gradually into the air.

When he was about halfway up, Coyote shouted at him, "I am smart too! You could not catch me!" The Stump-Man arrived at the sky through an opening that Coyote saw. He went back to the old woman, and told her that he had found out where the people had gone.

Then he assembled all the survivors, and asked them to suggest plans of reaching the sky. For five days they twisted a rope whereby to make the ascent. Coyote tried to go up first; but every time he reached halfway, the rope fell down. Similar attempts by other people proved of no avail. Finally Coyote pointed out to Bumblebee the place whence Stump-Man had started his journey to the sky. Bumblebee began to spin around from the same place, and rose until he disappeared into the sky.

Pretty soon Bumblebee came back, and was asked by Coyote to tell what he had seen there. Bee, however, replied, "I am tired and want to rest." Upon being urged, he related the following: "I came to the residence of Stump-Man. He was sound asleep and broken-hearted, because he had lost an opportunity of killing you." Coyote wanted to know how they could get up there; and Bee said, "I can climb up myself, but cannot take up any one else. Suppose you try Spider."

Coyote laughed at this, saying, "Oh! He does not have a rope." But the people insisted upon Spider making a trial. Spider arrived with a piece of rope, and began to spin. He rose slowly, and finally reached the sky. He made his rope fast there, and the people used it as a ladder. Coyote came last. They arrived at the house of Stump-Man, where they found a boy whose body consisted of flesh only, and who was eating all the people Stump-Man had killed.

Upon seeing the new-comers, the boy tried to awaken Stump-Man; but he was sound asleep. Then Coyote and his friends set fire to Stump-Man's house, while the boy looked on helplessly. The fire grew bigger, and the boy's shouts became louder, until he burst, making the sound "Boom!" Soon the legs of Stump-Man caught fire. This woke him up, and he started to run; but, being deprived of the use of his feet, he died.

All over the world it was announced that Coyote had killed the Bad Man. The people descended by means of Spider's rope.

THE KILLING OF THE DUTCHMAN

Tradition Bearer: James E. Twadell

Source: Banister, Manly Andrew C. "Interview of James E. Twadell." American Life Histories: Manuscripts from the Federal Writers' Project, 1936–1940. Manuscript Division, Library of Congress. 12 October 2005. http://memory.loc.gov/ammem/wpaintro/wpahome.html.

Date: 1939

Original Source: Oregon

National Origin: European American

Violence was an aspect of frontier life that came to be romanticized in the **legends** arising from the exploits of historically famous or notorious characters. Rather than resulting from a larger-than-life epic adventure, the following **personal experience narrative** tells of the murder of an ordinary man by another ordinary man, seen through the eyes of an ordinary boy.

I'm not a pioneer, but I come to this country in pretty early days, all right. I landed in the Grande Ronde Valley the nineteenth of September, 1865. I crossed the plains with my parents with an ox-team, starting from Missouri, on May 3rd, 1865, the year the Civil War closed. I was at the first Fourth of July Celebration ever held in the Grande Ronde Valley. That was at Uniontown in 1867, located in the south end of the valley, near the canyon that cuts through the mountain there going to Baker.

I lived up there eleven years all told and saw six killings. Four men shot and two hung—the last two for killing a man and civil law took care of them. Of course there were lots more killings, but none that I saw with my own eyes. I recall there was a man name of Reed killed another man in a butcher shop. I was standing in the doorway at the time. He got away and killed another man later in Linn County when I was there. They caught him that time and hung him.

Then there was a fellow named Martin that killed a Dutchman. The Dutchman had been working for Martin, and Martin owed him some wages. Well, the Dutchman asked for his money, and Martin said he didn't have it, and got nasty with the Dutchman and said something or other—I don't know what—and the Dutchman slapped him. That angered the old man and he drew himself up straight and told the Dutchman, "I'll kill you before the sun sets tonight." Then he turned around and walked away. He got on his horse and rode to Uniontown and there he began to liquor up.

Now there was a little store down at Hendershott's Point a little ways away, and the folks sent me down with some eggs to barter to get coffee. While I was at the store, a pack train came in and camped down by the creek where it bends around the point. Of course, the sight of a pack train was a great sight to me as it was to all the folks who had just come from the east. We had never seen nothing like it before.

This Dutchman was there at the store, and he took my arm and said, "Come on, kid, let's go down and see the pack train."

So we went down there and I sat down on a box or a chunk of wood or something, and the Dutchman, he squatted alongside and began to talk with one of the packers. I don't know what we were talking about ... just passing the time of day, or talking about the pack train or something. Then the Dutchman looked up and saw old Martin coming down the trail. You could see he was drunk the way he staggered along over the rough ground.

"There comes my boss now," said the Dutchman. "He made me mad this morning and I slapped his face; then he threatened to kill me before sunset tonight." The Dutchman kind of laughed, because evidently he wasn't afraid of the old man and didn't think he would carry out his threat.

The old man come on down and walked up to the Dutchman squatting there. The Dutchman didn't stand up, and Martin sort of swayed as he stood there, looking down at him, and there was a mean look on the old man's face, and his eyes was bloodshot with the whiskey he had drunk.

"Know what I told you this morning?" he said.

"Yes, I do," said the Dutchman, and grinned up at him.

The old man didn't say another word but drew his gun then and there shot him before he could move. The ball struck the Dutchman just below the left collar bone and come out above the right hip. Martin was sent to the penitentiary for life.

Then there was another man, who lived in the cove where I did, shot and killed his brother-in-law over a bottle of whiskey. Cawhorn was the name of the man that was killed, but I didn't see any of the doings.

THUNDER AND HIS SON-IN-LAW

Tradition Bearer: Klamath Billie

Source: Farrand, Livingston, and Leo J. Frachtenberg. "Shasta and Athapascan Myths from Oregon." *Journal of American Folklore* 28 (1915): 211–12.

Date: 1900

Original Source: Shasta

National Origin: Native American

Polygyny (multiple wives)—especially sororal polygyny (marriage to two or more sisters)—was permitted among Northwest Coast Native American cultures. In fact, the only prohibiting factor in most instances was the husband's wealth, since his resources needed to sustain a household composed of multiple wives and their children. The bestowal of a daughter as a wife often required the payment of "bride-price" to the new father-in-law. The test of the son-in-law story that follows may echo this practice. At any rate, the young man is saved by wit and preparation, without falling back on the deception that his father-in-law attempts to use to get rid of him.

The Thunder had two daughters who were courted by many men. But he was mean, and tried to kill the suitors of his daughters. In vain the girls remonstrated with their father, telling him that they wanted a husband. One day a good-looking man arrived to court the girls. The girls told their father, and he asked to see the young man. The suitor was smart, and, as he went to see Thunder, he said to himself, "I wish the old man would like me!"

Thunder looked at the young man, and said to his daughters, "I like him. He is the kind of man I have been looking for. Do you two take him for your husband!" So the girls married the young man.

The next day Thunder said to his son-in-law, "I want to eat salmon. Go and spear some! You will find a big red salmon in the river. This is the one I want you to spear." The young man took his spear and went to the river. He had a small brother whom he was in the habit of taking along everywhere. Pretty soon he saw a red salmon, and he said to his little brother, "You sit here and watch me spear this salmon." He hit the salmon; but the salmon started down-stream, and the young man followed him. His brother waited for him all day, and at last gave him up as lost. The salmon took him all the way to the ocean, where the young man succeeded in hooking him. On the third day he returned and gave his father-in-law the salmon.

Thunder was surprised, and said, "I'll cook it outside." He said this because he was mean and did not want to share the meat with any one else.

Soon afterwards Thunder asked his son-in-law to go with him to the sweat-house. The young man consented, and Thunder said, "You go in first!" He did so, taking along a small stick. Pretty soon rattlesnakes came at him, but he killed them with his stick.

He tied up the rattlesnakes and took them to his father-in-law. "Here," he said to him, "I found these in the sweat-house." Thunder said nothing.

The next morning Thunder pointed out a cliff to his son-in-law, and asked him to fetch some bird-eggs from there. The cliff could be ascended by means of steps, which Thunder had made. The young man climbed up; but when he came to the top and looked down, the steps had disappeared, and there was nothing but a steep precipice. He thought, "Verily, I shall die now." He stayed there five nights, and the girls gave him up as dead. Thunder was glad, because he was sure he had at last rid himself of his son-in-law. But the young man did not give up. He threw his stick down, and noticed that it fell down fast. Then he threw some lichens, and, behold! They were falling down slowly. So he picked all the lichens he could reach, (wove them into a mat,) sat down on it, and descended slowly with the eggs in his hands.

He gave the eggs to his father-in-law, who said, "I'll make a fire and boil them over there."

The next day Thunder invited his son-in-law to play spring-board with him. The young man consented, and they went in quest of a suitable log. Having found one, Thunder sat down near the butt-end, while the young man took a position near the spring-end. After a while he persuaded his father-in-law to sit at the very end, where-upon he jumped off suddenly, and the tree swung Thunder clear into the sky, where he has been staying ever since. The young man taunted his father-in-law.

WHEN RAVEN WANTED TO MARRY SNOWBIRD AND FLY WITH THE GEESE

Tradition Bearer: Unavailable

Source: Kroeber, A. L. "Tales of the Smith Sound Eskimo." *Journal of American Folklore* 12 (1899): 173–74.

Date: 1897–1898

Original Source: Eskimo

National Origin: Native American

Raven served as **trickster** and **culture hero** for both the Eskimo and for many other Native cultures along the Northwest Coast. Despite his gift of fire, the tales of Raven also depict him with the common flaws of **trickster** figures—in this case they include lying to satisfy his selfish impulses and intruding where his company is not wanted.

A small snowbird was crying because she had lost her husband. While she was crying, the raven, who had no wife, came along. When the raven reached her he said, "Why are you crying?" "I am crying for my husband, because he has been away so long a time," said the snowbird. "My husband went out to look for food for me, and has not come back." The raven told her that her husband was dead; that he had been sitting on a rock, when this became loosened and fell through the ice, and that he had fallen with it. "I will marry you," he said. "You can sleep here under my armpit. Take me for a husband; I have a pretty bill; I have a pretty chin; I have good enough nostrils and eyes; my wings are good and large, and so are my whiskers."

But the little snowbird said, "I don't want you for my husband." Then the raven went away, because the snowbird did not want to marry him.

After a while the raven, who was still without a wife, came to some geese who had become persons. The geese were just going away. The raven said, "I too, I who have no wife, I am going." The geese, because they were about to leave, now became birds again. One of them said, "It is very far away that we are going. You had better not go with us. Don't come with us."

The raven said, "I am not afraid to go. When I am tired, I shall sleep by whirling up." Then they started, the raven going with them. They flew a great distance (having now become birds), passing over a large expanse of water, where there was no land to be seen. Finally, when the geese wanted to sleep, they settled and swam on the water, and there they went to sleep. The raven also grew very tired, and wanted to sleep, but of course could not swim. So he whirled upwards towards the sky. But as soon as he went to sleep, he began to drop from up there.

When he fell into the water he woke up and said, "Get together, so that I can climb on your backs and go to sleep there." The geese did as he told them, and he was soon asleep on their backs.

Then one of the geese said, "He is not light at all. Let us shake him off, because he is so heavy." Then they shook him off their backs into the water.

"Get together," cried the raven. But they did not do so, and thus the raven was drowned.

BLUE JAY AND HIS SISTER

Tradition Bearer: Charles Cultee

Source: Boas, Franz. Pages 158–82 in *Chinook Texts*. Smithsonian Institution Bureau of American Ethnology Bulletin 20. Washington, DC: U.S. Government Printing Office, 1894.

Date: 1890–1891

Original Source: Chinook

National Origin: Native American

Death among the Chinook is highly serious and hemmed in with ritual. Blue Jay's behavior toward the dead goes to the extremes that only a **trickster** could conceive. He takes a dead wife, seeks out his sister who has married the chief of a village of the dead, and plays the practical joke of switching body parts on the corpses of his brother-in-law's village. The living are also not safe from his absurd inversions of appropriate behavior. In a culture in which his older sister should be obeyed, he not only disobeys her, but he also deliberately misconstrues her orders.

There were Blue Jay and his elder sister [Iô'i]. The latter went every day digging roots.

Once upon a time she said to her brother: "Make some arrows; the ducks, the geese, the tail-ducks always lick my buttocks."

"Yes, I will do so," said Blue Jay. The next day she went again digging. Then Blue Jay made the arrows. When he had finished them he went and searched for his elder sister. When he came to the place Iô'i always dug roots he heard her scratching her anus. She looked back, turning her head over her shoulder. Now Blue Jay spanned his bow and shot her in her buttocks.

"Anah, Squint-eye," she said. She took away his bow and said: "These here are the birds," and she shot them. She killed a male mallard duck, which was very fat. Then she said to her younger brother: "Go home, and when you get home give them the nose ornament to eat, keep for me only a stone and its rope."

"I will do so," said Blue Jay. Iô'i had five children. He went home. Now he plucked the duck. He finished plucking it. Now he cut the fat of the duck and tied it to the noses of Iô'i's children. He made a fire and said: "Go near the fire. Look into the fire in the middle of the house." Now he put a stone aside; a stone of that size. Now they looked into the fire and the fat became warm. Then they licked it off. Iô'i went home.

She opened the door and saw her children. Their faces had become flushed by the heat. Then she jumped into the house. The stone, which Blue Jay had put aside, hit her right on her forehead and she fell down. She lay there a long time; she recovered, arose, and said: "Anah, Squint-eye, what did I tell you? I told you to give them a little and to keep the stomach for me." Then she took her children away from the fire.

Blue Jay replied: "I thought so; why do you not speak plainly when you speak to me?"

Another time Iô'i said to her brother. "Make me a canoe large enough for one leg."

"I will do so," replied Blue Jay. Iô'i said: "When there are no roots here I shall always go to the other side when you have finished the canoe."

"I think so," replied Blue Jay. Early next morning Blue Jay went and hollowed out a piece of cedar wood. He put his leg into the canoe to measure it and made it just as large as his leg. He finished the canoe and went to his sister.

He said: "I have finished the canoe." They carried it to the water and went to the canoe. When she saw it and noticed that it was just large enough for one leg she said: "Anah, Squint-eye, what did I tell you? I told you to make a canoe large enough for one man."

Blue Jay replied: "I thought so; why do you not speak plainly when you speak to me?" On the next day Blue Jay made a large canoe. It was good, large enough to carry one person. He brought it to his sister.

After a while his sister said to him: "You ought to get married. Take a wife. She shall help me dig roots. But take a dead one."

"I will do so," said Blue Jay. Now the daughter of the chief of a town had died. Blue Jay went to the grave at night and took her out. Early the next morning he landed and said to his elder sister. "Here, I bring the dead one ashore, as you told me."

"Anah, Squint-eye, I told you to bring an old one. Quick! Take her to the supernatural beings and ask them to cure your wife."

Now Blue Jay went. He cut off all his hair and began to cry. He went to the place where the supernatural beings lived. They heard somebody crying and went outside.

They spoke: "Oh, see; that is poor Blue Jay who is crying there; perhaps his sister died."

But he cried all the time: "O, my wife; O, my wife."

"Perhaps his sister died, but he said his wife." He landed and they tried to cure her. They asked him: "How long has she been dead?"

He replied: "She died yesterday."

Then the supernatural beings said: "Then you must go to another town where they can cure those who have been dead one day."

Blue Jay said: "She died on the same day when I bought her." He traveled on, and when he had gone some distance he lay down to sleep. On the next morning he went on and came to the town of the supernatural beings. They heard someone crying and went outside.

They spoke: "Oh, see; that is poor Blue Jay who is crying there; perhaps his sister died." But he always said his wife, died. Blue Jay landed and the supernatural people went down to meet him.

He told them: "She died on the same day when I bought her. I bring her to you to cure her."

They looked at her and asked him: "When did she die?" He replied: "She died two days ago." "Then you must carry her to another town where they know how to cure people who have been dead two days."

Then Blue Jay traveled on, and after he had gone a distance he lay down to sleep. Early the next morning he awoke and traveled on. After some time he reached a town, and the people heard him crying.

They ran outside and said: "Oh, see; that is poor Blue Jay; perhaps his sister died." He cried. He landed, and the supernatural people came down to meet him. Now the body of that woman was stinking.

They asked him: "When did she die? "O," he replied, "three days ago." They took water and washed her face. Then they said: "You must carry her to another town where they know how to cure those who have been dead three days." Blue Jay went on, and after some time he lay down to sleep. Early the next morning he started again, and reached the town of the supernatural people.

They heard him crying and said: "Oh, that is poor Blue Jay who is crying there; perhaps his sister died." But he always said his wife had died.

He landed. "O, my wife has died."

They said to him: "When did she die?"

"O," he replied, "four days ago." Now they washed the whole body and bathed her. The bad smell disappeared. They said: "Carry her to another town." Blue Jay went. When he had gone some distance and had almost reached the town he lay down to sleep. Early the next morning he awoke and traveled on to the place of the supernatural beings.

They heard somebody crying and went outside and said: "Oh, see; that is poor Blue Jay; perhaps his sister died."

He landed and the supernatural people went down. He said: "She died on the same day when I bought her."

"When did she die?"

"Oh, five days ago." They tried to cure her there on the beach. Her heart began to move and they carried her up to the house. There they continued to cure her. And Blue Jay's wife resuscitated. Her hair was so long that it hung down below her buttocks. Now they brought Blue Jay into the house of the oldest one of the supernatural people, they worked over him and made his hair grow until it hung down to his thighs. They said to him: "Remain here; you shall do as we do. When a person has been dead five days you shall cure him." Early the next morning the supernatural man arose. He sat down with Blue Jay and said: "Spit as far as you call." Blue Jay tried to spit, but his saliva fell down nearby. Then the supernatural being spat, and his saliva struck the other side of the house.

Five days Blue Jay tried, then he spat, and his saliva struck the other side of the house. Now he became a chief. He stayed there some time and then he became homesick. The supernatural people told him: "When you go home never give your hair in payment for a wife." Blue Jay went home. He arrived at his elder sister's house with his wife.

The younger brother of the woman had grown up. One day he went some distance and reached Blue Jay's house. He peeped into the house through a hole and he saw his elder sister sitting with Blue Jay. Blue Jay's hair reached down to his thighs. The boy came home, but he did not tell anything. Early the next morning he went again to the house and peeped into it, and again he recognized his sister.

Five times he went and then his elder sister saw him. She called him: "Come in, come in, brother." He entered and she gave him to eat.

Then the boy went home and said to his mother: "My elder sister is staying with Blue Jay." The people took a stick and whipped him. He cried: "Indeed, indeed, she gave me to eat. She called me; I went into the house and she fed me."

Then the people went to the burial-ground and saw that she had disappeared. Only the canoe was there. They sent a young man to Blue Jay's house, and, indeed, there was the chief's daughter. Then the chief said: "Go to Blue Jay and tell him that he must give me his hair in payment for his wife."

The messengers went and said to Blue Jay: "The chief wants your hair." Blue Jay did not reply. Five times they spoke to him. Then the chief said to his people: "Let us go, we will take her back." Now the people went. They took hold of her, one at each arm. They put her on her feet and dragged her out of the house. Then Blue Jay began to fly. He became a Blue Jay and flew away.

The, woman collapsed right there. Then they called him: "Blue Jay, come back, she shall be your wife." But he did not return. Now they buried her again. She had died again.

* * *

There were Blue Jay and Iô'i. One night the ghosts when out to buy a wife. They bought Iô'i. Her family kept the dentalia that they had given and at night they were married. On the following morning Iô'i had disappeared. Blue Jay stayed at home for a year, then he said: "I shall go and search for my sister."

He asked all the trees: "Where do people go when they die?" He asked all the birds, but they did not tell him. Then he asked an old wedge.

It said: "Pay me, and I shall carry you there." Then he paid it, and it carried him to the ghosts.

The wedge and Blue Jay arrived near a large town. There was no smoke rising from the houses. Only from the last house, which was very large, they saw smoke rising. Blue Jay entered this house and found his elder sister.

"Ah, my brother," said she, "where do you come from? Have you died?"

"Oh, no, I am not dead. The wedge brought me hither on his back." Then he went and opened all those houses. They were full of bones.

A skull and bones lay near his sister. "What are you doing with these bones and this skull?" asked Blue Jay.

His sister replied: "That is your brother-in-law; that is your brother-in-law." "Pshaw! Iô'i is lying all the time. She says a skull is my brother-in-law!" When it grew dark the people arose and the house was quite full. It was ten fathoms long. Then he said to his sister: "Where did these people come from?"

She replied: "Do you think they are people? They are ghosts." He stayed with his sister a long time. She said to him: "Do as they do and go fishing with your dipnet."

"I think I will do so," replied he. When it grew dark he made himself ready. A boy whom he was to accompany made himself ready also. Those people always spoke in whispers. He did not understand them.

His elder sister said to him; "You will go with that boy; he is one of your brother-in-law's relations." She continued: "Do not speak to him, but keep quiet."

Now they started. They almost reached a number of people who went down the river singing in their canoes. Then Blue Jay joined their song. They became quiet at once. Blue Jay looked back and saw that in place of the boy there were only bones in the stern of his canoe. They continued to go down the river and Blue Jay was quiet. Then he looked back towards the stern of the canoe. The boy was sitting there again.

He said to him in a low voice: "Where is your weir?" He spoke slowly.

The boy replied: "It is down the river." They went on.

Then he said to him in a loud voice: "Where is your weir?" And only a skeleton was in the stern of the canoe. Blue Jay was again silent. He looked back and the boy was sitting again in the canoe. Then he said again in a low voice: "Where is your weir?" "Here," replied the boy. Now they fished with their dip-nets. Blue Jay felt something in his net. He lifted it and found only two branches in his net. He turned his net and threw them into the water. After a short while he put his net again into the water. It became full of leaves. He turned his net and threw them into the water, but part of the leaves fell into the canoe. The boy gathered them up. Then another branch came into Blue Jay's net. He turned his net and threw it into the water. Some leaves came into it and he threw them into the water. Part of the leaves fell into the canoe. The boy gathered them up. Blue Jay was pleased with two of the branches, which had caught in his net. He thought: "I will carry them to Iô'i. She may use them for making fire." These branches were large. They arrived at home and went up to the house. Blue Jay was angry, because he had not caught anything. The boy brought a mat full of trout up to the house and the people roasted them.

Then the boy told them: "He threw out of the canoe what we had caught. Our canoe would have been full if he had not thrown it away."

His sister said to him: "Why did you throw away what you had caught?"

"I threw it away because we had nothing but branches."

"That is our food," she replied. "Do you think they were branches? The leaves were trout, the branches fall salmon."

He said to his sister: "I brought you two branches, you may use them for making fire." Then his sister went down to the beach. Now there were two fall-salmon in the canoe. She carried them up to the house and entered carrying them in her hands. Blue Jay said, to his elder sister: "Where did you steal these fall salmon!"

She replied: "That is what you caught."

"Iô'i is always lying."

On the next day Blue Jay went to the beach. There lay the canoes of the ghosts. They had all holes and parts of them were moss-grown. He went up to the house and said to his sister: "How bad are your husband's canoes, Iô'i."

"Oh, be quiet," said she; "the people will become tired of you." "The canoes of these people are full of holes."

Then his sister said to him: "Are they people? Are they people? They are ghosts." It grew dark again and Blue Jay made himself ready. The boy made himself ready also. They went again. Now he teased the boy. When they were on their way he shouted, and only bones were there. Thus he did several times until finally they arrived. Now they fished with their dipnets. He gathered the branches and leaves, which they caught, and when the ebb-tide set in their canoe was full. Then they went home. Now he teased the ghosts. He shouted as soon as they met one, and only bones were in the canoe. They arrived at home. He went up to his sister. She carried up what he had caught; in part fall salmon, in part silver-side salmon.

On the next morning Blue Jay went into the town. He found many bones in the houses. When it grew dark somebody said: "Ah, a whale has been found." His sister gave him a knife and said to him: "Run! A whale has been found." Blue Jay ran and came to the beach. He met one of the people whom he asked, speaking loudly: "Where is that whale?" Only a skeleton lay there. He kicked the skull and left it. He ran some distance and met other people. He shouted loudly. Only skeletons lay there. Several times he acted this way toward the people. Then he came to a large log. Its bark was perhaps that thick. There was a crowd of people who peeled off the bark. Blue Jay shouted and only skeletons lay there. The bark was full of pitch. He peeled off two pieces, I do not know how large. He carried them on his shoulder and went home.

He thought: "I really believed it was a whale, and, behold, it is a fir." He went home. When he arrived he threw down the bark outside the house. He entered and said to his sister: "I really thought it was a whale. Look here, it is bark."

His sister said: "It is whale meat, it is whale meat; do you think it is bark?" His sister went out and two cuts of whale lay on the ground. Iô'i said: "It is a good whale; its blubber is very thick." Blue Jay looked. A whale lay on the beach. Then he turned back. He met a person carrying bark on his back. He shouted and nothing but a skeleton lay there. He took that piece of bark and carried it home on his shoulder. He came home. Thus he did to the ghosts. In course of time he had much whale meat.

Now he continued to stay there. He went again to that town. He entered a house and took a child's skull, which he put on a large skeleton. And he took a large skull, which he put on that child's skeleton. Thus he did to all the people.

When it grew dark the child rose to its feet. It wanted to sit up, but it fell down again because its head pulled it down. The old man arose. His head was light. The next morning he replaced the heads. Sometimes he did thus to the legs of the ghosts. He gave small legs to an old man, and large legs to a child. Sometimes he exchanged a man's and a woman's legs. In course of time they began to dislike him.

Iô'i's husband said: "These people dislike him, because he mistreats them. Tell him he shall go home. These people do not like him."

Iô'i tried to stop her younger brother. But he did not follow her. On the next morning he awoke early. Now Iô'i held a skull in her arms. He threw it away: "Why do you hold that skull again, Iô'i?"

"Ah, you broke your brother-in-law's neck." It grew dark. Now his brother-in-law was sick. A man tried to cure him and he became well again.

Now Blue Jay went home. His sister gave him five buckets full of water and said: "Take care! When you come to burning prairies, do not pour it out until you come to the fourth prairie. Then pour it out."

"I think so," replied Blue Jay. Now he went home. He reached a prairie. It was hot. Red flowers bloomed on the prairie. Then he poured water on the prairie and one of his buckets was half empty. He reached the woods and soon he came to a prairie, which was burning at its end.

He reached another prairie, which was half on fire. "That is what my sister spoke about." He poured out on his road the rest of the bucket. He took another bucket and when it was half empty he reached the woods on the other side of the prairie.

He reached still another prairie, the third one. One half of it burned strongly. He took one of his buckets and emptied it. He took one more bucket and emptied one-half of it. Then he reached the woods on the other side of the prairie. Now he had only two buckets and a half left.

He reached another prairie, which was almost totally on fire. He took that half bucket and emptied it. He took one more bucket and when he reached the woods at the other side of the prairie he had emptied it. Now only one bucket was left.

He reached another prairie, which was all over on fire. He poured out his bucket. When he had come nearly across he had emptied his bucket. He took off his bearskin blanket and beat the fire. The whole bearskin blanket was burnt. Then his head and his hair caught fire and he was burnt.

Now Blue Jay was dead. When it was just growing dark he came to his sister, Iô'i," he said.

His sister cried: "Ah, my brother is dead." His trail led to the water on the other side of the river. She launched her canoe and went to fetch him. She reached him. Iô'i's canoe was pretty. She said to him: "And you said that canoe was moss-grown."

"Ah, Iô'i is always telling lies. The other ones had holes and were moss-grown." She said to him: "You are dead now, therefore you see them differently."

"Iô'i is always telling lies." Now she carried her brother across to the other side. He saw the people. They sang, they gambled, they played dice with beaver teeth; they played hoops; they played dice with ten disks. Farther in the town they sang conjurers' songs. Blue Jay heard them. They were dancing, kumm, kumm, kumm, kumm. He wanted to go to these singers. He tried to sing and to shout, but he was laughed at. He went and tried to shout but they all laughed at him.

Then he entered his brother-in-law's house. There was a chief; Iô'i's husband was good looking. She said: "And you broke his neck."

"Iô'i is always telling lies. Whence came these canoes? They are pretty."

"And you said they were moss-grown."

"Iô'i is always telling lies. The others had all holes. Part of them were moss-grown."

"You are dead now, therefore you see everything differently," said his sister. "Iô'i is always telling lies." He tried to shout at the people, but they laughed at him. Then he gave it up and became quiet. His sister forgot him for a moment. When she went to look for him, he stood near the dancers. After five nights he entered their house. His sister opened the door and saw him dancing on his head, his legs upward. She turned back and cried. Now he had again really died. He had died a second time.

* * *

There were Blue Jay and his elder sister Iô'i. "Let us go visiting, Iô'i," he said to his sister. "Let us visit the Magpie."

Early the next morning they went. They came near his house and saw him on the roof. They landed and went up to the house. Then they saw Magpie on his house. After a little while he swept his house and found one salmon egg. He put it into his topknot, made a fire, and heated some stones. When they were hot he took a kettle, poured water into it, and threw the dry salmon egg into the kettle; then he boiled it. The kettle came to be full of salmon eggs. He placed it before Blue Jay and his sister and they ate. When they had half emptied the kettle they were satiated. They carried away what was left and started to go home.

Iô'i said to her brother: "Let us go to the beach; you go down first."

Blue Jay said: "You go first down to the beach." His sister went down.

Then Blue Jay said to Magpie: "Come to-morrow and fetch your kettle." Magpie said: "I shall go." Then Blue Jay and his sister went home. Early in the morning Blue Jay made a fire and went up to the roof of his house, where he stayed. After awhile he said to his elder sister: "A canoe is coming."

She replied: "It comes because you told him to come." Now Magpie landed and went up to the house. Blue Jay arose and swept his house. He found a salmon egg. He put it into his top-knot. He finished sweeping his house and he heated stones. When they were hot he took his kettle and poured water into it. He took that salmon egg and threw it into the water. Then he threw the hot stones into the kettle and the water began to boil. Then he covered it.

He imitated all Magpie had done. After awhile he uncovered it, but nothing was in the kettle. "Blue Jay can do only one thing," said Magpie. He took the stones and threw them out of the kettle. He threw one dry salmon egg and hot stones into the kettle. When the water began to boil he covered it and when he uncovered it the kettle was quite full of salmon eggs. Then Magpie left them and went home.

After several days Blue Jay and his sister became hungry. "Let us go and visit the Ducks," said Blue Jay.

"To-morrow we will go," said Iô'i. The latter had five children. On the following morning they started and went visiting. After awhile they landed at the beach of the Duck. They came up to the house.

The Duck said to her five children: "Go and wash yourselves." They went to the water and washed themselves. They dived. Soon they emerged again, each carrying a trout. Ten times they dived and their mat became full of trout. They went up to the house, made a fire, and roasted them. Then they gave Blue Jay and his sister to eat. Now the fish that they were roasting were done. They fed Blue Jay, and he and his sister ate.

They ate part and were satiated. Iô'i said to her brother: "You go down first, else you will talk ever so much."

He replied to his sister: "Ah, you would always like to stay here, you go down first."

His sister went down first and as soon as she had left he said to the Duck: "Come to my house tomorrow and get your mat." Now Blue Jay went down to the beach. The Duck said: "We shall all go to-morrow." Then they went home.

They arrived at home. Early the next morning Blue Jay arose and went up to the roof of the house.

He said to his sister: "A canoe is coming."

She remarked: "It comes because you invited them." Then the Duck landed with her five children and went up to the house.

After awhile Blue Jay said to his sister's children: "Go and wash yourselves." Then Blue Jay and his sister's children went down to the beach. They tried to dive, but their backs remained over water. Ten times they dived and were almost dead with cold. They came up to the house empty-handed.

"Blue JayJay does one thing only," said the Duck. She told her children: "Go and wash yourselves. We will give them food." The Duck's children went down to the beach and washed themselves. They dived ten times and their mat was full. They went up to the house. "That trout is thrown at your feet." Now the Ducks went home.

After a number of days Blue Jay and his sister became again hungry. "Let us go and visit the Black Bear," he said. The next morning they went. They arrived at the Bear's house. The Bear heated stones.

Blue Jay said to his sister: "What may he give us to eat, Iô'i?" When the stones were hot the Bear sharpened his knife and cut his feet here all around the sole and cut his thigh. Then he rubbed over the wounds, and they were heated. Then he cut the flesh, which he had cut from his feet and from his body, into small pieces and boiled it. When it was done, he placed it before them, and after a little while they were satiated.

Iô'i said to her brother: You go down first, else you will talk ever so much." Blue Jay said: "You go down first."

His sister went, and then Blue Jay said: "Come to-morrow and fetch your mat." Then he went home with his sister. They came home. Early the next morning Blue Jay arose and made a fire. He went up to the roof of his house.

He said to his sister: "A canoe is coming."

And she replied: "It comes because you invited him." Then the bear landed and came up to the house. Blue Jay heated stones, and when they were hot he sharpened his knife and cut his feet. He fainted right away. They blew on him until he recovered.

The Bear said: "You can do only one thing, Blue Jay." The Bear took his foot and slowly cut it. He cut his thigh. Then he cut the flesh into small pieces. He boiled it. When he had finished cooking and it was done he threw it before them and went home. Blue Jay's feet were sore.

After several days they again got hungry. Then Blue Jay said to his elder sister: "To-morrow we will go and visit the Beaver." Early in the morning they started to visit him, and they arrived at the Beaver's house.

The Beaver was in his house. After a little while he went out and carried willows into the house, which he placed before them. He took a dish and went out. Then he carried it back filled with mud. Blue Jay and his sister could not eat it and started to go home.

As they set out homeward his elder sister said to him: "You go down first else you will talk ever so much." Blue Jay said to his elder sister: "You go down first." She went to the beach first. Then Blue Jay said: "Come to my house tomorrow to fetch your dish."

The Beaver replied: "I will come tomorrow."

Early the next morning Blue Jay made a fire and went up to the roof of his house. He said to his sister: "A canoe is coming."

"It comes because you told him to come."

The Beaver landed and entered the house. Blue Jay went out and when he had been away a little while he brought that many willows. He threw them before the Beaver, who began to gnaw and ate them all. Then Blue Jay ran to the beach. He went to get some mud, which he put before the Beaver. He ate it all and went home.

Blue Jay said again to his sister: "Tomorrow we will go and visit the Seal."

On the next morning they started and arrived at the house of the Seal, who had five children. The Seal said to her young ones: "Go to the beach and lie down there." They went and lay down at the edge of the water. The Seal took a stick and went down. When she reached her children she struck the youngest one upon its head. The others dived and when they came up again they were again five. Then she pulled up to the house the one that she had killed. She singed it. When she had finished singeing it she cut it. Its blubber was three fingers thick. She boiled it and when it was done she gave it to Blue Jay and his sister. Soon they had enough.

Then Iô'i said to her brother: "You go down first."

He replied: "You go down first, else you will always want to stay where they give its food." He said: "Go to the beach." His elder sister went to the beach. Then Blue Jay said to the Seal: "Come to-morrow and fetch your kettle."

"I shall come," replied the Seal.

They went home. Early next morning Blue Jay made a fire and went up to the roof of his house. He said to his elder sister: "A canoe is coming."

She replied: "It comes because you invited him."

The canoe came ashore. The Seal and her children landed and they came up to the house.

Then Blue Jay said to Iô'i's children: "Go to the beach and lie down there." Then Iô'i's children went and lay down at the edge of the water. Blue Jay took a stick. He went down and struck the youngest one; he struck it twice and it lay there dead.

Then he said to the other children: "Quick, dive!" They dived, and when they came up again one was missing. Five times they dived, but the one that was struck remained dead.

The Seal said: "Blue Jay knows to do one thing only." She struck one of her daughters and said: "Quick; dive!" And when they came up again all five of them were there. She singed her daughter. When she had finished singeing her she cut her and threw her down before Blue Jay and his sister, saying: "You may eat this." Then they tied up and buried the dead child of Iô'i, and the Seal went home.

After a while they got hungry again. "Let us go and visit the shadows." "To-morrow we will go."

Early next morning they started and arrived at the house of the shadows. They went up to the house. The house was full of provisions, and on the bed there were large dentalia. There were coats, blankets of deer skin, of mountain goat, and of ground-hog. Blue Jay said: "Where may these people be?"

His elder sister replied: "Here they are, but you can not see them." Blue Jay took up one of the large dentalia.

"Ahahaha, my ear, Blue Jay," cried a person. They heard many people tittering. He took up a ground-hog blanket and pulled at it.

"Ahahaha, my ground-hog blanket, Blue Jay." He searched under the bed for the person who had spoken and again the people tittered. He took up a coat of mountain-goat wool.

The person cried, "Why do you lift my coat, Blue Jay?"

He took a nose ornament and the person cried: "Ahahaha, my nose-orna-ment, Blue Jay." Then a basket fell down from above. He took it and put it back. Then a salmon roe fell down. He put it back, and again he searched under the bed for persons. Then, again, the people tittered and laughed at him.

His sister said to him: "Stay here quietly. Why should they be called shad-ows if they would not act as they do?" They looked around. There was salmon roe put up in a bag for winter use, and they ate it.

Blue Jay said again: "Where may these people be?"

His elder sister replied: "Here they are, here they are; but you do not see them." When it got dark Blue Jay said: "We will sleep here." Now they slept dur-ing the night. Blue Jay awoke and went out. He tried to urinate standing. It ran down his legs. Blue Jay's elder sister went out. She sat down on the ground and urinated. There stood her urine.

Blue Jay spread his legs: "Look here, Iô'i, what became of me!"

He pulled his groins and his sister cried much. "Ahahaha, that hurts me, Squint-eye!"

"Is it Iô'i's body, and it hurts her?" After some time she took revenge upon him. She pulled the penis; "Anah," cried Blue Jay, "it hurts me Iô'i."

"Is it his body, and he feels sick?" Then they went to sleep again. Blue Jay awoke early. Then he was a man again as before. His elder sister awoke. Now she was again a woman as before. She was well again.

Thus they took revenge on Blue Jay, because he had teased the people. "Let us go, else they will tease us again," said Blue Jay.

His sister replied: "You did not believe me and they teased us."

Then Blue Jay went home. He arrived at home. His sister said: "Now we have gone visiting enough."

ROBIN AND BLUE JAY

Tradition Bearer: Charles Cultee

Source: Boas, Franz. Pages 151–52 in *Chinook Texts*. Smithsonian Institution Bureau of American Ethnology Bulletin 20. Washington, DC: U.S. Government Printing Office, 1894.

Date: 1890–1891

Original Source: Chinook

National Origin: Native American

Blue Jay confines his antics as **trickster** primarily to deceiving the sleeper fish and dominating an elder brother, which violates Chinook norms, as well as those of the general Native Northwest Coast. Most of this narrative, though, is devoted to Blue Jay demonstrating his powers of supernatural sight and healing.

There were Blue Jay and Robin. Once upon a time they were hungry. Blue Jay said: "Make yourself ready, Robin." And they went to the sea where a slough was left by the receding tide. They were in their canoe.

Blue Jay called: "Come ashore, sleeper!" [name of a large fish]. The sleeper shouted in reply, but it was far away from the shore.

Blue Jay called again: "Why do you stay far from the, shore? Only the heron can carry food to you if you stay that far from the shore."

Again the sleeper shouted; he was nearer the shore now.

Blue Jay repeated: "Why do you stay far from the shore? Only the heron can carry food to you if you stay that far from the shore."

Blue Jay called him five times; then he came ashore. Blue Jay speared him and he and his brother went home after they had thrown the fish into their canoe. They reached their home and went ashore.

Blue Jay said to his brother, "Make a fire." Robin made a fire. Blue Jay went and carried the fish up to the house.

He cut it and Robin said: "I will have its tail, I will have its breast, I will have its head."

Then Blue Jay became angry: "You want to have everything for yourself; the Q!tê'nse [imaginary tribe] are going to eat what at has been killed for you."

Then Robin cried; he took his work and left the house. He cried outside.

Blue Jay finished cutting the fish. Then he called his elder brother and said: "Come in, come in, you poor one, you shall have the breast, you shall have the head, you shall have the tail." Then Robin came in. When the fish was roasted they began to eat.

After some time Blue Jay dreamed, and he said to his elder brother, "Robin, I dreamed people sent for us; I was to cure a sick person." After some time people came in a canoe, wailing. When they had almost reached the shore they (Robin and Blue Jay) recognized the duck.

She landed and said to Blue Jay: "O, your brother-in-law is choking. I came to fetch you; you shall cure him."

Blue Jay replied: "We shall go." They made themselves ready to go. They went, and he said to his elder brother: "Robin, you must say, 'She shall give us in payment one lake and one-half of another lake.' Thus you must say when I cure her."

Robin said: "All right."

They landed. The duck's husband was breathing heavily. Now Blue Jay began to cure him and Robin sang: "You shall pay us both sides of one lake and one side of another lake."

One of the ducks who sat at some distance sang differently: "One side shall be yours, my nephews." Then Blue Jay took out the morsel that was choking the duck and made him well. He recovered.

Now Robin and his brother dug roots on the place that they had received in payment. They gathered two canoes full and went home. They arrived at home. They carried their roots up to the house. They stayed there for some time. They ate all their roots.

Then Blue Jay dreamed again. He said to his elder brother: "Robin, I dreamed that people sent for us; I was to cure a sick person." In the afternoon they saw a canoe coming; two persons were in it. They landed and two young men came up to the house. They were the young wolves.

They said to Blue Jay: "We come to call you; a girl of our family is choking." Blue Jay replied: "We shall go." After some time he and his brother made themselves ready, and he said to his elder brother: "When I cure her you must point to the largest basket and say, 'There is the spirit of the disease.'"

"All right," replied Robin.

They landed, and when they came to the house the girl was almost suffocated. Then Blue Jay began to cure her. He sang: "What is it that is in this girl? Her throat is all twisted up."

Then Robin said, pointing to the largest basket: "It is in that large basket." The wolves took it down and placed it near Robin. Robin continued to do so, and pointed to all the large baskets. Then Blue Jay took out what had choked the girl; it was the kneepan of an elk. Then they gave them in payment two canoes full of meat and grease. They went home and now they were satisfied and carried the meat up to the house. Their house became full.

THE BEAVER AND THE WOODRAT

Tradition Bearer: Unavailable

Source: Gatschet, Albert S. "Oregonian Folklore." *Journal of American Folklore* 4 (1891): 139–40.

Date: 1891

Original Source: Modoc

National Origin: Native American

The wood rat, in Modoc oral tradition, is a trouble-maker—quarrelsome and vicious. In other tales, he initiates arguments with his neighbors—such as cottontail rabbit—for no apparent reason. He then ambushes, kills, and sometimes eats them. Beaver's retaliation here, then, undoubtedly would bring satisfaction to the original Native American audiences.

Abeaver rowed a dug-out canoe, and had two young going with him. A wood rat came up to him, asking what was the news.

"I cannot tell you any news, but you can; tell me quick what you know!" the beaver replied.

Then the wood rat said, "The rat was married to his mother, they say; that's the kind of news I know!"

Then the rat went away to watch the canoe upon an ambush; it then attacked and shot at the canoe, and when it was upset it saved the two young beavers, while the old one plunged to the bottom of the lake.

Then the wood rat went straight home and hid itself in its mother's lodge, to avoid the beaver's wrath.

But when the beaver arrived, he discovered the rat and inquired of him, "Whither did you flee?"

"Why do you want to know? I went to get a neck-lace of beads to present to you," replied the rat. The beaver took the beads and indignantly threw them into the fire. Upon this the wood rat attacked him, and told its mother to make an open space in the midst of the camp-fire to throw the beaver into. "I am going to throw the beaver into the fire; when he is there, cover him up with earth!"

But things went off differently, for the beaver seized both the rat and his mother, and threw them into the fire. "Utututu!" cried the rat in the fire," so it whirled about in the fire, while its hair and flesh was singed.

The beaver then apostrophized it for its meanness, "I did not come to see you here for a mere child's play; you get a painful punishment now, and the Indians would certainly scoff at you if they could see where you are now. After your body is charred up, the people would not like to have a smell of you, and would call you simply the 'stinking one,' you miserable fellow, you who own nothing but a house of sticks, and are of no account!"

Hereupon the beaver set fire to the wooden lodge of the rat and its mother, took his two young under his arms, and went home.

So far goes the story.

THE STORY OF SKUNK

Tradition Bearer: Thomas Jackson

Source: Frachtenberg, Leo J. "Myths of the Alsea Indians of Northwestern Oregon." *International Journal of American Linguistics* 1 (1917): 65–69.

Date: 1910

Original Source: Alsea

National Origin: Native American

The Alsea were a wealthy maritime culture whose members lived on the coasts and riverbanks of Oregon. Their seal hunting brought them wealth, accumulated through the dentalia shells used as currency and through slaves. "The Story of Skunk" was transcribed in English that imitated as closely as possible the indigenous style of performance. Although the archaic English and five-part repetition may prove difficult for modern readers, it is comparable to the European folktale with its descriptive conventions and three-part plot structures.

O nce there were five brothers. They were traveling all over the world. They did not travel long, when they came upon a person (Skunk). "Oh, dost thou live here, old man?"

"Yes, here is my place, here I grew into a man. Where are you going now?"

"We are not going anywhere. We just travel to look over the people everywhere." "And have you seen any people already?"

"No."

"If you want to look at people, I will constantly go with you where the people come together."

"All right, this our eldest brother will go with thee first."

And then, indeed, they two started. They two were not going long, when they two rested. Then they two started again. And now Skunk began to try repeatedly his own power. He was constantly looking back at the man who followed him. "Thou shalt follow right behind me, thou shan't be dodging here and there." Then, indeed, he would do it. And Skunk would just open his anus. Then again they two would take a rest. Once more they two would start, but just similarly it would happen.

At last they two started out for the fifth time. "We two are now about to arrive at where there are many people. Thou shalt always follow me close behind."

And then, indeed, the man did it, whereupon Skunk broke wind at him suddenly. He killed him, and dragged him to one side.

He turned back and went home. And then, when he came home, he was asked, "Where is our oldest brother?"

"Oh, he remained at the place to which we two came. Those people there are doing all sorts of things—they play shinny-ball, they throw spears through hoops, they play the guessing-game—all sorts of things are done by them."

"Oh, all right, we shall go together."

"You will come with me one at a time."

"All right, I will go with him." And then, verily, they two went. They two did not go long, when they two took a rest. Then they two started out again, but soon the same thing would happen as before. For the fifth time they two started out again, whereupon Skunk once more broke wind at him suddenly. Again he carried him to one side, and went back home once more.

Then he arrived home again. "Oh, didst thou come back?"

"Yes, I came back alone."

"And where are they two?"

"Oh, they two remained there. All sorts of things are done at where we two came."

"All right, art thou going back again?"

"Yes, I am going back once more."

"May I go with thee?"

"Certainly, we two shall go." Then they two, verily, started out. They two did not go long, when they two took a rest and sat down.

"Let me have this thy bow. He is referring to Skunk's deadly anus!" Then, indeed, he gave it to him. The man began to examine it. "Thy bow is good."

"Yes, I have inherited it," said Skunk. The man tried it several times, he pulled it a little.

"Hey! Do not pull it hard, it is my heirloom. It is the bow of my father's father." Again they two started out. The same thing was done as before.

Finally, after their fifth start, Skunk said to him several times, "Keep thou right behind me! Thou shalt not dodge back and forth; because, if thou keepest on dodging here and there, perchance somebody will hurt thee." Then the man did it, indeed.

Thereupon again he quickly broke wind at him, after which he went home once more. And then, when he came back, he told the two remaining brothers, "I left them behind."

"All right, art thou going back again?"

"Yes, I am going back." Then they two (Skunk and the fourth brother) went back again. They two did not go long, when they two took a rest. "Let me have thy bow!" So he gave him his bow.

"Verily, thy bow is good."

"Yes, it is my heirloom." Then the boy began to pull its string. "Hey! Do not pull it hard!" Nevertheless he kept on pulling it harder. "Hey! Do not pull it hard! Thou wilt spoil it. It is my heirloom, it is the bow of my father's father and also of my father."

Then they two started out again. "Keep right behind me! Thou shalt not twist thyself here and there." He looked back at him once in a while. "Hey! Thou art twisting thyself here. Follow close behind me, follow close behind me, follow close behind me!"

Then the boy walked right behind him, although his anus was all the time repulsive to his sense of smell. Skunk was continually opening his anus. Finally, after their fifth start, Skunk did the same thing as before. He kept on saying, "Keep right behind me! Thou shalt not dodge here and there." Then at last he again broke wind at him suddenly. The boy died.

Then he went home. And when he came back, he was asked by the last brother, "Where are thy former companions?" "Oh, I left them behind. They refused to come home. All sorts of things are done there—shinny-playing, guessing, running, wrestling, throwing spears through hoops."

"All right, wilt thou go back?"

"Yes, I am going back once more."

"All right, I will go back with thee."

Then, verily, they two went. They two did not go long, when they two took a rest. "Let me have this thy bow!" said the young man.

Thereupon, indeed, Skunk gave it to him.

So then he tried to pull it. "Hey! Do thou not pull it hard! Thou wilt break my ancient heirloom, the thing that was left to me. This is the bow of my father's father, and then of his father."

"Now, verily, thy bow is good." Again he would begin to pull it.

"Hey! Do thou not pull it hard! Thou wilt break it, per-chance."

Again they two started out. Once more then similarly it was done thus. Then they two would start out again. "Follow me close right behind, perchance somebody might hurt thee."

Nevertheless, the young man would not do this; he just kept ongoing alongside of him. "Hey! Thou art not walking behind me. Keep right behind me!"

Then the boy would pretend to walk behind him, whereupon Skunk began to open his anus.

At the fifth time they two rested again. "Let me see this thy bow! I am going to carry thy bow."

"No. Thou mayst not know what to do with it. Thou art young yet."

Finally the boy persuaded Skunk to part with his bow. And then he began to pull it again. He would pull it quickly just a little.

"Hey! Do thou not pull it! Hey! Do thou not pull it!" He pulled it a little harder. "Hey do not pull it! Give me back my bow!"

"No! Thou shalt first give me back my elder brothers, then I will return to thee thy bow."

"All right, but give me back my bow!"

"No! First bring back here my elder brothers, then I will return to thee thy bow." "All right." Then, indeed, he went. He was not absent long, when they all came back. He brought them all back. "Here are thy elder brothers."

"Is this here thy bow?"

"Yes."

"Hm! No, my friend! It is thy anus, not thy bow." So he began to pull it. Only this much was necessary. As he kept on pulling it, Skunk just whined all the time. Finally his bow broke. Then Skunk just straightened out again, and died.

Only now the story ends.

BIG FRED

Tradition Bearer: Fred Roys

Source: Walden, Wayne. "Interview of Fred Roys." American Life Histories: Manuscripts from the Federal Writers' Project, 1936–1940. Manuscript Division, Library of Congress. 12 October 2005. http://memory.loc.gov/ammem/wpaintro/wpahome.html.

Date: 1938

Original Source: Northwest

National Origin: European American

The following group of narratives is intended to represent the style and repertoire of a Northwestern logging camp raconteur. Invoking the name of Paul Bunyan seems to set the first story up as a **tall tale**, but it quickly becomes fiction best characterized as comic **anecdote**. This narrative comments on the bosses of the camps in which Big Fred worked "in the old days." The tale then transitions into Big Fred's **personal experience narrative**, finally concluding with the expected **tall tale**.

Big Fred and several others were indulging in reminiscences of by-gone times. The talk was of the Northwest logging camps, and Big Fred, a former lumberjack, was doing most of the talking. Despite his years, Big Fred seems still capable of bucking big logs and, more certain, possesses the faculty of telling tales, the veracity of which may be questioned.

Fred claims that years ago he sometimes "chased around with Paul Bunyan," that Paul "wasn't a bad plug," that modern phases of the lumber industry require more up-to-date methods.

"Paul Bunyan was all right in his time, but he didn't have the big shots of today to deal with—and he never was able to get rid of the crumbs. It was the Wobblies—and you got to give 'em credit for it—that really done something about the crumbs. That was one of their big fights.

"In Bunyan's day the camps was crummy, the bunks was crummy, and the men wus so used to being crummy that they wouldn't of knowed what to do without 'em. After the Wobs begun to have some say-so on the jobs they begun to holler for clean bedding, and that sort of put the skids under the crumbs—a lot of 'em anyway.

"A crumb is what you'd call a louse," said Big Fred, with a tone of pity, for one so ignorant as I seemed to be. "They was called 'cooties' by the soldiers during the war, but they're the same thing; we always called 'em crumbs. Anyhow—as I was going to say—one time when one of the big shots come out to look things over, he stuck his head in one of the bunk-house doors. Before he could duck back again he heard a bunch of voices yelling at him, 'Hello Brother'. It kinda puzzled him. After a while, when he seen that the crumbs were coming to meet him, and was actually calling him their brother, the boss got mad. He figured that that was an insult to his dignity, you see.

"'What do you mean by calling me your brother?' he says to them. 'Well, we are, ain't we?' they says. 'We don't need no interpreter,' they says, 'we may be a little different looking on the outsides, but we got the same souls, ain't we?' they says to him. 'We get our livin' from the same source, don't we?' they says, 'It's the blood of the guys you get workin' for you,' they says, 'You bleed 'em by day, and we bleed 'em by night,' they says, 'that makes you and us blood-brothers,' they says to the boss. 'Yeah?' says the boss, 'well as you weaken 'em and rob 'em of some of their energy, I'm going to kill you,' the boss says to the crumbs."

"'All right,' says the crumbs—'hop to it, but you'll lose the best ally you got, or ever had.' 'How so?' says the boss. 'Well,' says the crumbs, 'ain't it our gouging into the hides of your slaves that keeps 'em so busy scratching they can't do any thinking? And as long as they can't think,' they says, 'your slaves won't bother to organize,' they says. 'They won't demand any improvements,' they says.

"And, well, by that time, I was kind of tired with their damned propaganda," Fred says.

"Them religious revivals they used to have, you don't see much of that sort of goings-on nowadays; but in them days they was great doings. When I was a kid we used to look forward to 'em like we did the circus. Sometimes they was as good as a circus. It was a case of some to Jesus everybody. You had to come in or they'd hound the hell out of you if you didn't. The woods was full of Billy Sundays, and if you could stand out against their persuading you, you was a good one. You had to have what they call stamina. Generally when some of those old hens got a hold of a guy, he was a goner, 'cause the women then went into the revival business with both feet. When they took out after you, there wasn't much use o' running.

"But there was one old codger they had a devil of a time a-snaring. He wouldn't fall for their bait at all. They tried every which way to get him, but old Rufe—Rufus Gray his name was—was one guy they couldn't bring into the fold. He had read Bob Ingersoll, I guess, and didn't seem to give a damn if his soul was saved or not. Pie in the sky couldn't move him. The chase went on for years, revival after revival, and still old Rufe couldn't be swayed from the paths of wickedness he preferred to travel. His soul was getting blacker and blacker with accumulating sins, but still the old cuss hung back. The stubborn old geezer seemed sure as hell bound for hell, and the betting was odds against his ever being corralled.

"Well, it finally happened that a revival came on and, whether the Bible-pounder was more convincing, or whether the sisters put on greater pressure in their persuading whatever it was, old Rufe—maybe he thought it was better to get it over with, but anyhow the old guy shows signs of weakening. He give up arguing and told 'em O-Kay, that he was ready to submit at last.

Well, of course, landing a hard-shell old sinner, the likes of him, caused a lot of rejoicing among the sisters and the brethren. It was a great triumph, something to holler about. All that was lacking now was the baptism. And for old Rufus it'd need more'n a little sprinkling. It'd need a whole damned puddle of water for him to be made pure and radiant!

"The baptisings was most of the time done in a lake, about a mile and a half from town. The preacher, and whoever would be his helpers, would lead the converts out to where the water was about arm-pit deep, and them dip 'em under. That's what they done to old Rufe too—they leads him out to where the water was up to his whiskers and then topples him under. But he wasn't counting on being ducked. So he comes up sputtering, and pawing, and madder'n hell. Soon as he untangles himself from their hanging on to him, he starts out swimming to beat the devil himself, and when he gets out in about the middle of the lake he turns his head and hollers out: 'Yeah, you would, would you? You'd try to drown somebody, would you? You Gawd-damned fools.'

Big Fred speaking-something of a drawl:

"Talkin' bout speed, I'd liked to had some of you guys with me a couple of months ago. I don't know what kind of a car it was, but it sure could go. The fellow driving the car was a Jap, and there was only me and him in it. We left town here and was out fifty miles in less than an hour, that was makin' pretty good time I thought, but when we got out where the traffic thinned down, the Jap steps on it. We had the radio going to kind of occupy our minds as we went along, and every so often he had to slow down to let the waves catch up."

"But," put in an incredulous member of the group, "but do you know that radio waves travel thousands of miles in a second, way up in the thousands?"

"Well, we must of been beatin' that," said Fred, "cause we couldn't get the drift of what the program was 'cept by slowing down once in a while.

"Years ago, in the mountains of Colorado, lived an old veterinarian whose name was 'Doc' Squires. He was something of a local character, and characteristic of him were some of the oddest word formations that I have ever heard. Given to raillery, the old man upon an occasion when cigarettes were being discussed, said: 'I cannot see why boys will go on smoking those founcounded cigareets when they know that it is conjorious to their institutions—why it's utterly rickydoodulous.'

"Then too, there was old Jack, a tall, lanky, and grizzled prospector, whom I remember as quite a character of those same parts. Relating on experience he had, when suddenly confronted with a bear, he said:

'I was coming down the trail when all of a sudden I see this here bar spending on his hind feet lookin' at me. The only thing I could do was to hit for the nearest tree I could find. The nearest tree was a scrubby little pinion, but I lit out for it and climbed it. But when I'd climbed it as fer as I could go, I looked down and seen that my feet was still on the ground.' What happened to the bar I never learned, or have forgotten.'"

THE GOLD BRICK

Tradition Bearer: George Estes

Source: Sherbert, Andrew C. "Interview of George Estes." American Life Histories: Manuscripts from the Federal Writers' Project, 1936–1940. Manuscript Division, Library of Congress. 12 October 2005. http://memory.loc.gov/ammem/wpaintro/wpahome.html.

Date: 1938

Original Source: Oregon

National Origin: European American

The following **personal experience narrative** is offered as validation for the narrator's claims of extraordinary luck. It serves as a cautionary tale as well, however, given his comments, "I hadn't heard that the Brooklyn Bridge was being 'sold' by prosperous-looking New Yorkers to bucolic-looking strangers on an average of once a week."

As I review the incidents of my past life I can but conclude that luck played a major role in all that I ever did or in all that ever happened to me. A case in point. As a young telegrapher in Portland, I had a great many acquaintances. At the time of which I speak, Burnside street was a busy thoroughfare—the cross-roads of the Oregon country, where one might meet anyone he had ever met or known before. In those few short blocks there congregated people of all types, from the more or less dandified Portland sophisticates, to the rough, uncouth wranglers of the hinterland. The gold miner from eastern or southern Oregon rubbed elbows with the almond-eyed Chinese. The farmer from Tualatin Valley walked the length of Burnside street a time or two, before he started for home with the new plow he had purchased. There was only one Burnside street on the face of the earth, and that was in Portland.

One day I was approached by an acquaintance, a young fellow of no means, who asked to speak to me confidentially. He said that he had made the acquaintance of a miner, who at that very moment was waiting for him in a room in a Burnside street lodging house, and who had possession of a gold brick worth twelve thousand dollars, which could be bought for three thousand. He said the miner was badly in need of money and had come by the brick "never mind how."

It looked like a splendid investment. Now as it happened, my bank balance—because of frugal personal habits—stood at a sum just about ample enough to take care of such an investment. Three thousand dollars becomes twelve thousand dollars—just like that. No long, tedious, slaving, scraping, and waiting for slowly amassed principal and small, annual interest accruing to do the job. I hastened to the bank and drew out the three thousand.

My acquaintance and I hurried down to the miner's room, anxious to get there before someone else did, or before he changed his mind. He was there. I bought the brick. Certainly I was excited. My eyes bulged. The brick was golden yellow and heavy as lead. I left the miner's room and with the winged heels of a Mercury ran over to the shop of a jeweler and goldsmith who was a very good friend of mine. I wanted him to appraise, and perhaps buy, my twelve-thousand-dollar brick. My friend was out when I entered. It was some little time before he returned. I jumped up and hurriedly told him of my good fortune. His face turned ashen. He clamped his head with both hands in anguish and cried, "George, George, what have you done? You bought a gold brick down an Burnside Street? Oh, George! You damned fool! Give me the brick. Run down to Burnside Street and see if you can find the fellow that sold it to you! Get the Marshal! Hurry! Run!"

Needless to say, I ran, but I arrived there too late. My miner had checked out and disappeared in the brief interim that followed the transaction. And here is why I say "luck" played a major role in all of the incidents of my life: whether for good or ill. I mended my way slowly back to the shop of my friend, the goldsmith. I was callow. I had never heard of anyone being gold-bricked. At that time I hadn't heard that the Brooklyn Bridge was being "sold" by prosperous-looking New Yorkers to bucolic-looking strangers on an average of once a week.

I walked into the shop of my friend—beaten, defeated, despondent. He jumped up excitedly at my entrance, shouting. "George, you're the luckiest damn fool in the world. I've tested your gold brick and it's solid gold to the core. An ingot worth pretty near what your miner said it was."

THE POWERS THAT BE: SACRED TALES

COYOTE CREATES TABOOS

Tradition Bearer: Charles Cultee

Source: Boas, Franz. Pages 102–6 in *Chinook Texts*. Smithsonian Institution Bureau of American Ethnology Bulletin 20. Washington, DC: U.S. Government Printing Office, 1894.

Date: 1890–1891

Original Source: Chinook
National Origin: Native American

The following Chinook **myth** enumerates and validates taboos concerning their food sources. Such ritualized behavior is common. It is noteworthy that even Coyote, who at the outset of the narrative demonstrates the power to control the environment, observes taboos. While it is hardly surprising that, even when operating in **culture hero** mode, a **trickster** figure such as Coyote should speak to his excrement, there is a logic behind this act. In order to understand those things that are taboo, he seeks answers from the "physically dirty" substance that emanates from a supernaturally powerful figure—himself.

Coyote was coming. He came to Gôt'a't. There he met a heavy surf. He was afraid that he might be drifted away and went up to the spruce trees. He stayed there a long time. Then he took some sand and threw it upon that surf: "This shall be a prairie and no surf. The future generations shall walk on this prairie." Thus Clatsop became a prairie. The surf became a prairie.

At Niâ'xaqcê a creek originated. He went and built a house at Niâ'xaqcê. He went out and stayed at the month of Niâ'xaqcê. Then he speared two silver-side salmon, a steel-head salmon, and a fall salmon. Then he threw the salmon and the fall salmon away, saying: "This creek is too small. I do not like to see here salmon and fall salmon. It shall be a bad omen when a fall salmon is killed here; somebody shall die; also when a salmon is killed. When a female salmon or fall salmon is killed a woman shall die; when a male is killed a man shall die."

Now he carried only the silver-side salmon to his house. When he arrived there he cut it at once, steamed it and ate it. On the next day he took his harpoon and went again to the mouth of Niâ'xaqcê. He did not see anything, and the flood tide set in. He went home. On the next day he went again and did not see anything. Then he became angry and went home. He defecated and said to his excrements: "Why have these silver-side salmon disappeared?"

"Oh, you with your bandy legs, you have no sense. When the first silver-side salmon is killed it must not be cut. It must be split along its back and roasted. It must not be steamed. Only when they go up river then they may be steamed." Coyote went home. On the next day he went again and speared three. He went home and made three spits. He roasted each salmon on a spit. He had three salmon and three spits. On the next day he went again and stood at the month of the creek. He did not see anything until the flood tide set in. Then he became angry and went home.

He defecated. He spoke and asked his excrements: "Why have these silver-side salmon disappeared?"

His excrements said to him: "I told you, you with your bandy legs, when the first silver-side salmon are killed spits must be made, one for the head, one for the back, one for the roe, one for the body. The gills must be burnt."

"Yes," said Coyote.

On the next day he went again. He killed again three silver-side salmon. When he arrived at home he cut them all and made many spits. He roasted them all separately. The spits of the breast, body, head, back, and roe were at separate places. Coyote roasted them. On the next morning he went again. He speared ten silver-side salmon. Coyote was very glad. He came home and split part of the fish. The other part he left and went to sleep. On the next morning he roasted the rest. Then he went again and stood at the mouth of the river. He did not see anything before the flood tide set in. He went home. On the next morning he went again, but again he did not see anything. He went home angry.

He defecated and asked his excrements: "Why have these silver-side salmon disappeared?"

His excrements scolded him: "When the first silver-side salmon are killed, they are not left raw. All must be roasted. When many are caught, they must all be roasted before you go to sleep." On the next morning Coyote went and stood at the mouth of the river. He speared ten. Then he made many double spits, and remained awake until all were roasted that he had caught.

Now he had learned all that is forbidden in regard to silver-side salmon when they arrive first at Niâ'xaqcê. He remained there and said: "The Indians shall always do as I had to do. If a man who prepares corpses eats a silver-side salmon, they shall disappear at once. If a murderer eats silver-side salmon, they shall at once disappear. They shall also disappear when a girl who has just reached maturity or when a menstruating woman eats them. Even I got tired."

Now he came this way. At some distance he met a number of women who were digging roots. He asked them: "What are you doing?"

"We are digging camas."

"How can you dig camas at Clatsop? You shall dig a root, species, and thistle roots in this country. No camas will be dug here." Now they gathered a root, species, and thistle roots. He left these women and spoiled that land. He transformed the camas into small onions.

Then he came to Clatsop. It was the spring of the year. Then he met his younger brother the snake. He said to him: "Let us make nets."

The snake replied: "As you wish." Now they bought material for twine, and paid the frog and the newt to spin it. Now Coyote cleaned all the material for twine while the snake was crawling about. Then the frog and the newt spun it. Then Coyote said to his younger brother: "Clean it, clean it. You crawl about all day." Thus he spoke to the snake. Coyote continued: "You shall make one side of the net, I make the other." Coyote finished his twine and said to the snake: "Quick! Quick! You let me wait. Make your net." The snake replied: "You let me wait." Thus he spoke to Coyote. Now, Coyote made his net. He finished it all. The two women made the ropes, Coyote made the net buoys; while the snake crawled about.

Coyote said: "Make your net buoys; you let me wait." Thus he said to the snake. The snake replied: "Make haste! You let me wait." Coyote finished his net buoys. Then he went to look for stones, and the snake accompanied him. They went for stones to Tongue point. The snake crawled about among the stones, while Coyote carried them down. They went home.

After they reached home Coyote went to gather spruce roots. The snake accompanied him. Coyote dug, up the ground and the snake crawled about at the same place. They went home.

Coyote split the spruce roots. "Go on; work," he spoke to the snake; "you let me wait."

The snake replied: "Quick, quick; work! You let me wait."

Now Coyote tied his net to the buoys and laid it down flat on a large mat. Then he tied it to the buoys. The snake crawled about at the same place. Coyote finished his net and hung it up outside. Early the next morning he stepped out of the house, and there hung already the net of the snake.

"Oh, brother," he said, "you got the better of me." Coyote was ashamed. The snake had won over him.

Coyote said: "When a person makes a net, he shall get tired before he finishes it. It would not be well if he would not get tired."

The snake said to him: "I told you that you would let me wait."

It got day. Then they went to catch salmon in their net. They laid the net and caught two in it. Coyote jumped over the net. Now they intended to catch more salmon, but the flood-tide set in. They had caught only two before the flood-tide set in. Now they went home. Coyote said that he was hungry, and he split the salmon at once. They roasted them. When they were done they ate.

The frog and the newt were their cousins. The next morning they went fishing with their net. The newt looked after the rope, the snake stood at the upper end of the net, Coyote at the lower end. They intended to catch salmon, but they did not get anything until the flood-tide set in. They went home.

Coyote was angry. He defecated and spoke to his excrements: "You are a liar." They said to him: "You with your bandy-legs. When people kill a salmon they do not jump over the net. You must not step over your net. When the first salmon are killed, they are not cut until the afternoon."

"Oh," said Coyote, "You told me enough."

On the next morning they went fishing. When they had killed a salmon they did not jump over the net. They laid their net twice. Enough salmon were in the net.

Then he ordered the newt: "Bail out the canoe, it is full of water." She bailed it out. Then they intended to fish again, but the flood-tide set in. They went home and put down what they had caught in the house.

In the afternoon Coyote split the salmon. He split them in the same way as the silver-side salmon. He placed the head, the back, the body, and the roe in separate places and on separate double spits. They were done. The next morning they went fishing. They did not kill anything.

Coyote became angry and defecated.

He said to his excrements: "Tell me, why have these salmon disappeared?"

His excrements scolded him: "Do you think their taboo is the same as that of the silver-side salmon? It is different. When you go fishing salmon and they go into your net, you may lay it three times. No more salmon will go into it. It is enough then. Never bail out your canoe. When you come home and cut the salmon, you must split it at the sides and roast belly and back on separate double spits. Then put four sticks vertically into the ground so that they form a square and lay two horizontal sticks across them. On top of this frame place the back with the head and the tail attached to it."

He said to his excrements: "You told me enough."

On the next morning they went fishing and killed three salmon. They did not bail out their canoe. Then he said to the newt: "Fetch a stick from the woods. We will make a club." She went and brought a stick. Then they laid their net again. Again a salmon was in it and he killed it with his club. They intended to continue fishing, but the flood-tide set in. They killed four only. They put down their salmon. In the afternoon Coyote cut them and put four sticks into the ground. Now he did as his excrements had told him. When they were done he broke the backbone at once. On the next morning they went fishing. They did not kill anything before the flood-tide set in. They went home.

Coyote was angry and defecated. "Why have these salmon disappeared?" he asked his excrements.

"I told you," they said to Coyote; "do you think their taboo is the same as that of the silver-side salmon? It is different. When you kill a salmon you must never strike it with a stick. When they may be boiled, then you may strike them with a stick. When it is almost autumn you may strike them with a stick. Do not break a salmon's backbone when they just begin to come. When you have killed a salmon, take sand, strew it on its eye, and press it with your fist. Do not club it."

Coyote said: "You have told me enough." On the next morning they went fishing. Salmon went into the net; three went into the net immediately. He strewed sand on each and pressed each. He killed many salmon. They went home and roasted them. When they were done he distributed them among the people of the town above Clatsop. Now they dried them. On the next morning they went fishing. They tried to fish but did not catch anything before the flood-tide set in. They went home. Coyote was angry.

He defecated: "Why have these salmon disappeared?"

"I told you, you lean one, with your bandy-legs. There are many taboos relating to the salmon. When you have killed many salmon you must never carry them outside the house. You must roast and eat them at the same place. When part is left they must stay it the same place. When you want to dry them you must do so when the flood-tide sets in on the day after you have caught them."

He said to them: "You have told me enough." On the next morning they went fishing again. They killed many salmon. They roasted them all. When they were done he invited the people. The newt was sent out. They came to eat in Coyote's house. They finished eating. Then they left there what they had not eaten. Now it was low water in the morning. They went out early to lay their net, but they did not catch anything. They fished until the flood-tide set in. They did not kill anything. They were unsuccessful. Twice they tried to go fishing early in the morning, but they were unsuccessful; they did not catch anything.

Coyote defecated and said to his excrements: "Why have the salmon disappeared?"

Coyote received the answer: "I told you, you lean one, that the salmon has many taboos. When you go fishing and it is ebb-tide early in the morning, you must not lay your net before sunrise. The salmon must not be carried outside until a crow takes one and carries it outside. Then it must be distributed raw. No fire must be made until daylight; the breast must not be eaten before the next day. When salmon are roasted at a tire and they are done, water must be poured into the fire."

He said to his excrements: "You have told me enough. The Indians shall always do this way. Thus shall be the taboos for all generations of Indians. Even I got tired."

Thus spoke Coyote about the taboos of Clatsop. He said to his cousins: "We will move to the other side." The newt made herself ready. Then the snake looked at the frog, who was growling. The snake reached her, struck, and killed her.

Now they arrived here on this side. They went fishing and killed salmon. He did the same way as in Clatsop. He strewed sand on the eye of that salmon. He pressed its eye. Then they intended to fish again, but they did not kill anything. They went home. On the following morning they went fishing again, but they did not kill anything. On the next morning they went fishing again, but they did not kill anything.

Coyote scolded. He defecated: "Why have these salmon disappeared?"

"Oh, you foolish Coyote. When you kill a salmon you must kick it. Do you think it is the same here as at Clatsop?"

"Oh," said Coyote. On the next morning they went fishing again. They laid their net and caught two salmon. They laid their net again and caught three salmon. He threw one ashore. It fell down head first so that the mouth struck the sand. They tried to lay their net again but they did not kill anything. They tried to fish until the flood tide set in. They had not killed anything. They had caught five only. They went home. In the evening Coyote cut the salmon and roasted them. They were done. The following morning they went fishing, but did not kill anything.

Coyote scolded. He defecated: "Why have these salmon disappeared?"

"Oh, you foolish Coyote. Do you think it is the same here as at Clatsop? Do not throw salmon ashore so that the head is downward. It is taboo. When you kill a salmon go and pick salmonberries. When you have caught many salmon put salmonberries into the mouth of each."

"Oh, you have told me enough," he said to his excrements. The next morning they again went fishing. They killed many salmon. He sent the newt to pick salmonberries. The newt brought salmonberries. Now they put those berries into the mouths of those salmon.

It got day and they went fishing again. They met fishermen on the water. A short distance down river they laid their net. They laid it several times and went up the river a short distance. They passed the canoes of those fishermen. They laid their net and intended to fish, but they did not kill anything. They were unsuccessful. They went home. Coyote scolded. He defecated: "Why have these salmon disappeared?"

"You lean one! When yon kill a salmon, and you have laid your net at one place and you kill one more, you must lay your net at the same place. You must not pass a canoe with fishermen in it. It is taboo."

"Yes," said Coyote. On the next day they went again fishing. Coyote said: "Even I got tired. The Indians shall always do in the same manner. Murderers, those who prepare corpses, girls who are just mature, menstruating women, widows and widowers shall not eat salmon. Thus shall be the taboos for all generations of people."

THE DOOM OF THE KATT-A-QUINS

Tradition Bearer: Unavailable

Source: Deans, James. "The Doom of the Katt-a-quins: From the Aboriginal Folk-lore of Southern Alaska." *Journal of American Folklore* 5 (1892): 233–35.

Date: 1862

Original Source: Tlingit

National Origin: Native American

The Tlingit, like the other cultures of the Northwest Coast, attained an extremely high level of cultural complexity due to the abundance and dependability of food resources, and because of the presence of thick jungle-like forests that provided building materials. The Tlingit were able to develop stable settlements and devote less time to the business of staying alive. Raven, who acts as an agent of justice in the following **myth**, was the **culture hero** of many Northwest Coast Native Americans, including the Tlingit.

Katt-a-quin was a chief among the Tlingit. He lived very long ago, our fathers tell us, so long that no man can count the time by moons nor by snows, but by generations. He was a bad man, the worst that ever lived among our people. Not only were he himself and his wife bad, but the whole family were like him. They were feared and shunned by everyone, even by little children, who would run away screaming when any of the family came near.

Nothing seemed to give them so much pleasure as the suffering of other people. Dogs they delighted to torture, and tore their young ones to pieces. Most persons love and fondle a nice, fat little puppy, but not so the Katt-a-quin family; when they got a nice puppy it was soon destroyed by hunger and ill-usage.

When the people met their neighbors from above, at Shakes-heit, if Katt-a-quin came there, he generally spoiled the market, and if he could not get what he wanted by fair means, he would take it by force. The people, seeing this, would pack up and leave. So tired had they grown of the family, that the rest of the tribe had decided to make them all leave the village, or, failing in that, endeavor to get clear of them by some other means. But before doing anything of that sort, they were delivered in a way terrible and unthought of. From old versions of the story, it appears that the people had become so disgusted with the family that when they wished to go hunting or to gather wild fruit, they would strictly conceal their object and the direction of their journey from those whom they disliked.

One morning, while all were staying at Shakes-heit, they made up their minds to go to the large flat where these rocks stand, and lay in a stock of wild fruits for winter use. So in order that none of the Katt-a-quin might come, they all left early and quietly. When the others got up, which was far from early, as they were a lazy lot, and found that they were left alone, they were displeased at not being asked to go along with the others. After a time they all got into a canoe, and went up the river in order to find the rest, which after a while they did, by finding their canoes hauled up on shore.

After this they also landed, and began to pluck berries, but finding that the people who preceded them had got the best of the fruit, they gave up picking in disgust, and were seated on the shore when the others returned, having, as might be expected, plenty of fine fruit. Seeing that the rest had a fine supply, and they themselves nothing but sour, unripe stuff, they asked for a few, which the others gave them; at the same time saying that they should not be so lazy, as they might also have got their share of good ones. After a while, the old fellow demanded more of the best fruit; this the people flatly refused, saying that the late comers ought to go picking for themselves.

Just then a number of the first party, who had gone in another direction, returned with baskets full of nice, large, and ripe fruit. Seeing this, the whole family of the Katt-a-quins went and demanded the whole; this the others refused, saying they had no idea of toiling all day gathering fruit for such a worthless, lazy set as they were. A scuffle began, which ended in the family upsetting all the fruit, and trampling it under foot in the sand, thus destroying the proceeds of a long and hard day's work.

Seeing all this, the people made a rush, some for their bows and arrows, others arming themselves with whatever came to hand, all determined to wreak vengeance on those who had caused the destruction of their day's labor, and whom all disliked.

Seeing this turn of affairs, and the determination of the people, the offenders knew that their only safety lay in getting aboard their canoe, and going down the river before the others could follow them. This they did, leaving in their hurry one or two of their children behind them. But a new and terrible retribution awaited them. When they reached the middle, Yehl (Raven), who had been watching their conduct, turned them in an instant to these stones, and placed them where they now stand, to be an eternal warning to evil-doers. The largest one is Katt-a-quip. The next is his wife, and the small stones in the land and in the water, his children. What is seen is only their bodies; their souls, which can never die, went to Seewuck-cow, there to remain for ages, or until such time as they have made reparation for the evil done while in the body. After this they will ascend to Kee-wuck-cow, a better land. Such was the doom of the Katt-a-quins. As our fathers told the story to us, said the Tlingit, so I tell it to you.

THE MARMOT WOMAN

Tradition Bearer: Unavailable

Source: Boas, Franz. "Traditions of the Ts'ets'ā´ut I." *Journal of American Folklore* 9 (1896): 263–64.

Date: 1894–1895

Original Source: Ts'ets'ā´ut

National Origin: Native American

The narratives of the Athabascan Ts'ets'ā´ut were profoundly influenced by the Tlingit. The most obvious evidence of such influence in this **myth** is seen in the Tlingit phrase used by Marmot Woman to bring her brother back to life. There is a belief reported by Franz Boas that before the arrival of human beings in the country, the land was inhabited by people wearing marmot skins. The donning of a magical skin is a well-known cross-cultural belief among European Americans, African Americans, and Native Americans (including the Southwestern Athabascans—the Navajo). The **motif** of recognizing a shape-shifter by a human token, such as the bracelet in this narrative, is common as well.

Once upon a time there was a widower who had a son. He had built his lodge near the upper end of a valley which abounded in marmots. Every day they went hunting, but he was unsuccessful. It so happened that one day the boy caught a young marmot. He did not kill it, but took it home.

Its mother saw what had happened, and followed the boy to his lodge. There she took off her skin, and was at once transformed into a stout woman. She stepped up to the entrance of the lodge, and said to the men: "Give me my child." They were surprised, for they did not know who she was, but the father invited her to enter. She said: "No, your lodge is not clean." Then he arose, gathered some grass, which he spread on the floor for her to sit on. She entered and sat down.

The boy gave her the young marmot, which she at once proceeded to suckle. Then the woman asked for eagle's down. After she had received this, she said to the hunter: "You are unsuccessful in hunting because you are unclean. I will cleanse you." She wiped the inside of his mouth and removed a vast quantity of phlegm. Now he was clean. She became his wife. Before he again went out hunting she ordered him to seek the solitude of the mountains, and to fast for three days. He went, and on his return the woman gave him a small stick with which to kill marmots.

The first day he went out hunting he saw numerous marmots, and killed twenty. He carried them home, and his wife at once began to skin and carve them. She hung up the meat to dry. While her husband had been away, she had gathered a vast quantity of salmon berries, and they lived on berries and on meat. On the following day the man again went hunting, and killed fifty marmots. The lodge was full of meat.

Often while he was out hunting he noticed that one marmot was following him all the time. It was tame, and played around him. Therefore he did not kill it. One day, however, when there were no, other marmots to be seen, he killed it and carried it home. When his wife opened the pouch and pulled out the game, she began to cry and to wail: "You have killed my brother! You have killed my brother!"

She put down the body, and laid all the other marmots that her husband had procured around it. Then she sang: "Brother, arise!" (goxde kuse khek! This is said to be Tlingit). When she had sung a little while, the body began to move. The dried meat began to assume shape. She threw on it the skins, and all the marmots returned to life and ran up the hills.

She followed them, crying. Her husband was frightened, but followed her, accompanied by his son. After they had gone some distance, they saw her disappearing in a fissure of the rocks, which opened and let her in. When they reached the fissure, the father told his son to stay outside while he himself tried to enter. The fissure opened, and on entering he found himself in a lodge. His brother-in-law had taken off his skin, which was hanging from the roof. He was sitting in the rear of the lodge. The women were seated in the middle of the floor, and were weaving baskets and hats.

The chief spoke: "Spread a mat for my brother-in-law." The people obeyed, and he sat down next to his wife. The chief ordered to be brought a cloak of marmot skins. When he put it on, he was transformed into a marmot. He was given a hole to live in, and a rock on which he was to sit and whistle as the marmots are in the habit of doing. The son saw all that had happened, and returned home in great distress.

Two years after these events, the brothers of the man who had been transformed into a marmot went hunting. They pitched their camp at the same place where their brother had lived. After having cleaned their bodies and fasted for four days, they set their traps. They were very successful. One day one of the brothers saw a marmot jumping into a crack of the rocks. He set his trap at the entrance of the fissure, and when he came back in the evening he found the animal in his trap. He put it into his pouch with the rest of his game, and went home. His wife began to skin the marmots, and to dress the meat.

She took up this particular animal last. When she cut the skin around the forepaws she saw a bracelet under the skin, and her nephew, who was staying with them, recognized it as that of his father. Then she put the animal aside. At midnight it threw off its skin, and resumed the shape of a man. On the following morning they recognized their brother who had been lost for two years. He told them of all that had happened since the time when he had left his son at the fissure of the rock, how he had become a marmot, and how he had lived as one of their race.

THE VISIT TO THE SKY

Tradition Bearer: Unavailable

Source: Boas, Franz. "Traditions of the Ts'ets'ā´ut I." *Journal of American Folklore* 9 (1896): 267–68.

Date: 1894–1895

Original Source: Ts'ets'ā´ut

National Origin: Native American

The following tale focuses on a man lacking in social responsibility, a trait that was crucial both to the Northern Athabascan Ts'ets'ā´ut and to the Tlingit whose culture profoundly influenced the former group. Deserting one family, he is transported in a dream to the Sky World. After bringing back the daughter of the Sky chief as his new wife, he lies to her (Tlingit cosmology reserves a special hell for liars). This leads to the destruction of his people, a holocaust he somehow escapes. The plot of the narrative more closely resembles a European **ordinary folktale** than a Native American **myth**. A particular European evidence is impossible to determine, however.

Once upon a time there was a man who had a large family. One morning his wife and children, upon awaking, were unable to find him. He had disappeared.

When he awoke he found himself in a strange lodge among strange people. The house stood on a vast open prairie. A young girl was lying at his side. It was very beautiful there. Now he heard the chief speaking. He looked around, but he did not see a soul. The girl said to him: "You are in the sky. My father is going to make you clean and strong."

Then he heard the chief saying: "Build a large fire and put stones on top of it." A giant arose, who built a fire and put on stones.

After a while the chief asked, "Are the stones red hot?" The giant replied, "They are hot." Then the wood was taken away, the red hot stones were piled up, and, after the man had been placed on top, a blanket was spread over him. Then the ashes were placed on top of the blanket, and a new fire was built over the whole pile. This was kept burning for a whole day.

In the evening the chief said to the giant, "I think he is done." The fire and the ashes were removed, and the man was found to be red hot, but not steamed. He was taken from the pile of stones with wooden tongs and placed on a plank, which was supported at each end.

The girl was crying all day, because she believed him dead. Early the next morning the chief sent the giant to see if the visitor was still alive. He lifted the blanket, which had been spread over the red hot body. Then the plank, which had been burned by con-tact with the body of the stranger, gave way, and he fell down. But he arose at once hale and well.

Then the chief had a mat spread for him in the rear of the house and said, "I burned you in order to make your body as hard as stone. Sit down with my daughter. She shall be your wife." He married her, and the young woman was glad.

The chief said: "If you so desire, you may take her down to the earth. She shall see what the people are doing." The chief's lodge was full of many kinds of food, which, however, were not known to the visitor.

When they prepared to descend to the earth, the chief gave his daughter a pot and a black tube, through which she drank of the liquid contained in the pot. Nobody except herself was allowed to use these, and she herself did not partake of any other kind of food. The chief ordered the giant to open the road that led to the earth. He opened a hole in the ground, took the rainbow at its one end, and placed the other end on the earth. Before they parted the chief forbade the man ever to tell where he had been and what he had seen and to talk to any woman except his present wife.

They departed, and reached the earth not far away from the village where the man had formerly lived. He did not recognize the country, but his wife showed him the way and told him that they would reach the village in the evening. When they approached the camp the people recognized him. All assembled and asked him where he came from.

He told them that he had been in the sky, and that his new wife was a daughter of the chief of the sky. He was invited to return to his former wife and to his children, but he did not go. He built a lodge outside the camp. He took a girl into his lodge to be a servant to his wife. Every day he himself had to fetch water for his wife in the pot that her father had given to her. This she drank through her tube. The latter had the property of swimming on the water as long as her husband was true to her. It went down when he had spoken to any other woman but her.

One day when he returned bringing the water his young wife asked him if he would like to talk to his former wife. He did not reply, thus intimating that he did not care for her. But when the young woman placed the tube into the water it sank. She knew at once that her husband had spoken to his former wife.

Then she said, "I came to take pity on you and on your friends, but since you do not obey my father's commands I must go back." She wept, and embracing her servant she said, "Hide in the woods under the roots of a large tree where the rays of the sun will not strike you, else you will perish with all the rest of the people." The girl did as she was bidden. Then the rainbow appeared. She climbed up and disappeared from view.

On the following day the man went hunting. Then the sun began to shine hotter and hotter. There was no cloud in the sky. The camp grew quiet, even the dogs ceased to howl. The rays of the sun had burned the whole camp. Only the man and the servant girl had escaped destruction. The man, when the sun was shining so fiercely, had cooled himself with the snow and the water of the mountains, while the servant girl was protected by the roots of the tree. When the sun set the fire went out and the girl returned to her friends, to whom she told what had happened. Nobody knows about the further fate of the man.

LEGEND OF SATTIK

Tradition Bearer: Unavailable

Source: Powers, Stephen. "North American Indian Legends and Fables." *Folk-Lore Record* 5 (1882): 107.

Date: ca. 1882

Original Source: Mattoal

National Origin: Native American

The Mattoal on the borders of California and Oregon relied primarily on a diet of acorns and salmon. The following **legend** emphasizes the importance of strict adherence to taboos (see "Coyote Creates Taboos," p. 127). A belief existed in traditional hunting cultures that animals in a sense "gave" themselves to the hunter, but violation of a taboo could block this generosity. Thus, failure to observe proper hunting practices was considered as serious a crime as murder in some cases. The violation of taboo in this narrative is swiftly punished. The character Frog in the myths of the Northwest was associated with fresh water and access to it; therefore, a prohibition existed against harming the animal.

Many snows ago there came up a white man out of the south land, journeying down Eel River to the country of the Mattoal. He was the first white man who had ever come into that land, and he lost his way and could not find it again. For lack of food through many days he was sore distressed with hunger and had fallen down faint in his trail, and he came near dying.

But there passed that way an Indian who was called Sattik, and he saw the white man fallen in the trail with hunger with his mouth in the dust, and his heart was touched because of him. He took him and lifted him up, and he brought him fresh water to drink in his hands, and from his basket gave him dried salmon to eat, and he spoke kind words to him. Thus the man was revived, and his soul cheered within him, but he could not yet walk.

Then the heart of Sattik was moved with pity for the white man, and he took him on his back and carried him on the way. They journeyed three sleeps down Eel River, but Sattik carried the white man on his shoulders, and often he sat down to rest. At the end of the third day they came to a spring wherein were many frogs; and Sattik dipped up water in his hands to drink, as the manner of Indians is, but the white man bowed down on his belly and drank of the waters, and he caught a frog in his hand and eat it, because of the hunger he had.

At the sight of this the Indian's heart became as water for terror, and he fled from the wrath of the Big Man, lest, because of this impious thing that was done, he should come down quick out of heaven and with his red right hand rend a tree to splinters and smite them both to the ground. He ran one day and two nights, and turned not his face back to look behind him, neither did he rest. Then he climbed up a redwood tree to the top of it, but the tree was hollow and he broke through at the top, and fell down on the inside to the bottom, and died there.

AMHULUK, THE MONSTER OF THE MOUNTAIN POOL

Tradition Bearer: Unavailable

Source: Gatschet, Albert S. "Oregonian Folklore." *Journal of American Folklore* 4 (1891): 141–42.

Date: 1891

Original Source: Kalapuya

National Origin: Native American

The Kalapuya lived in permanent winter homes and migrated throughout the Willamette Valley of Oregon during the summers. Subsistence was based on fishing, hunting, and gathering wild plant foods. As far as can be determined from the existing records of the traditions of the Native American cultures of the area, the **legend** of Amhuluk functioned primarily to frighten children away from dangerous bodies of water.

Amhuluk at first desired to establish his residence in the fertile plains of Atfalati [a Native American group that has ceased to exist as a cultural entity], but seeing that they were not large enough for him, he set out for a more extended region. Such a one he found at the Forked Mountain; he stopped there and has ever since occupied that spot. Every living being seen by him is drowned there, all the trees within his reach have their crowns upside down in his embrace, and many other things are gathered up in his stagnant waters. The monster's legs seem deprived of their hair, and several kinds of dogs he keeps near him. His horns are spotted and of enormous magnitude.

Three children were busy digging for edible roots, when Amhuluk emerged from the ground not far from them. When the children became aware of him, they exclaimed, "Let us take his beautifully spotted horns, to make digging-tools of them!" But the monster approached fast and lifted two of the children on his horns, while the eldest managed to escape. Wherever Amhuluk set his feet the ground was sinking.

When the boy returned home he said to his father: "Something dreadful has come near us, and has taken away my brother and my sister!" He then went to sleep, and when he lay on his couch his parents noticed that his body was full of blots.

Immediately the father put his girdle around his dress and started for the Forked Mountain, where his children had met their death. He found the tracks of the son who had been fortunate enough to escape the same fate, followed them, skirted the mountain, and there he saw the bodies of his children emerging from the muddy pool.

Then they disappeared for a while, to emerge again on the opposite slope of the mountain. This apparition occurred five times in succession, and finally the father reached the very spot where the children had been drowned. A pool of water was visible, which sent up a fog, and in the midst of the fog the children were seen lifted up high upon the horns of Amhuluk. With his hands he made signals to them, and the children replied, "Didei, didei, didei" ("we changed our bodies").

The father, painfully moved, set up a mourning wail and remained upon the shore all night. The next day the fog rose up again, and the father again perceived his children borne upon the horns of the monster. He made the same signals, and the children replied: "Didei, didei, didei." Full of grief, he established a camping lodge upon the shore, stayed in it five days, and every day the children reappeared in the same manner as before. When they appeared no longer, the father returned to his family and said, "Amhuluk has ravished the children. I have seen them; they are at the Forked Mountain. I have seen them upon the horns of the monster; many trees were in the water, the crown down below, the trunk looking upward."

THE BEWITCHED WIVES

Tradition Bearer: Unavailable

Source: Burrows, Elizabeth. "Eskimo Tales." *Journal of American Folklore* 39 (1926): 79–80.

Date: 1926

Original Source: Eskimo
National Origin: Native American

The cure for supernatural assault among the Eskimo is by recourse to a shaman, an individual who through personal power (as distinct from divine intervention) is able to discover the source of evil influence and remove it. In many cases, the shaman then sends the malevolent force from the victim to the original aggressor. This is the case in the following narrative when the ferns used to remove the girl's bewitchment are then used as the instrument of attacking the evil woman-spirit.

A little girl, who lived alone with her grandmother, followed tracks along the river till at a water-hole she found a house where a man was making arrows. He gave her no greeting, but warned her to be careful lest the door close upon her. She got away safely to the ceremonial house near-by, but here the door in closing upon her bit off a piece of her dress. On her return home her grandmother suspected her adventure from the torn garment, but the girl claimed that the rent was made by a fall on the ice.

Early next morning she returned to the Arrow-maker's with a plate of fish-heads. The house was empty. She lifted up the grass-mat on the wall and discovered another door. She went through it into a passage where she commenced sliding, first on her feet till her moccasins were worn out, then on one side, then on the other, then on her breasts, and then on her back, in each position wearing out the dress on that side. She held on to her plate of fish-heads, and at last came to a high cliff overlooking the water. She heard someone singing.

It was the Arrow-maker she had seen the previous day; he was sealing in his kayak. When he had speared the seal, lifted it on his raft, cut it up, and put it into the kayak, he came in close to the cliff, and told the girl to jump into the boat. She was afraid, but he pointed out that the place where she was covered with the bones of people who had starved to death there, and warned her that unless she obeyed, she would meet the same fate. The girl jumped, and the man took her home, warning her not to look behind at anyone who called to her. She heard people crying out, and he told her it was his wives making a great racket.

Finally they came to his home where there were two houses. He told her to go to the smaller one, where the head-man and the head-woman welcomed her with gifts of clothing and sent food to the ceremonial house for the man. Several times the girl heard someone calling, but each time she refused to look in the direction of the call.

In the course of a year, the girl married the Arrow-maker. One day as she carried his food to him at the ceremonial house, she at last looked behind her at the person whom she heard calling. At once she was in the power of this evil woman-spirit, and followed her to her house. There this evil spirit gave her snow-and-oil to eat, and immediately she began to cry out continuously like the other wives. Thereupon the evil woman threw her out of the house, where her husband found her and put her into the house with the other wives.

In the large village across the river an old woman lived with her grandson, and the girl had been accustomed to give them food. When the old woman knew that the girl had been bewitched, she sent her grandson to get her. She put her on a grass-mat, removed her clothes, and with a bunch of ferns whipped her from the feet to the face, until at last the girl sat up and asked why she had been awakened.

Then the old woman directed her to take the ferns and use them in the same way on the face of the evil woman-spirit. When she had done so, the bad woman began to call out continuously as she had made others do. In the same way the girl transformed also the evil woman's father and mother, and then took them all by the hair and threw them out of the house.

Meanwhile her husband searched for her, and when he found her cured in the house of the old woman, he took her home where they lived together and had children. He always took care of the old woman that had saved her life, but the rest of the villagers all died.

QAUTIPALUNG

Tradition Bearer: Unavailable

Source: Kroeber, A. L. "Tales of the Smith Sound Eskimo." *Journal of American Folklore* 12 (1899): 172.

Date: 1897–1898

Original Source: Eskimo

National Origin: Native American

The Arctic Eskimo bands relied heavily on a diet of protein and fat from animal sources. As a result the hunt, an exclusively male pursuit historically, was crucial to survival. This led to a relatively higher value being placed on males than females in Eskimo tradition. As a result, it is not uncommon to see cruel treatment meted out to female characters in their tales. In this case, the rejection of a suitor, who was obviously a shaman, leads to disaster.

There was a woman named Qautipalung, who had an unmarried daughter. One day some people came in a boat to get this daughter to be wife to one of them.

But when the girl saw the suitor, she said to her mother, "He is much too old; don't let him have me!"

When the man heard that his suit was rejected, he said that he would go away, but that the girl would be turned to stone.

Qautipalung now was frightened and asked him to stay, but he refused and went on his way. "The boat is going away," Qautipalung said to her daughter, and the girl made herself ready to go outdoors.

When she got outdoors the boat was already some distance away, and she began to run after it over the land to catch up with it. But as she ran her feet turned to stone, so that she fell down on her face, and the rest of her body turned to earth. As she fell, the bag she had in her hand was spilled, and the contents, falling out, turned into small auks, that flew away, crying tuu, tuu, tuu.

THE MAN AND WOMAN WHO BECAME SEA-OTTERS

Tradition Bearer: Mrs. C. A. Anderson

Source: Golder, F. A. "Aleutian Stories." *Journal of American Folklore* 18 (1905): 220–21.

Date: 1905

Original Source: Aleut

National Origin: Native American

The following is an Attu narrative widely distributed throughout the Aleutian Islands. Within the culture, marriages were, as a rule, informal and, in fact, abduction and marriage by force were common occurrences. The frailty of the institution of marriage, then, led easily to violent conflict. Within bands, social control was in the hands of its members, rather than codified in legal systems. An act such as the husband's "taking the law into his own hands" was one way of managing social conflict.

Once upon a time there lived in a certain village a married couple; and one day the husband told the wife, "We are going to make a feast, and we are going to invite your brother-in-law. Go and gather some herbs and roots, and then go to the beach and bring some moss from the rocks."

He himself went to get some seals or ducks. On his return he busied himself preparing the dishes. This done, he sharpened his knives, and commanded his wife to call the expected guest. She knew that her husband was jealous of her brother-in-law and planned to kill him, but was forbidden by her husband to say anything to him about it. She went and called him, and as they were coming toward the house she, walking behind, thought continually of the fate that was awaiting him, yet fear of her husband prevented her from saying anything.

When they came into the house she looked at the two men and saw how much the handsomer of the two the brother-in-law was. The husband turned to the invited guest, and said, "I prepared a feast for you; I have planned it for many years. Come and eat with me."

They sat down on the floor, having the food before them in a hollowed rock. In the meantime the woman was outside, weeping because the man she loved more than her husband was about to be killed. The meal started off pleasantly, but the husband was watching his chance, and once when the brother-in-law had an unusually full mouth and could not defend himself he jumped on him, seized him by the throat, cut his head off, and said, "Now you have your feast."

This done he left the house and sat down among the rocks, waiting to see what his wife would do. She went in and picked up the head, washed it, put it into an intestine bag finely trimmed with sea-otter fur, and, after observing the whereabouts of her husband, started off with it towards the cliff near the house.

She went quite a distance before her husband noticed her and started in pursuit, calling to her, "Where are you going?"

She answered: "You will see which way I am going; you killed him and you will never see me again." As he increased his speed she began to run until she reached the top of the cliff, from which she threw herself into the water below.

The husband arrived just in time to see her disappear. He stood there watching the spot, believing her drowned; but to his great surprise there emerged two sea-otters, and one went west while the other went east. He went back to the house, where he took his hunting gear and his bidarka (kayak) and said, "I will end their lives and mine too." Saying this he launched his skin boat, got into it, and paddled away from the shore, while singing to himself:

"I will end their life,
And I will end mine.
I hear the birds singing
That sing in the spring-time, So I am going,"

And he upset his bidarka and drowned himself.

THE BROTHER AND SISTER WHO BECAME HAIR-SEALS

Tradition Bearer: "Chief" of Unga Island

Source: Golder, F. A. "Aleutian Stories." *Journal of American Folklore* 18 (1905): 221–22.

Date: 1905

Original Source: Aleut

National Origin: Native American

As noted in the introduction to "Qautipalung" (p. 145), members of Arctic bands deemed nonproductive—whether due to gender, age, or social violations—often are expunged from the band. This tale has an ending very much like the conclusion of "The Man and Woman Who Became Sea-otters" (p. 146). The **motif** is known throughout the Aleutian Islands.

In a certain family there were twelve brothers and one sister. She lived in a hut away from the rest of the family. There were no other men living in the neighborhood, and so she was somewhat surprised when some man came to see her at night.

She did not know who it was, but suspected that it was one of her brothers, and in order to find out which one of them it was, she prepared some red paint, and when the man was about to leave she dipped her hands into the paint and put them on his shoulders.

The next day, as all her brothers were outside playing, she went among them and detected marks of paint on the shoulders of the oldest. Going back to her barrabara (indigenous dwelling), she sharpened her knife and placed it alongside of her. That night, as usual, the man came and slept with her, but as he started to leave she threw her knife at him and cut the sinews of one of his legs. The following morning she went about her work as customary, when someone came to announce that her oldest brother was sick, the sinews of one of his legs being cut.

She went to him, got him out of bed, and set off with him. Their mother, learning the state of affairs, said, "We reared them that they might be a help to us and work for us; but now they have gone and ruined themselves."

The two went a long distance until they arrived at the bluff, over which they threw themselves, and a short time after they appeared as hair-seals.

THE POWERS THAT BE: SECULAR TALES

THE WOMAN WHO WAS FOND OF INTESTINES

Tradition Bearer: Mrs. C. A. Anderson

Source: Golder, F. A. "Aleutian Stories." *Journal of American Folklore* 18 (1905): 215–20.

Date: 1905

Original Source: Aleut

National Origin: Native American

Historically, law among the Eskimo, Aleuts, and many other societies was customary law; it rested on custom, tradition, and taboo. The society at large would not move to settle grievances, rather it was the parties involved who sought justice. Just as the society would not act to insure justice, neither would it come between disputants. In the case of murder, the family of the victim sought revenge, as in the following narrative. While the avengers in this tale use supernatural power to convert themselves into wild animals, the major focus of the plot is on social justice for the wronged wife.

Once there lived an Aleut with his wife and little boy. The wife was very fond of intestines, and early each morning the husband would go out in his bidark (kayak) hunting, and return in the evening with a boat full of intestines which he gave to his wife, telling her to keep what she wanted for herself, and distribute the rest among her neighbors.

The wife was somewhat puzzled by the husband's actions; she could not understand why he went so early in the morning, where he got so many intestines, or his reasons for wishing to have them distributed among the villagers. She, of course, did not know that her husband had a mistress in the village, whom he went to see while his wife was asleep, and that he desired the intestines distributed in order that his wife's rival might have a share.

All of a sudden, without explanations, the man ceased going out early, and when he did go, he came back but lightly loaded. This did not in the least clear up the mystery to the wife. But one day, when he had gone somewhat later than usually, his mistress called on his wife, whom she found busy sewing a kamalayka (waterproof shirt) out of the intestines her husband brought. The two got into a conversation, and, among other questions, the mistress asked: "Does your husband love you?"

"Yes."

"Do you love him?"

"Yes."

"Do you know where he gets all the intestines?"

"No."

"Can you guess why he has them distributed over the village?"

"No."

"I will tell you," said the mistress, "but you must not tell him I told you. Every day your husband goes to the village where your parents and relatives live and where you lived before your marriage, and kills the people there and brings their intestines to you. Yesterday there were but five people remaining in the village: your mother, your two sisters, and two brothers. He killed your mother and sisters yesterday, and today he went to bring the intestines of your brothers. He is in love with another woman of this village, whom he visits nightly when you have fallen asleep."

With this parting shot she left the house, leaving the poor wife weeping so bitterly that the kamalayka was hot from her tears. For the rest of the day she did not stir from the house, but sat lamenting and sewing. Towards evening her little boy rushed in announcing the approach of his father, which she generally anticipated with pleasure, and always went down to the beach to meet him; but this time she neither answered nor made the least motion. A few minutes later the little son came again saying, "Father is here," but all the reply he got was a new outburst of weeping.

Missing the usual meeting and greeting of his wife, the father asked the little boy where his mother was, and when told of the state she was in, he hastened to the house, where he found her on the floor shedding bitter tears and sewing the kamalayka.

"Why do you weep? Has someone offended you?"

"No one has offended me."

"Why then this lamentation?"

"I was thinking of my mother, sisters, and brothers, and my other relatives in my native village, and I wondered how they were getting along, and this made me weep."

He did not attempt to cheer her, but after a pause he said, "I did not kill many animals today—two only."

This enraged her so that she jumped up from the floor, picked up the little boy, who was near her, and threw him at him, saying, "If my two brothers do not satisfy you, take him also." The boy's forehead came in contact with the edge of a sharp knife on the father's breast, making quite a gash from which the blood flowed freely. This the mother noticed before escaping out of the house.

Putting aside the boy, the man made a dash for the woman, but she got out of his reach, and being the better runner of the two he did not succeed in laying hands on her. She would let him come up quite close to her, and then dash away again until he saw the hopelessness of the chase and gave it up.

In a short time the boy's wound healed, but it left a very noticeable scar. Now that his mother was gone, his father placed him in the care of his sister, with instructions that he should under no circumstances be allowed to go very far from home. In this manner he passed a few years longer, until he became the proud possessor of a bow and arrows, with which he often amused himself.

One day, while indulging in his favorite sport, he began to wonder why his father and aunt forbade his going far from the house; and the more he thought about it the more anxious did he become to go, until he finally concluded "to go just a little distance beyond that hill to see what is there." On the way he noticed a hillock just ahead of him, at which he discharged his arrow, then ran and got it, aimed at another and another, and became so absorbed in this amusement that he did not observe how far from home it was taking him.

One hillock somewhat different from the others especially attracted his attention as offering a good mark. He took aim and sent his arrow flying right into the centre of it; but what was his surprise on approaching the supposed hillock to discover that it was a barrabara (dwelling), and that the arrow had gone inside through the hole in the top. When he peeped in, he was frightened at the sight of a very wild-looking woman who stared at him, and he began to cry. "Why do you cry?" the woman asked.

"I want my arrow."

"Come in and get it," the woman invited. But he was too scared to do that; he however got up courage enough to stick his foot in, hoping to draw it out that way, and he had nearly succeeded when he heard the woman move. At this he ran away in tears.

The woman called him back, saying: "Do not be afraid of me. I am your mother. It is I who threw you at your father, making the scar on your forehead. Come in, I will not harm you." When he saw that it was really his mother, he went to her and remained with her two days. During that time she told him his father's wicked deeds, how he mistreated and neglected her for another, and finally wrought on him so that he swore he would revenge her wrongs. She bade him go home, but attempt nothing for the present, and make no mention of what he had seen and heard.

During the boy's absence the father was away hunting, but the aunt was quite worked up over the long absence, and ran about the fields looking for him. When he returned she asked him all sorts of questions as to his whereabouts, but all the satisfaction she got from him was that he had lost his way and could not get back. She offered him food, which he refused to touch, and finally refused to answer her when spoken to.

Toward evening of the same day his father returned, and, when told that the boy would neither eat nor drink, asked what was the matter with him; but for an answer the boy turned his back on him and went to sleep. The father then inquired of the aunt whether anything unusual had occurred and whether the boy had been far from home, and to all this she replied that all during his father's absence, the boy's life had gone on as ordinarily, and that he was not out of sight of the house the whole time.

As the boy grew older he avoided his father more and more, and when he reached early manhood the father lost control over him and actually feared him. One day, while the older man was away hunting, the young man took his bow and arrows, some food and water, and set out to see his mother. Before going, he told his aunt that he intended going quite a distance from home, and not to be, therefore, uneasy over his long absence. He went to the place where he had last seen his mother, and, as she was not there, he wandered on until on the following day he came in sight of some barrabaras (native dwellings) and two men. They answered him when he spoke to them, but when he wished to enter into one of the barrabaras they barred his way. While they were thus disputing, his mother appeared on the scene and motioned to the men to let him pass.

When he came inside he was greatly surprised at the quantity of furs that was lying about in great disorder, and at the abundance of meats and other eatables that he found there. He was certain he had never seen anything like it before. After eating, his mother told him to spend the night there, and in the morning take as many of the best furs as he could carry and go back to the village of his father, in order to tempt him and his relatives to come hunting in this neighborhood, which would offer an opportunity to repay him for what he had done. The boy did as he was told, took with him a heavy load of precious furs, and started back.

In his absence, the mother and the people with whom she was living made elaborate and crafty preparations for the reception of the expected guests. In the large barrabara, where the feasts and dances were always held and where visitors were generally received, quantities of oil were sprinkled about and covered up with grass. Along the walls seal-bladders full of oil were concealed, and screened with straw mats. And in this place the visitors were to be received.

The young man's father was home on his return, and received the present of furs which his son made him with much pleasure, for the boy seemed so kindly disposed that the father hoped that his natural affection for his parent had returned. He inquired the whereabouts of the hunting grounds where the son had secured these skins, and the latter told him that it was not very far, and that it was very rich, and that he planned to go back the next day to the same place, and if he and his men cared to accompany him, he would be glad to show them the way. His offer was accepted, and the following morning a large party left the village for the hunting ground.

Some of the people of the mother's village had been on the look-out, and when they saw the large party approaching, they changed themselves into wild beasts: bears, wolves, foxes, etc. The hunters marked them and shot at them, but it had no other result than to drive the beasts nearer and nearer to the village. These tactics the men-beasts repeated until the hunters were decoyed into the village. Seeing so many barrabaras, the men asked the boy who the people were that lived in them. "They are friendly people," he replied, "with whom I spent the night the last time I was in this neighborhood. Tomorrow morning we will go to the other side of the village, where there is a great deal of game."

The people of the village greeted them very cordially, and assigned a place for the night to each one of them; the father and son were given the barrabara where the latter had been entertained on his previous visit. Although the mother was in the same room with them, they were not aware of it, for she had concealed herself. Everywhere about them were scattered the richest furs, and the food before them was the choicest and best, and so much of it that it rather made the older man uneasy, for, though an old hunter, he had never seen anything like it before.

In the evening, all the people of the village, including the guests, went to the large dance-hall, where the formal reception was held and the guests entertained as was customary. One by one they descended through the hole in the roof, the only entrance there was. The interior was lighted up by two rows of stone lamps filled with oil, and grass wicks. On one side of the room sat the local men, while the visitors faced them from the other; the centre was occupied by the women, and on the two sides sat seven or eight men with drums in their hands, on which they played and accompanied their singing. They would take turns; first the local men would sing their local songs, and then the visitors sang theirs. To this music the women danced with men whom they invited from either side.

Everything moved along smoothly and joyfully until the father recognized his wife among the women. She was dancing and moving towards him. At this sight he turned pale and looked for away to get out, but the ladder had been removed. The woman moved up to him, grasped his hand, and dragged him to dance, but he resisted. The boy, who sat near, urged him and pushed him on, but all in vain.

Then the woman began to sing him a song in which she went over all his misdeeds, his unfaithfulness, his cruelties, his falsehoods, as well as many of his other shortcomings, and concluded with these words, "You and your men shall never leave this place alive."

When she had said this, all the local people, including the mother and son, were turned into birds or flying insects and flew out through the hole in the roof. The visitors, unable to follow them, remained behind.

On the outside grass and wood were ignited and thrown in, which set on fire the grass and oil inside. Then the smoke hole was stopped up, and in this way all those who were inside were smothered to death. A few days later the son went to his father's village, destroying it as completely as his father had destroyed his mother's. He spared, however, his aunt, whom he brought back with him.

THE MADDEST MAN IN TOWN

Tradition Bearer: Charles Imus

Source: Haight, Willliam C. "Interview of Charles Imus." American Life Histories: Manuscripts from the Federal Writers' Project, 1936–1940. Manuscript Division, Library of Congress. 14 October 2005. http://memory.loc.gov/ammem/wpaintro/wpahome.html.

Date: 1939

Original Source: Oregon

National Origin: Irish American

Although the church is charged with sacred power, in most contexts it wields considerable secular power as well. The following **personal experience narrative** reveals the reason for and means by which a quarrel between a local priest and member of his congregation lead to a family's being ostracized.

Are ya religious? If ya are I won't tell this story. Awright, I guess it won't hurt ya none to hear it. It's about old man Donovan. He was as good a Catholic as I ever knew, until he got mad once. Then he was mad for 17 years—the maddest man in town. Ye-up, dingblasted mad and powerful mizzur'ble. Considering all in all, I reckon his being mad so long set a record of sorts for the whole danged county.

You're right, the old duffer was an Irishman. Being Irish, it didn't take much to start his blood a-boilin'. A kinda small man, inclined to be delicate, with long gray whiskers and a sizable mustache, he was quite a Injun on the warpath. His long gray chin whiskers would wave in the air sorta like they was fannin' the cuss words to take the heat offa them an they came out.

Well, among other things he had two kids, Harry and Joe. Harry was the little bugger and Joe was the big one. Joe was might nigh six-four. Joe bein' so tall and me bein' considerable shorter didn't no way effect our fightin' nearly every day at school. I reckon that was mainly why I went—so I could wallop Joe up; an' then got walloped up by Joe. We both seemed to like it.

One day I went to school prepared to give Joe a walloping, since he'd done walloped me the day before. But Joe wasn't there. Right away, I figgered somethin' mighty darned important musta happened to keep Joe from coming to school that day.

Sure 'nuff, school hadn't been took up more'n a little while when somebody came by and told us old man Donovan had died. Soon's the teacher heard this she dismissed school. Seems like the widow Donovan was a-needin' some help at the house, so the teacher asked my side-kick, Bill, the long 'un, and me to go up there. Seein' as how my old man was the undertaker and had already loaned her

157

the money to send for the priest to come and pray Donovan out of purgatory, I guess the teacher thought I was the one to send. Bill allus went where I did, him and me bein' the long an' short of it, as folks'd say.

Mrs. Donovan had to send to Vancouver for a priest, and the fellow that come was purty old and mighty set in his ways. I reckon he figgered he was close to God and didn't mind to allow he knew purty near as much.

And he did his job all right. After he got settled he put on all his robes and started to work. Him and Dad laid Donovan out on a board supported by two chairs, threw a sheet over him and put the required number of candles at his head and feet. Then the priest prayed and sprinkled water, and prayed and sprinkled water some more, till old man Donovan was prayed and sprayed out of purgatory.

Soon's the priest left, Bill and me was delegated to sit in the kitchen and watch the corpse, which was in the next room.

Donovan, bein' an Irishman, his passin' naturally allowed for a make. So every Irishman and German within forty miles came to set up for the night. The Germans in our part was not much on wakin' the dead, but because they was mighty thick with the Irish they was willing to help the Irish wake their dead 'uns. All foreigners in them days stuck purty close together, ya know. These wakers set around in another room with the family, and were a-passin' a sociable evenin'. Most of 'em were drinkin' out of a couple of demijohns I saw on the table when some Irishman stuck his head out the door to see if Donovan was a-lyin' out right. The rest of the people were a-playin' cards and talkin' to the widow. Seems as though they'd drink, play cards awhile, then the widow'd wail a bit.

Me and Bill bein' too young to wake had to pass the time tryin' to read in the kitchen. This was kinda hard to do. The house was built on a hill, almost the crest, causin' the shakes to catch all the wind. That old wind would howl a mighty bit when she'd hit the shakes. The wind a-howlin', coupled with the wail of the wakers, sort of discommoded Bill and me. Bill was plenty scairt anyhow. Donovan was the first corpse he'd ever been around. So's all that howlin' had Bill a-settin' mighty uncomfortable like in his chair, and kept me kinda on the uneasy side.

All of a sudden Bill and me heard the consarndest noise I've ever heard, or expect to hear. Bill jumped from his chair scairt like and says, kind of quavery like, "What's that?" By this time I'm a-standin' on my feet and a-listenin'. Sure 'nuff! 'Tweren't the mind nor the wakers—the sound was a-comin' from that corpse.

Now, Bill, not a-takin' his job none too good no ways, decided he wanted to leave. "Shucks," I says to Bill, tryin' to calm him, "its probably the cat." God! I thought that was terrible. Here them wakers were a-dependin' on Bill and me to watch the corpse and we'd done let the cat in! I told Bill to be real quiet like and we wouldn't disturb nothin', and to bring the metal-plated lamp along so's we could see.

Bill and me sort of crept into the room. Soon's the light hit that corpse we could see the sheet a goin' up and down, up and down, with the awfullest noise a-comin' out from under it. Bill takes a good look, tries to hand me the rattlin' lamp, shakin' his hands, and says, "By God, I'm a-gettin' out of here!" He shoves the lamp in my hand and runs like a scairt rabbit for home. I figgers him bein' so much bigger'n me, there's a lot more of him scairt than there is of me, so I goes up closer.

For a spell I watched. Then I goes over and gingerly lifts up the sheet, sort of expectin' to see the cat. By that time some of the wakers heard the noise and came edging in to see what it was all about.

Well, I'll be dingblasted if old man Donovan wasn't a-breathin'. Yes air, the old coot was as alive as you or me right now. That peculiar noise we'd been hearin' under the sheet was him a-breathin'. Right away the fellers picked him up and toted him into the bedroom. They wrapped warm blankets-round him and nursed him back to full breath. Purty soon he took a pull at the demijohn hisself. And was his wife happy! Everybody was real excited.

In a few days Donovan was out on the streets again, a well man. He lived for 17 years more.

And here's what made him mad all that time:

The priest, bein' mighty set in his ways, wouldn't let Donovan nor his family go to church no more. He figgered Donovan had pulled the trick of playin' possum on him. And even if he hadn't it looked like God thought the old cuss was such a sinner that he had to be sent back to earth. Anyway, the priest said he had prayed old Donovan out of purgatory and now he was beyond the jurisdiction of the Church.

Mad? I reckon there never was a madder Irishman than old man Donovan. You could just see it boiling out of him as he walked down the street. If you wanted to see them chin whiskers of his fan the air, you only had to mention purgatory or the priest to him. His old lady got to swearin' like a trooper, and between the two of 'em I guess they really told the priest off.

Ye-up. Donovan stayed mad for 17 years. Maybe be still is, I don't profess to know. A freight train finally put an end to his mortal life; it took that to kill him. But he had to die sometime.

APPENDIX

Cyberspace

In terms of the concept of region that has been advanced so far in *The Greenwood Library of American Folktales*, the texts offered in this appendix do not circulate within a contiguous, geographically defined region of the United States, although many do speak to regional concerns or articulate local stereotypes (see, for example, "How Many Aggie Foremen Does It Take," p. 187). These electronically circulated traditions do, however, articulate the hopes and anxieties of our contemporary computer-connected society. A certain familiarity with the issues and contexts of each of the following examples is taken for granted. Therefore, although the following tales are categorized in the same fashion as the traditional tales, no introductions are given; the examples will be allowed to speak for themselves.

ORIGINS

KENTUCKY FRIED CHICKEN BECOMES KFC

Tradition Bearer: Unavailable

Source: E-mail Forward

Date: 2000

Original Source: E-mail

National Origin: Unavailable

This is Very Disturbing—this was sent to me so I'm just sharing the information. KFC has been a part of our American traditions for many years. Many people, day in and day out, eat at KFC religiously. Do they really know what they are eating? During a recent study of KFC done at the University of New Hampshire, they found some very upsetting facts.

First of all, has anybody noticed that just recently, the company has changed their name? Kentucky Fried Chicken has become KFC. Does anybody know why? We thought the real reason was because of the "FRIED" food issue. It's not. The reason why they call it KFC is because they can not use the word chicken anymore. Why? KFC does not use real chickens.

They actually use genetically manipulated organisms. These so-called "chickens" are kept alive by tubes inserted into their bodies to pump blood and nutrients throughout their structure. They have no beaks, no feathers, and no feet. Their bone structure is dramatically shrunk to get more meat out of them. This is great for KFC because they do not have to pay so much for their production costs. There is no more plucking of the feathers or the removal of the beaks and feet.

The government has told them to change all of their menus so they do not say chicken anywhere. If you look closely you will notice this. Listen to their commercials, I guarantee you will not see or hear the word "chicken." I find this matter to be very disturbing. I hope people will start to realize this and let other people know. Please forward this message to as many people as you can. Together we make KFC start using real chicken again.

JOHN KERRY'S MEDALS

Tradition Bearer: Unavailable

Source: E-mail Forward

Date: 2004

Original Source: E-mail

National Origin: Unavailable

This was written by a retired admiral and Annapolis graduate. The item offers no direct testimony about Kerry, but it does provide informed background useful in assessing what Kerry seems to have claimed for himself. It confirms information I have received from other sources.

Our media should be demanding that Senator Kerry open his service records in the same way they demanded that of President Bush regarding his National Guard service.

I was in the Delta shortly after he [Kerry] left. I know that area well. I know the operations he was involved in well. I know the tactics and the doctrine used. I know the equipment. Although I was attached to CTF-116 (PBRs) I spent a fair amount of time with CTF-115 (swift boats), Kerry's command.

Here are my problems and suspicions:

(1) Kerry was in-country less than four months and collected a Bronze Star, a Silver Star, and three purple hearts. I never heard of anybody with any outfit I worked with (including SEAL One, the Sea Wolves, Riverines, and the River Patrol Force) collecting that much hardware so fast, and for such pedestrian actions. The Swifts did a commendable job. But that duty wasn't the worst you could draw. They operated only along the coast and in the major rivers (Bassac and Mekong). The rough stuff in the hot areas was mainly handled by the smaller, faster PBRs.

(2) Three Purple Hearts, but no limp. All injuries so minor that no time lost from duty. Amazing luck. Or he was putting himself in for medals every time he bumped his head on the wheel house hatch? Combat on the boats was almost always at close range. You didn't have minor wounds. At least not often. Not three times in a row. Then he used the three purple hearts to request a trip home eight months before the end of his tour. Fishy.

(3) The details of the event for which he was given the Silver Star make no sense at all. Supposedly, a B-40 was fired at the boat and missed. Charlie jumps up with the launcher in his hand, the bow gunner knocks him down with the twin .50, Kerry beaches the boat, jumps off, shoots Charlie, and retrieves the launcher. If true, he did everything wrong.

(a) Standard procedure when you took rocket fire was to put your stern to the action and go balls to the wall. A B-40 has the ballistic integrity of a Frisbee after about 25 yards, so you put 50 yards or so between you and the beach and begin raking it with your .50's.

(b) Did you ever see anybody get knocked down with a .50 caliber round and get up? The guy was dead or dying. The rocket launcher was empty. There was no reason to go after him (except if you knew he was no danger to you just flopping around in the dust during his last few seconds on earth, and you wanted some derring-do in your after-action report). And we didn't shoot wounded people. We had rules against that, too.

(c) Kerry got off the boat. This was a major breach of standing procedures. Nobody on a boat crew ever got off a boat in a hot area. EVER! The reason was simple. If you had somebody on the beach your boat was defenseless. It couldn't run and it couldn't return fire. It was stupid and it put his crew in danger. He should have been relieved and reprimanded. I never heard of any boat crewman ever leaving a boat during or after a firefight.

Something is fishy.

Here we have a JFK wannabe (the guy Halsey wanted to court martial for carelessly losing his boat and getting a couple people killed by running across the bow of a Jap destroyer) who is hardly in Vietnam long enough to get good tan, collects medals faster than Audie Murphy in a job where lots of medals weren't common, gets sent home eight months early, requests separation from active duty a few months after that so he can run for Congress, finds out war heroes don't sell well in Massachusetts in 1970 so reinvents himself as Jane Fonda, throws his ribbons in the dirt with the cameras running to jump start his political career, gets Stillborn Pell to invite him to address Congress and Bobby Kennedy's speechwriter to do the heavy lifting, winds up in the Senate himself a few years later, votes against every major defense bill, says the CIA is irrelevant after the Wall came down, votes against the Gulf War, a big mistake since that turned out well, decides not to make the same mistake twice so votes for invading Iraq, but oops, that didn't turn out so well so he now says he really didn't mean for Bush to go to war when he voted to allow him to go to war.

I'm real glad you or I never had this guy covering our flanks in Vietnam. I sure don't want him as Commander in Chief. I hope that somebody from CTF-115 shows up with some facts challenging Kerry's Vietnam record. I know in my gut it's wildly inflated. And fishy.

RED BULL

Tradition Bearer: Unavailable

Source: E-mail Forward

Date: 2000

Original Source: E-mail

National Origin: Unavailable

Ever wondered what's in a can of Red Bull Energy drink? The small print lists a host of ingredients and among them is Glucuronolactone, an artificially manufactured stimulant developed in the early '60s by the American Government.

Glucuronolactone was first used in the Vietnam conflict to boost morale amongst GI's who were suffering from stress and fatigue, but was banned after a few years following several deaths and hundreds of cases involving anything from severe migraines to brain tumors in personnel prescribed the stimulant.

That was in 1973 and Glucuronolactone is still banned for commercial consumption in America this day. The bad news is that the substance never found it's way to Europe in the early days and was therefore never banned by the EU community. An article in this month's edition of the British Medical Journal has highlighted a growing number of cases reported by doctors and surgeons involving the very same side effects from the '70s.

All of the patients examined were regular drinkers of Red Bull and it is believed that the safety of Glucuronolactone is currently under review in at least three major European countries.

Please pass this on to any Red Bull drinkers you know, and next time you get a headache after drinking the stuff, you'll know why!

CHRONIC DEHYDRATION

Tradition Bearer: Unavailable

Source: E-mail Forward

Date: 2004

Original Source: E-mail

National Origin: Unavailable

Hi all. This came from one of my wellness groups and thought I'd pass it on. Especially true after exercise, injury, massage, etc. that release poisons into the system. Remember what I said about chronic low-level dehydration. But I won't say I told you so....

75% of Americans are chronically dehydrated.

In 37% of Americans, the thirst mechanism is so weak that it is often mistaken for hunger.

Even mild dehydration will slow down one's metabolism as much as 3%.

One glass of water shut down midnight hunger pangs for almost 100% of the dieters studied in a U-Washington study.

Lack of water is the number one trigger of daytime fatigue.

Preliminary research indicates that 8 to 10 glasses of water a day could significantly ease back and joint pain for up to 80% of sufferers.

A mere 2% drop in body water can trigger fuzzy short-term memory, trouble with basic math, and difficulty focusing on the computer screen or on a printed page.

Drinking 5 glasses of water daily decreases the risk of colon cancer by 45%, plus it can slash the risk of breast cancer by 79%, and one is 50% less likely to develop bladder cancer.

Are you drinking a healthy amount of water each day?

SPIELBERG'S CRUSADE (PARODY?)

Tradition Bearer: Unavailable

Source: E-mail Forward

Date: 2004

Original Source: E-mail

National Origin: Unavailable

Hollywood megahit producer and director Steven Spielberg has decided to fight fire with fire. He's announced that since Mel Gibson is fueling the fires of anti-Semitism in the world with his movie about the last hours of Christ, Spielberg will make a graphic movie about the Crusades.

"In order to get Jews and Moslems to convert to Christianity," Spielberg commented, "Christians went through Europe and into the Middle East forcing conversions on nonbelievers. Along the way they raped, beat, bludgeoned, maimed, tortured, and killed hundreds of thousands of innocent men, women, and children. I will show Christian brutality in a realistic and most graphic and gory way."

Spielberg went on to add that the movie will have a well-deserved anti-Christian tone. "Let's face it, Gibson wants to blame the Jews for the death of one person we didn't even kill. I will show the inhuman brutality of thousands of Christians against hundreds of thousands of people of other faiths, about which historically there is no ambiguity as to who is to blame."

Spielberg said that if this movie is successful, he is likely to follow it up with The Spanish Inquisition, a historical film on the torture and murder of the Jews of Spain by the Catholic Church. "To complete the trilogy," Spielberg announced, "in 2006 I will be filming Hitler and the Pope: A Team Formed in Hell." That should generate some heated debate.

LIFE WITHOUT BLACK PEOPLE

Tradition Bearer: Unavailable

Source: E-mail Forward

Date: 2005

Original Source: E-mail

National Origin: Unavailable

A very humorous and revealing story is told about a group of white people who were fed up with African Americans, so they joined together and wished themselves away. They passed through a deep dark tunnel and emerged in sort of a twilight zone where there is an America without black people.

At first these white people breathed a sigh of relief. At last, they said, "No more crime, drugs, violence, and welfare. All of the blacks have gone!"

Then suddenly, reality set in. The "NEW AMERICA" is not America at all—only a barren land.

1. There are very few crops that have flourished because the nation was built on a slave-supported system.
2. There are no cities with tall skyscrapers because Alexander Mils, a black man, invented the elevator, and without it, one finds great difficulty reaching higher floors.
3. There are few if any cars because Richard Spikes, a black man, invented the automatic gearshift, Joseph Gambol, also black, invented the Super Charge System for Internal Combustion Engines, and Garrett A. Morgan, a black man, invented the traffic signals.
4. Furthermore, one could not use the rapid transit system because its procurer was the electric trolley, which was invented by another black man, Albert R. Robinson.
5. Even if there were streets on which cars and a rapid transit system could operate, they were cluttered with paper because an African American, Charles Brooks, invented the street sweeper.
6. There were few if any newspapers, magazines, and books because John Love invented the pencil sharpener, William Purveys invented the fountain pen, and Lee Barrage invented the Type Writing Machine and W. A. Love invented the Advanced Printing Press. They were all, you guessed it, Black.
7. Even if Americans could write their letters, articles, and books, they would not have been transported by mail because William Barry invented the Postmarking and Canceling Machine, William Purveys invented the Hand Stamp and Philip Downing invented the Letter Drop.
8. The lawns were brown and wilted because Joseph Smith invented the Lawn Sprinkler and John Burr the Lawn Mower.
9. When they entered their homes, they found them to be poorly ventilated and poorly heated. You see, Frederick Jones invented the Air Conditioner and Alice Parker the Heating Furnace. Their homes were also dim. But of course, Lewis Later invented the Electric Lamp, Michael Harvey invented the Lantern and Granville T. Woods invented the Automatic Cut-off Switch. Their homes were also filthy because Thomas W. Steward invented the Mop and Lloyd P. Ray the Dust Pan.
10. Their children met them at the door—barefooted, shabby, motley, and unkempt. But what could one expect? Jan E. Matzelinger invented the Shoe

Lasting Machine, Walter Sammons invented the Comb, Sarah Boone invented the Ironing Board and George T. Samon invented the Clothes Dryer.

11. Finally, they were resigned to at least have dinner amidst all of this turmoil. But here again, the food had spoiled because another Black Man, John Standard, invented the refrigerator.

Now, isn't that something? What would this country be like without the contributions of Blacks, as African Americans?

Martin Luther King, Jr., said, "by the time we leave for work, Americans have depended on the inventions from the minds of Blacks." Black history includes more than just slavery, Frederick Douglass, Martin Luther King, Jr., Malcolm X, Marcus Garvey, and W. E. B. Du Bois.

PLEASE SHARE, ABUNDANTLY.

WHY WE LOVE CHILDREN

Tradition Bearer: Unavailable

Source: E-mail Forward

Date: 1999

Original Source: E-mail

National Origin: Unavailable

A kindergarten pupil told his teacher he'd found a cat, but it was dead.
"How do you know that the cat was dead?" she asked her pupil.
"Because I pissed in its ear and it didn't move," answered the child innocently.
"You did WHAT?!?" the teacher exclaimed in surprise.
"You know," explained the boy, "I leaned over and went 'Pssst!' and it didn't move."

2. A small boy is sent to bed by his father.
Five minutes later ... "Da-ad...."
"What?"
"I'm thirsty. Can you bring drink of water?"
"No, You had your chance. Lights out."

Five minutes later: "Da-aaaad...."

"WHAT?"

"I'm THIRSTY. Can I have a drink of water??"

"I told you NO! If you ask again, I'll have to spank you!!"

Five minutes later ... "Daaaa-aaaad...."

"WHAT!"

"When you come in to spank me, can you bring a drink of water?"

3. An exasperated mother, whose son was always getting into mischief, finally asked him:

"How do you expect to get into Heaven?"

The boy thought it over and said, "Well, I'll run in and out and in and out and keep slamming the door until St. Peter says, 'For Heaven's sake, Dylan, come in or stay out!'"

4. One summer evening during a violent thunderstorm a mother was tucking her son into bed.

She was about to turn off the light when he asked with a tremor in his voice, "Mommy, will you sleep with me tonight?"

The mother smiled and gave him a reassuring hug. "I can't dear," she said. "I have to sleep in Daddy's room."

A long silence was broken at last by his shaky little voice: "The big sissy."

5. It was that time, during the Sunday morning service, for the children's sermon. All the children were invited to come forward.

One little girl was wearing a particularly pretty dress and, as she sat down, the pastor leaned over and said, "That is a very pretty dress. Is it your Easter Dress?"

The little girl replied, directly into the pastor's clip-on microphone, "Yes, and my Mom says it's a bitch to iron."

6. When I was six months pregnant with my third child, my three year old came into the room.

I was just getting ready to get into the shower. She said, "Mommy, you are getting fat!"

I replied, "Yes, honey, remember Mommy has a baby growing in her tummy."

"I know," she replied, but what's growing in your butt?"

7. A little boy was doing his math homework.

He said to himself, "Two plus five, that son of a bitch is seven.

Three plus six, that son of a bitch is nine...."

His mother heard what he was saying and gasped, "What are you doing?"

The little boy answered, "I'm doing my math homework, Mom."

"And this is how your teacher taught you to do it?" the mother asked.

"Yes," he answered.

Infuriated, the mother asked the teacher the next day, "What are you teaching my son in math?"

The teacher replied, "Right now, we are learning addition."

The mother asked, "And are you teaching them to say two plus two, that son of a bitch is four?"

After the teacher stopped laughing, she answered, "What I taught them was, two plus two, THE SUM OF WHICH, is four."

8. One day the first grade teacher was reading the story of Chicken Little to her class.

She came to the part of the story where Chicken Little tried to warn the farmer. She read, "... and so Chicken Little went up to the farmer and said, "The sky is falling, the sky is falling!"

The teacher paused then asked the class, "And what do you think that farmer said?"

One little girl raised her hand and said, "I think he said: 'Holy Shit! A talking chicken!'"

The teacher was unable to teach for the next 10 minutes.

9. A certain little girl, when asked her name, would reply, "I'm Mr. Sugarbrown's daughter."

Her mother told her this was wrong, she must say, "I'm Jane Sugarbrown."

The Vicar spoke to her in Sunday School, and said, "Aren't you Mr. Sugarbrown's daughter?"

She replied, "I thought I was, but mother says I'm not."

10. A little girl asked her mother, "Can I go outside and play with the boys?"

Her mother replied, "No, you can't play with the boys, they're too rough."

The little girl thought about it for a few moments and asked, "If I can find a smooth one, can I play with him?"

Now keep that smile on your face and pass it on to someone else!!

Heroes, Heroines, Tricksters, and Fools

MR. JONES'S ADVICE

Tradition Bearer: Unavailable

Source: E-mail Forward

Date: 2005

Original Source: E-mail

National Origin: Unavailable

A 92-year-old, petite, well-poised, and proud man, who is fully dressed each morning by eight o'clock, with his hair fashionably coifed and shaved perfectly applied, even though he is legally blind, moved to a nursing home today. His wife of 70 years recently passed away, making the move necessary. After many hours of waiting patiently in the lobby of the nursing home, he smiled sweetly when told his room was ready.

As he maneuvered his walker to the elevator, I provided a visual description of his tiny room, including the eyelet sheets that had been hung on his window. "I love it," he stated with the enthusiasm of an eight-year-old having just been presented with a new puppy.

"Mr. Jones, you haven't seen the room; just wait."

"That doesn't have anything to do with it," he replied. "Happiness is something you decide on ahead of time. Whether I like my room or not doesn't depend on how the furniture is arranged ... it's how I arrange my mind. I already decided to love it.

"It's a decision I make every morning when I wake up. I have a choice; I can spend the day in bed recounting the difficulty I have with the parts of my body that no longer work, or get out of bed and be thankful for the ones that do. Each day is a gift, and as long as my eyes open I'll focus on the new day and all the happy memories I've stored away. Just for this time in my life. Old age is like a bank account. You withdraw from what you've put in. So, my advice to you would be to deposit a lot of happiness in the bank account of memories. Thank you for your part in filling my memory bank. I am still depositing."

Remember the five simple rules to be happy:

1. Free your heart from hatred.
2. Free your mind from worries.
3. Live simply.
4. Give more.
5. Expect less.

Pass this message to 7 people except me. You will receive a miracle tomorrow.

Now, STOP! Did you hear what I just said. You WILL receive a miracle tomorrow. So send it right now!

AN ACT OF KINDNESS

Tradition Bearer: Unavailable

Source: E-mail Forward

Date: 2005

Original Source: E-mail

National Origin: Unavailable

Subject: Let's see if you send it back. We all know or knew someone like this!! One day, when I was a freshman in high school, I saw a kid from my class was walking home from school. His name was Kyle. It looked like he was carrying all of his books. I thought to myself, "Why would anyone bring home all his books on a Friday?

He must really be a nerd. I had quite a weekend planned (parties and a football game with my friends tomorrow afternoon), so I shrugged my shoulders and went on.

As I was walking, I saw a bunch of kids running toward him.

They ran at him, knocking all his books out of his arms and tripping him so he landed in the dirt. His glasses went flying, and I saw them land in the grass about ten feet from him.

He looked up and I saw this terrible sadness in his eyes. My heart went out to him. So, I jogged over to him and as he crawled around looking for his glasses, and I saw a tear in his eye.

As I handed him his glasses, I said, "Those guys are jerks. They really should get lives."

He looked at me and said, "Hey thanks!" There was a big smile on his face. It was one of those smiles that showed real gratitude.

I helped him pick up his books, and asked him where he lived. As it turned out, he lived near me, so I asked him why I had never seen him before. He said he had gone to private school before now.

I would have never hung out with a private school kid before. We talked all the way home, and I carried some of his books. He turned out to be a pretty cool kid. I asked him if he wanted to play a little football with my friends. He said yes.

We hung out all weekend and the more I got to know Kyle, the more I liked him, and my friends thought the same of him.

Monday morning came, and there was Kyle with the huge stack of books again. I stopped him and said, "Boy, you are gonna really build some serious muscles with this pile of books everyday!

He just laughed and handed me half the books.

Over the next four years, Kyle and I became best friends.

When we were seniors, we began to think about college.

Kyle decided on Georgetown, and I was going to Duke.

I knew that we would always be friends, that the miles would never be a problem.

He was going to be a doctor, and I was going for business on a football scholarship. Kyle was valedictorian of our class. I teased him all the time about being a nerd. He had to prepare a speech for graduation. I was so glad it wasn't me having to get up there and speak.

Graduation day, I saw Kyle. He looked great. He was one of those guys that really found himself during high school. He filled out and actually looked good in glasses. He had more dates than I had and all the girls loved him. Boy, sometimes I was jealous.

Today was one of those days. I could see that he was nervous about his speech. So, I smacked him on the back and said, "Hey, big guy, you'll be great!"

He looked at me with one of those looks (the really grateful one) and smiled. "Thanks!" he said.

As he started his speech, he cleared his throat, and began "Graduation is a time to thank those who helped you make it through those tough years. Your parents, your teachers, your siblings, maybe a coach ... but mostly your friends ... I am here to tell all of you that being a friend to someone is the best gift you can give them. I am going to tell you a story."

I just looked at my friend with disbelief as he told the story of the first day we met. He had planned to kill himself over the weekend. He talked of how he had cleaned out his locker so his Mom wouldn't have to do it later and was carrying his stuff home.

He looked hard at me and gave me a little smile. "Thankfully, I was saved. My friend saved me from doing the unspeakable."

I heard the gasp go through the crowd as this handsome, popular boy told us all about his weakest moment.

I saw his Mom and dad looking at me and smiling that same grateful smile. Not until that moment did I realize its depth.

Never underestimate the power of your actions. With one small gesture you can change a person's life. For better or for worse. God puts us all in each other's lives to impact one another in some way. Look for God in others.

You now have two choices, you can: 1) Pass this on to your friends or 2) Delete it and act like it didn't touch your heart. As you can see, I took choice number 1.

"Friends are angels who lift us to our feet when our wings have trouble remembering how to fly."

There is no beginning or end. Yesterday is history.

Tomorrow is mystery.

Today is a gift.

It's National Friendship Week. Show your friends how much you care. Send this to everyone you consider a FRIEND.

If it comes back to you, then you'll know you have a circle of friends.

WHEN YOU RECEIVE THIS LETTER, YOU'RE REQUESTED TO SEND IT TO AT LEAST 10 PEOPLE, INCLUDING THE PERSON WHO SENT IT TO YOU.

THE NAVY SEAL AND THE ATHEIST

Tradition Bearer: Unavailable

Source: E-mail Forward

Date: 1999

Original Source: E-mail

National Origin: Unavailable

Two things Navy SEALS are always taught:
1. Keep your priorities in order
2. Know when to act without hesitation

A college professor, an avowed atheist and active in the ACLU, was teaching his class. He shocked several of his students when he flatly stated that once and for all he was going to prove there was no God. Addressing the ceiling he shouted: "GOD, if you are real, then I want you to knock me off this platform. I'll give you exactly 15 minutes!!!!!"

The lecture room fell silent. You could hear a pin drop.

Ten minutes went by. "I'm waiting, God, if you're real knock me off this platform!!!"

Again after 4 minutes, the professor taunted God saying, "Here I am, God!!! I'm still waiting!!!"

His count down got down to the last couple of minutes when a SEAL, just released from the Navy after serving in Afghanistan and Iraq and newly registered in the class, walked up to the Professor.

The SEAL hit him full force in the face, and sent the Professor tumbling from his lofty platform. The Professor was out cold!!

The students were stunned and shocked. They began to babble in confusion. The SEAL nonchalantly took his seat in the front row and sat silent. The class looked at him and fell silent ... waiting.

Eventually, the professor came to and was noticeably shaken. He looked at the SEAL in the front row. When the professor regained his senses and could speak he asked: "What the hell is the matter with you? Why did you do that"?

"God was really busy, protecting America's soldiers, who are protecting your right to say stupid shit and act like an asshole, so he sent me!!"

T-BONE STEAK

Tradition Bearer: Unavailable

Source: E-mail Forward

Date: 2005

Original Source: E-mail

National Origin: Unavailable

Here's to T-bone steaks, yellow roses, and friendship.

READ THIS!!!! And then reread it. Especially the last part...

I walked into the grocery store not particularly interested in buying groceries. I wasn't hungry. The pain of losing my husband of 57 years was still too raw. And this grocery store held so many sweet memories.

He often came with me and almost every time he'd pretend to go off and look for something special. I knew what he was up to. I'd always spot him walking down the aisle with the three yellow roses in his hands.

He knew I loved yellow roses. With a heart filled with grief, I only wanted to buy my few items and leave, but even grocery shopping was different since he had passed on.

Shopping for one took time, a little more thought than it had for two.

Standing by the meat, I searched for the perfect small steak and remembered how he had loved his steak.

Suddenly a woman came beside me. She was blonde, slim, and lovely in a soft green pantsuit. I watched as she picked up a large package of T-bones, dropped them in her basket, hesitated, and then put them back. She turned to go and once again reached for the pack of steaks.

She saw me watching her and she smiled. "My husband loves T-bones, but honestly, at these prices, I don't know."

I swallowed the emotion down my throat and met her pale blue eyes. "My husband passed away eight days ago," I told her. Glancing at the package in her hands, I fought to control the tremble in my voice. "Buy him the steaks. And cherish every moment you have together."

She shook her head and I saw the emotion in her eyes as she placed the package in her basket and wheeled away.

I turned and pushed my cart across the length of the store to the dairy products. There I stood, trying to decide which size milk I should buy. A quart, I finally decided, and moved on to the ice cream. If nothing else, I could always fix myself an ice cream cone.

I placed the ice cream in my cart and looked down the aisle toward the front. I saw first the green suit, then recognized the pretty lady coming towards me. In her arms she carried a package. On her face was the brightest smile I had ever seen. I would swear a soft halo encircled her blonde hair as she kept walking toward me, her eyes holding mine.

As she came closer, I saw what she held and tears began misting in my eyes. "These are for you," she said and placed three beautiful long stemmed yellow roses in my arms. "When you go through the line, they will know these are paid for." She leaned over and placed a gentle kiss on my cheek, then smiled again. I wanted to tell her what she'd done, what the roses meant, but still unable to speak, I watched as she walked away as tears clouded my vision.

I looked down at the beautiful roses nestled in the green tissue wrapping and found it almost unreal. How did she know? Suddenly the answer seemed so clear. I wasn't alone.

"Oh, you haven't forgotten me, have you?" I whispered, with tears in my eyes. He was still with me, and she was his angel.

Every day be thankful for what you have and who you are.

(Please read all of this, it is really nice)

This is a simple request. If you appreciate life, send this to your friends, including the person that sent it to you.

Even though I clutch my blanket and growl when the alarm rings. Thank you, Lord, that I can hear. There are many who are deaf.

Even though I keep my eyes closed against the morning light as long as possible. Thank you, Lord, that I can see. Many are blind.

Even though I huddle in my bed and put off rising. Thank you, Lord, that I have the strength to rise. There are many who are bedridden.

Even though the first hour of my day is hectic, when socks are lost, toast is burned, tempers are short, and my children are so loud. Thank you, Lord, for my family. There are many who are lonely.

Even though our breakfast table never looks like the picture in magazines and the menu is at times unbalanced. Thank you, Lord, for the food we have. There are many who are hungry.

Even though the routine of my job often is monotonous. Thank you, Lord, for the opportunity to work. There are many who have no job.

Even though I grumble and bemoan my fate from day to day and wish my circumstances were not so modest. Thank you, Lord, for life.

Pass this on to the friends you know. It might help a bit to make this world a better place to live, right? A friend is someone we turn to when our spirits need a lift. A friend is someone to treasure.

For friendship is a gift. A friend is someone who fills our lives with Beauty, Joy, and Grace and makes the world we live in a better and happier place.

YOU ARE MY FRIEND!

God bless you and yours.

Now send this to every friend you have and don't forget me! "IN GOD I TRUST"

GRANDMOTHER'S REVENGE

Tradition Bearer: Unavailable

Source: E-mail Forward

Date: 2005

Original Source: E-mail

National Origin: Unavailable

Hey, I just got this in an E-mail and thought you might want to work this into your Intro to Folklore class somehow!

Gun-toting granny Ava Estelle, 81, was so ticked-off when two thugs raped her 18-year-old granddaughter that she tracked the unsuspecting ex-cons down—and shot their testicles off. "The old lady spent a week hunting those bums down—and when she found them, she took revenge on them in her own special way," said admiring Melbourne police investigator Evan Delp.

"Then she took a taxi to the nearest police station, laid the gun on the sergeant's desk and told him as calm as could be: 'Those bastards will never rape anybody again, by God.'"

Cops say convicted rapist and robber Davis Furth, 33, lost both his penis and his testicles when outraged Ava opened fire with a 9–mm pistol in the seedy hotel room where he and former prison cellmate Stanley Thomas, 29, were holed up.

The wrinkled avenger also blew Thomas' testicles to kingdom come, but doctors managed to save his mangled penis, police said.

"The one guy, Thomas, didn't lose his manhood, but the doctor I talked to said he won't be using it the way he used to," Detective Delp told reporters. "Both men are still in pretty bad shape, but I think they're just happy to be alive after what they've been through."

The Rambo Granny swung into action August 21 after her granddaughter Debbie was carjacked and raped by two knife-wielding creeps in a section of town bordering on skid row.

"When I saw the look on my Debbie's face that night in the hospital, I decided I was going to go out and get those bastards myself 'cause I figured the police would go easy on them," recalled the retired library worker. "And I wasn't scared of them, either—because I've got me a gun and I've been shootin' it all my life."

So, using a police artist's sketch of the suspects and Debbie's description of the sickos' car, tough-as-nails Ava spent seven days prowling the wino-infested neighborhood where the crime took place till she spotted the ill-fated rapists entering their flophouse hotel.

"I knew it was them the minute I saw 'em, but I shot a picture of 'em anyway and took it back to Debbie and she said sure as hell, it was them," the ornery oldster recalled. "So I went back to that hotel and found their room and knocked on the door—and the minute the big one, Furth, opened the door, I shot 'em, got right square between the legs, right where it would really hurt 'em most, you know. Then I went down to the police station and turned myself in."

Now, baffled lawmen are tying to figure out how to deal with the vigilante granny. "What she did was wrong, but you can't really throw an 81-year-old woman in prison." Det. Delp said, "especially when all 3 million people in the city want to nominate her for sainthood."

A PATRIOT'S ANSWER TO AN IRAQI

Tradition Bearer: Unavailable

Source: E-mail Forward

Date: 2005

Original Source: E-mail

National Origin: Unavailable

Letter From A Mom:
One of my dear sons serves in the military. I'm a very proud Mom. He is still stateside here in California. He called me yesterday to let me know how warm and welcoming people were to him and his troops everywhere he goes. Telling me how people shake their hands, and thank them for being willing to serve and fight, for not only our own freedoms, but so that others may have them also.

But he also told me about an incident in the grocery store where he stopped yesterday, on his way home from the base. He said that ahead of several people in front of him stood a woman dressed in a burka. He said when she got to the cashier she loudly remarked about the U.S. flag lapel pin the cashier wore on her smock.

The cashier reached up and touched the pin, and said, "Yes, I always wear it."

The woman in the burka then asked the cashier when she was going to stop bombing her countrymen, explaining that she was an Iraqi.

A gentleman standing behind my son stepped forward, putting his arm around my son's shoulders, and nodding towards my son, said in a calm and gentle voice to the Iraqi woman, "Lady, hundreds of thousands of men and women like this young man have fought and died so that you could stand here, in MY country and accuse a checkout cashier of bombing your Countrymen. It is my belief that, had you been this outspoken in YOUR OWN country, we wouldn't need to be there today. But, hey! If you have now learned how to speak out so loudly and clearly, I'll gladly pay your way back to Iraq so you can straighten out the mess you are obviously here to avoid."

Everyone in line, and within hearing distance, cheered the older Gentleman, coming forward as they reached for their wallets. The woman in the burka left the store in silence.

I am, like at least some that were in the store, outraged! But it also warmed my heart to know that we as Americans are speaking out, calmly and succinctly (finally) to those that enjoy the freedoms here in the U.S.

God Bless America and Our Troops!

TEAMSTER BOYCOTT

Tradition Bearer: Unavailable

Source: E-mail Forward

Date: 2005

Original Source: E-mail

National Origin: Unavailable

Good Morning Friends,

I have spoken with a few independent truckers in the past 24 hours, and they ALL have indicated to me that there will be a nationwide trucker strike by the Teamsters Union & Major Independents commencing between 8 & 12 September 2005. They will be protesting the high price of fuel nationwide, and intend to bring the Nation to her knees, as they did in the early seventies. I have no reason to doubt these individuals, as their grapevine is usually accurate, and this poses a serious problem for the Nation at large. Almost everything moves by truck across this country, and it won't take very long for our merchants' shelves and gasoline storage tanks to empty resulting in serious shortages in food and fuel. So, be prepared ... fill your pantries and autos prior to the eighth of September!!!!

Unlike the contrived oil and gasoline shortages of the early seventies, the U.S. is not in the position of turning open the spigot and allowing the oil and refined products to flow. Because of the hurricane, the lack of new refineries, and the lack of an ingenious national energy policy, these shortages are real and will be exploited by the Teamsters Union. Every domestic refinery is producing gasoline and home heating oil at maximum capabilities, and combined with the shut down of the refineries in the Gulf due to the hurricane, along with the inability to pump crude oil from the Gulf region, there will be serious shortages for approximately two months. This is a serious National emergency!!!! There have already been long gasoline lines in the South this Labor Day weekend, as many with whom I have spoken from that region have stated to me that in some areas of Alabama, Georgia, Mississippi, North and South Carolina, Louisiana, and Florida, gasoline is already being rationed. These individuals are being allowed only 10 gallons each ... just enough to get by during this shortage. Every Governor of the above mentioned states have asked their citizens to stay at home over the holiday, thus trying to avoid a disaster in the making.

Wal-Mart has announced that their entire fleet of trucks will stop moving good and services effective Tuesday, September 6th ... they know that something is in the making, and don't want to jeopardize either their trucks or personnel during the National Strike. Every independent trucker with whom I have spoken has stated to me that they will not roll during this time frame, as the Teamsters mean business!!!!

Terry ... Teamster Union Member

WAL-MART BOYCOTT

Tradition Bearer: Unavailable

Source: E-mail Forward

Date: 1999

Original Source: E-mail

National Origin: Unavailable

For those of you that have not heard, Planned Parenthood is planning a boycott of Wal-Mart because Wal-Mart will not sell Preven. Preven is being called the "day after" contraceptive. It is not a contraceptive. The egg will have already been fertilized. This is an abortion device and Wal-Mart refuses to sell it.

Planned Parenthood is asking all women and the men who agree with a woman's right to choose (to kill) to boycott Wal-Mart and to write them letting them know why they are being boycotted.

Wal-Mart officials gave an E-mail address for us to write to. Please let them know we appreciate their stand. We mustn't let them down. They are standing up for what is right.

The address is: letters@wal-mart.com. Put re: Preven

Please forward this to everyone and let's let them know that the majority still supports Right to Life. Thanks. We really need to support businesses that take a moral stand on an issue.

"It is a very great poverty that a child must die so that you may live as you wish." —Mother Teresa

HOME DEPOT BOYCOTT

Tradition Bearer: Unavailable

Source: E-mail Forward

Date: 2002

Original Source: E-mail

National Origin: Unavailable

HOME DEPOT REFUSES TO SELL TO THE FEDERAL GOVERN-MENT OR SUB-CONTRACTORS DOING BUSINESS WITH THE FEDERAL GOVERNMENT! When I went to the Depot I spoke with the store manager on duty at the time. I asked if it was true that they would not sell to the U.S. government.

He said that their corporate office sent a letter that day stating that they could not sell to any Federal Government agency or contractors that were doing business with the U.S. Gov. I asked if I could see the letter that Home Depot corporate sent. He showed it to me but would not give me a copy.

I asked him to call HD's corporate office for permission. He declined. I told him I would not leave without a copy of the letter. He called. After he talked he gave me the phone I spoke to their public affairs office.

She confirmed that they would not sell to us, would not give a reason, but said it had nothing to do with Iraq. I asked if she realized what an impact this decision would have on their business and she stated that any loss of business they would suffer as a result of this policy was worth it.

I then asked her to tell the manager to give me a copy of the letter and she did. He made a copy for me and asked for my name. As I left I told him he should be ashamed to work at that store and that they should quit selling the U.S. flag or any item that had the flag on it.

HOW MANY AGGIE FOREMEN DOES IT TAKE

Tradition Bearer: Unavailable

Source: E-mail Forward

Date: 1999

Original Source: E-mail

National Origin: Unavailable

This is classic. We may be going through some rough times now, Aggies, but we stick together through thick and thin. This was sent to me by an Aggie in the office.

* * *

Please excuse the language, I used direct quotes where available...

My brother, Geoff is a construction site foreman for Del-Ware Companies. They build large public buildings (schools, city halls, utilities, etc.).

Geoff's job is to travel to all the sites they have under construction and to monitor the progress of their various projects.

He showed up Friday morning at a school under construction down near Victoria. He was wearing his A&M hat. When he got out of the truck, he began to inspect the steel framework that was going up. One of the foreman came down from the structure, walked over to him and said, "So, how many Aggies does it take to put together a stack of logs anyway ... Apparently more than twelve!!"

He and the guys gathered around thought this was hilarious until Geoff told him to "GET THE FUCK OFF MY JOB SITE!" He then fired the entire steel contracting company, told them to "pick up your shit and get it off my company's site, now! This guy just flushed your $250,000 contract." He called HIS boss (a t.u. grad) to make sure he had the authority to throw all these guys out. After telling him what was said his boss's response was classic:

"Geoff, I may not know how many Aggies it takes to build a Bonfire, but I do know it only takes one Aggie Foreman to fire a bunch of assholes."

PRICELESS

Tradition Bearer: Unavailable

Source: E-mail Forward

Date: 2000

Original Source: E-mail

National Origin: Unavailable

You guys will die laughing!
PRICELESS...
This actually IS true! It was in the local newspaper and even Jay Leno mentioned it. This is a true story about a recent wedding that took place at Clemson University:

It was a huge wedding with about 300 guests. After the wedding, at the reception, the groom got up on stage at the microphone to talk to the crowd. He said that he wanted to thank everyone for coming, many from long distances, to support them at their wedding. He especially wanted to thank the bride's and groom's families for coming and to thank his new father-in-law for providing such a fabulous reception. To thank everyone for coming and bringing gifts and everything, he said he wanted to give everyone a special gift from just him. So taped to the bottom of everyone's chair was a manila envelope, including the wedding party. He said that this was his gift to everyone, and told everyone to open the envelopes. Inside each manila envelope was an 8x10 picture of his best man having sex with the bride. He had gotten suspicious of the two of them and hired a private detective to trail them weeks prior to the wedding.

After he stood there and watched the people's reactions for a couple of minutes, he turned to the best man and said, "F— you!" He turned to his bride and said, "F— you!" and then he turned to the dumbfounded crowd and said, "I'm out of here."

He had the marriage annulled first thing that Monday morning. While most of us would have broken off the engagement immediately after finding out about the affair, this guy goes through with it anyway, as if nothing was wrong.

His revenge: Making the bride's parents pay over $32,000 for 300 guests for a wedding and reception. Letting everyone know exactly what did happen. And best of all, trashing the bride's and best man's reputations in front of all of their friends and their entire families. This guy has balls the size of church bells.

Do you think we might see one of those MasterCard "Priceless" commercials out of this?

Elegant wedding for 300 family and guests, $32,000. Photographers for the wedding $3,000. Accommodations in Maui for 2 weeks $8,500. The look on everyone's faces after seeing a photo of the Bride and Best Man having sex...

Priceless.

JANE FONDA NOMINATION

Variant A

Tradition Bearer: Unavailable

Source: E-mail Forward

Date: 2000

Original Source: E-mail

National Origin: Unavailable

I usually do not forward emails that I receive but I thought this one was important enough to share with all of you. Please take the time to read and remember and if you have a bit of extra time please send it to your friends so they too can remember. Jane Fonda is being honored as one of the "100 Women of the Century."

Unfortunately many have forgotten and still countless others have never known how Ms. Fonda betrayed not only the idea of our country but specific men who served and sacrificed during Vietnam. Part of my conviction comes from personal exposure to those who suffered her attentions.

The first part of this is from an F-4E pilot. The pilot's name is Jerry Driscoll, a River Rat. In 1978, the former Commandant of the USAF Survival School was a POW in Ho Lo Prison-the "Hanoi Hilton." Dragged from a stinking cesspit of a cell, cleaned, fed, and dressed in clean PJs, he was ordered to describe for a visiting American "Peace Activist" the "lenient and humane treatment" he'd received. He spat at Ms. Fonda, was clubbed, and dragged away. During the subsequent beating, he fell forward upon the camp commandant's feet, which sent that officer berserk. In '78, the AF Col. still suffered from double vision (which permanently ended his flying days) from the Vietnamese Col.'s frenzied application of a wooden baton.

From 1983–1985, Col. Larry Carrigan was in the 47FW/DO (F-4Es). He spent 6 years in the "Hilton"—the first three of which he was "missing in action." His wife lived on faith that he was still alive. His group, too, got the cleaned/fed/clothed routine in preparation for a peace delegation visit. They, however, had time and devised a plan to get word to the world that they still survived. Each man secreted a tiny piece of paper, with his SSN on it, in the palm of his hand. When paraded before Ms. Fonda and a cameraman, she walked the line, shaking each man's hand and asking little encouraging snippets like: "Aren't you sorry you bombed babies?" and "Are you grateful for the humane treatment from your benevolent captors?"

Believing this HAD to be an act, they each palmed her their sliver of paper. She took them all without missing a beat. At the end of the line and once the camera stopped rolling, to the shocked disbelief of the POWs, she turned to the officer in charge ... and handed him the little pile of papers. Three men died from the subsequent beatings. Col. Carrigan was almost number four but he survived, which is the only reason we know about her actions that day.

I was a civilian economic development advisor in Vietnam, and was captured by the North Vietnamese communists in South Vietnam in 1968, and held for over 5 years. I spent 27 months in solitary confinement, one year in a cage in Cambodia, and one year in a "black box" in Hanoi. My North Vietnamese captors deliberately poisoned and murdered a female missionary, a nurse in a leprosarium in Ban me Thuot, South Vietnam, whom I buried in the jungle near the Cambodian border. At one time, I was weighing approximately 90 lbs. (My normal weight is 170 lbs.). We were Jane Fonda's "war criminals."

When Jane Fonda was in Hanoi, I was asked by the camp communist political officer if I would be willing to meet with Jane Fonda. I said yes, for I would like to tell her about the real treatment we POWs were receiving, which was far different from the treatment purported by the North Vietnamese, and parroted by Jane Fonda, as "humane and lenient." Because of this, I spent three days on a rocky floor on my knees with outstretched arms with a large amount of steel placed on my hands, and beaten with a bamboo cane till my arms dipped. I had the opportunity to meet with Jane Fonda for a couple of hours after I was released. I asked her if she would be willing to debate me on TV. She did not answer me.

This does not exemplify someone who should be honored as part of "100 Years of Great Women." Lest we forget... "100 years of great women" should never include a traitor whose hands are covered with the blood of so many patriots. There are few things I have strong visceral reactions to, but Hanoi Jane's participation in blatant treason, is one of them.

Please take the time to forward to as many people as you possibly can. It will eventually end up on her computer and she needs to know that we will never forget.

If having Jane Fonda named one of the woman of the century bothers you as much as it does me, then mail this to everyone on your list.

Variant B

Date: 2001

HONORING A TRAITOR... :(JUST SO YOU KNOW, EVEN TO THIS DAY I WILL NOT WATCH A MOVIE OR LISTEN TO WHAT SHE HAS TO SAY BECAUSE I REMEMBER OH SO VERY WELL THAT TIME IN MY YOUNG LIFE.

AS AN ADULT I UNDERSTAND MORE OF WHAT SHE DID AND SAID. I COULD AND NEVER WILL FORGIVE HER FOR HER RECKLESS BELIEF IN THE NORTH VIETNAM.

KEEP THIS MOVING ACROSS AMERICA.

HONORING A TRAITOR.

This is for all the kids born in the '70s that do not remember this, and didn't have to bear the burden that our fathers, mothers, and older brothers and sisters had to bear.

BUSH REFUSES TO SELL HOME TO BLACKS

Tradition Bearer: Unavailable

Source: E-mail Forward

Date: 2000

Original Source: E-mail

National Origin: Unavailable

Brothers and Sisters, please read and pass along. We must remember this at the polls, and choose wisely. Whites-only covenant shows Bush's true colors.

Texas governor and Republican presidential candidate, George W. Bush recently sent waves through the Black community following a discovery that a Dallas house he sold in 1995 carries a racial covenant, which restricts the sale of the house to white people only. Bush and his wife, Laura, bought the house in 1988. How is this legal? It isn't.

The Fair Housing Act prevents the enforcement of racial covenants. However, many houses still carry them as a remnant of the Jim Crow era when it was common practice to exclude Blacks from buying houses and living in white neighborhoods. The Bush campaign responded with an online statement saying that the racial covenant was void and that Bush was unaware of it when he sold the house. Yeah right! It's extremely irresponsible for a public figure to accidentally overlook such a stipulation. Did Bush really know but just didn't care to do anything about it? The real estate agent who prepared the papers for the sale said that she notified Bush of the racial covenant but that he signed the papers anyway.

Perhaps equally shocking as the racial covenant is the fact that the media has swept this story under the rug.

Have you heard about it in any of the newspapers you read or on any of the news programs you watch?

ATTACKER IN THE BACKSEAT

Tradition Bearer: Unavailable

Source: E-mail Forward

Date: 2000

Original Source: E-mail

National Origin: Unavailable

ALL LADIES BEWARE, THIS IS AWFUL! MEN TELL YOUR WIFE, SISTER, AUNT, MOTHER, ETC. BE CAREFUL AND LOCK YOUR CARS NO MATTER WHAT! WATCH YOUR SURROUNDINGS. This was forwarded to me, it happened in Austin!

This actually happened to my friend's niece last week right here near downtown. It was after dark and she stopped to get gas at a QuikTrip. She filled her tank and walked into the store to pay for her gas. The cashier told her "don't pay for your gas yet ... walk around the store a while and act as if you're picking up some other things to buy. A man just got into the back of your car. I've called the police and they're on their way." When the police arrived, they found the man in the back seat of the girl's car and asked him what he was doing. He replied, he was joining a gang and the initiation to join is to kidnap a woman and bring her back to the gang to be raped. According to the police that night, there is a new gang forming here originating from Chicago. Part of the scary part of this is because the guy didn't have a weapon on him the police could only charge him with trespassing ... he's back on the streets and free to try again.

Please be aware of what's going on around you, ladies. This could happen to anyone. Please forward this on to anyone you care about!

BODY PART INITIATION

Variant A

Tradition Bearer: Unavailable

Source: E-mail Forward

Date: 1999

Original Source: E-mail

National Origin: Unavailable

I am passing this along because I know of an incident similar to this. My girlfriend was getting some gas and when she attempted to return to her car the gas station attendant starting yelling at her and telling her she did not pay yet.

When she went back in to argue about having already paid the attendant told her he just wanted to get her back in because he saw someone crawl in the back-seat of her car, and that he had already called the police.

So it's worth taking to heart.

This is a true story. It has been "ritual" of gang members to take one body part from women as an initiation into gangs. The rule is that is has to be in a well-lit area and at a gas station, so be careful.

They tend to lay under the car, and slash females' ankles when she goes to get in her car, causing her to fall and then they cut off a body part and roll and run. They are known to hide behind the gas pumps too, so be careful. It might sound bizarre and gross, but the bigger the body part the higher the initiation they receive.

This was communicated by a person who works in law enforcement in the South.

She has investigated and been called to a number of these scenes. She has also confirmed the above statement as true and not an Internet "hoax."

Please pass these on to as many people you know ... mothers, sisters, grandparents, daughters, nieces, and friends. It seems the world has become a crazy place to live.

Let's be careful out there and make stuff like this known so we are better protected.

Variant B

Subject: Attn: ALL LADIES!!!!
Tell all of the women in your life about this.
Be Careful.

I am passing along because I know of an incident similar to this. My girlfriend was getting some gas and when she attempted to return to her car the gas station attendant starting yelling at her and telling her she did not pay yet. When she went back in to argue about having already paid the attendant told her he just wanted to get her back in because he saw someone crawl in the back-seat of her car, and that he had already called the police. So it's worth taking to heart.

This is a true story. It has been "ritual" of gang members to take one body part from women as an initiation into gangs. The rule is that is has to be in a well-lit area and at a gas station, so be careful.

They tend to lay under the car, and slash the female's ankles when she goes to get in her car, causing her to fall and then they cut off a body part and roll and run. They are known to hide behind the gas pumps too, so be careful.

It might sound bizarre and gross but the bigger the body parts the higher the initiation they receive. This info. was communicated by a female law enforcement person that works in the South. She has investigated and been called to several of these scenes. She has also confirmed the following state-ment below as true and not an Internet "hoax."

Please pass these on to as many people you know, mothers, sisters, grand-parents, daughters, nieces, and friends. The world it seems has become a crazy place to live in but let be careful out there and make stuff like this known so we are better protected.

Here is an example of a true case—a gas station attendant yelled at a lady to come back and pay for her gas, if she did not he would call the cops if she tried to drive away (this was right after she had been in and paid for the gas.) She returned into the station upset and angry at the attendant, only to realize that he had called the cops after spotting a man roll under her car. She was about to be a victim of the above initiation.

Bless Your Spirit.

Rev. ———

Variant C

Date: 2000

Subject: FW: YOUR SAFETY—WARNING FROM U.S.A. MILITARY POLICE SCHOOL

IMPORTANT MESSAGE FOR SAFETY FROM THE DIRECTOR OF TRAINING AT THE U.S. ARMY MILITARY POLICE SCHOOL—PLEASE TAKE TIME TO READ AND PASS ALONG!

A friend stopped at a pay-at-the-pump gas station to get gas. Once she filled her gas tank after paying at the pump and started to leave the attendant inside came over the speaker. He told her that something happened with her card and that she needed to come inside to pay.

The lady was confused because the transaction showed complete and approved.

She told him that and was getting ready to leave but the attendant once again urged her to come in to pay or else. She proceeded to go inside and started arguing with the attendant about his threat.

He told her to calm down and listen carefully: He told her that while she was pumping gas, a guy slipped into the back seat of her car on the other side and he had called the police.

She immediately became scared and looked out there in time to see her car door open and the guy slip out.

The report is that the new gang initiation thing is to bring back a woman's body part. One way they are doing this is crawling under girls/women's cars while they're pumping gas or at grocery stores in the nighttime. Then, they are cutting the lady's ankles to disable them in order to kidnap them, kill and dismember them. The other way is slipping into unattended cars and kidnapping the women to kill and dismember them.

Please pass this on to other women, young and old alike.

BE extra careful going to and from your car at night. If at all possible, don't go alone!

This is for real!!

THE MESSAGE:

1. ALWAYS lock your car doors, even if you're gone for just second.
2. Check underneath your car when approaching it for reentry, and check in the back before getting in.
3. Always be aware of your surroundings and other individuals in your general vicinity, particularly at night!

Send this to your friends so as many females as possible can be made aware of this new threat, & so your friend will not be the next victim.

Thanks,

Ms. ——, Secretary

Directorate of Training

U.S. Army Military Police School

MALL ABDUCTION PLOYS

Tradition Bearer: Unavailable

Source: E-mail Forward

Date: 2000

Original Source: E-mail

National Origin: Unavailable

ubject: FW: Abduction Scams
        I don't usually pass this kind of thing along but this is so logical and easy to fall for—especially during a busy holiday season.

Make sure you read the entire thing. Towards the end is really important!!!!!

The notice below was posted on JCPenney's E-mail this morning to all female associates. I wanted to pass the information on to you. Recently on Inside Edition there was an article about several new scams to abduct women.

In one, a man comes up to a woman in a mall or shopping center and asks if she likes pizza. When she says she does, he offers her $10,000 to shoot a commercial for pizza, but they need to go outside where the lighting is better. When the woman goes out of the mall she is abducted and assaulted.

Another ploy is a very nicely dressed man asks a woman if she would be in a public service announcement to discourage drug use. The man explains that they don't want professional actors or celebrities; they want the average mother to do this. Once she leaves the mall she is a victim.

The third ploy, the most successful, a frantic man comes running in to the mall and asks a woman to please help him, his baby is not breathing. She runs out of the mall following him and also becomes a victim.

These have been happening in well-lit parking areas, in daylight as well as nighttime, all over the country. The abductor usually uses a van to abduct the woman.

Inside Edition set up a test in a mall and 10 out of 15 women went out of the mall on the pizza and the PSA scam. And all of them went out of the mall on the baby scam. Please pass this along to your friends and family as now that it has been shown on nationwide TV there are bound to be copycats of this.

The third one, I think, is the scariest. You might resist pizza or becoming a commercial celebrity ... but who would be able to resist a frantic father asking for help for his child? I'm sure that one would get me.

A woman was shopping at the Tuttle Mall in Columbus. She came out to her car and saw she had a flat. She got her jack and spare out of the trunk. A man in a business suit came up and started to help her. When the tire had been replaced, he asked for a ride to his car on the opposite side of the mall. Feeling uncomfortable about doing this, she stalled for a while, but he kept pressing her.

She finally asked why he was on this side of the mall if his car was on the other.

He claimed he had been talking to friends. Still uncomfortable, she told him that she had just remembered something she had forgotten to pick up at the mall and she left him and went back inside the mall. She reported the incident to the mall security and they went out to her car. The man was nowhere in sight.

Opening her trunk, she discovered a briefcase the man had set inside her trunk while helping her with the tire. Inside were rope and a butcher knife. And, when she took the tire to be fixed, the mechanic informed her that there was nothing wrong with her tire, that it was flat because the air had been let out of it.

Send this to any woman you know that may need to be reminded that the world we live in has a lot of crazies in it ... better safe than sorry.

PLEASE BE SAFE AND NOT SORRY! JUST A WARNING TO ALWAYS BE ALERT AND USE YOUR HEAD!!!

Pass this along to every woman you have access to. Never let your guard down.

SOMETIMES THAT FEELING IN YOUR GUT IS THE VOICE OF GOD. TRUST YOURINSTINCTS!!

Sincerely,

————, PHR

JCPenney Direct Marketing Services

Human Resources

Sincerely,

————, Senior Project Manager

JCPenney Direct Marketing Services

POISON PERFUME

Variant A

Tradition Bearer: Unavailable

Source: E-mail Forward

Date: 2001

Original Source: E-mail

National Origin: Unavailable

I feel that it is important to inform you of very important information that I was told. Seven women have died after smelling a free perfume sample that was mailed to them. The product was poisonous.

If you receive free samples in the mail such as lotions, perfumes, diapers, etc., throw it away. The government is afraid that this might be another terrorist act. They will not announce it on the news because they do not want to alarm us of any danger.

Variant B

Date: 2003

Seven women have died after inhaling a free perfume sample that was mailed to them. The product was poisonous. If you receive free samples in the mail such as lotions, perfumes, diapers etc. throw them away.

The government is afraid that this might be another terrorist act. They will not announce it on the news because they do not want to create panic or give the terrorists new ideas.

Send this to all your friends and family members. Please pass on to all women you know.

PERFUME MUGGER

Variant A

Tradition Bearer: Unavailable

Source: E-mail Forward

Date: 1999

Original Source: E-mail

National Origin: Unavailable

I DON'T THINK ANY OF US WOULD BE SNIFFING AROUND OUTSIDE THE MALL, BUT JUST IN CASE. What will people think of next to try and get over on honest folks!?!?!

I just heard on the radio about a lady that was asked to sniff a bottle of perfume that another woman was selling for $8 (in a mall parking lot). She told the story that it was her last bottle of perfume that regularly sells for $49 but she was getting rid of it for only $8, sound legitimate? That's what the victim thought, but when she awoke she found out that her car had been moved to another parking area and she was missing all of the money that was in her wallet (total of $800). Pretty steep for a sniff of perfume!

Anyway, the perfume wasn't perfume at all, it was some kind of ether or strong substance to cause anyone that breathes the fumes to black out.

So beware....

Christmas time is coming and we will be going to malls to shop and we will have cash on us. Ladies, please don't be so trusting of others and be aware of your surroundings-ALWAYS! Obey your instincts!

Please pass this on to your friends, sisters, mothers and all the women in your life that you care about ... we can never be too careful!!!

Variant B

Date: 2000

This was forwarded to me by a friend.

TO ALL MY WOMEN FRIENDS—PASS IT ALONG TO YOUR WOMEN FRIENDS!!!

I just wanted to pass along that I was approached yesterday afternoon around 3:30 p.m. in the Wal-Mart parking lot at Forest Drive, by 2 males, asking what kind of perfume I was wearing. I didn't stop to answer them, and kept walking toward the store. At the time, I remembered this E-mail. The men continued to stand between parked cars, I guess to wait for someone else to hit on. I stopped a lady going toward them, pointed at them, and told her about how I was sent an E-mail at work about someone walking up to you at the malls or in parking lots, and asking you to SNIFF PERFUME that they are selling at a cheap price!

THIS IS NOT PERFUME—IT IS ETHER! YOU WILL PASS OUT, AND THEY WILL TAKE YOUR WALLET AND ALL OF YOUR VALUABLES.

This is not a prank email; this is true because I was stopped in the Governors Square parking lot today. A maroon van pulled up to me with two females in it. The female on the passenger side rolled down the window and asked me if I would be interested in "sniffing" some perfume they were selling.

I remembered the E-mail that I had received, and said, "NO".

She asked me a second time, I kept on walking and said "NO" once again, and they pulled away.

If it were not for this E-mail, I probably would have sniffed the "perfume."
PASS THIS ALONG TO ALL YOUR WOMEN FRIENDS, AND PLEASE
BE ALERT, AND AWARE!!

Variant C

Date: 2001

B E CAREFUL. PLEASE READ AND PASS ON!
At a gas station recently, I was approached by a young woman, who was
obviously with another woman, and was asked what kind of perfume I wore.
I told her I did not wear perfume.

The attendant came out and told them to leave. Apparently, they had been
bothering other people.

At the time, I thought it was odd, and then forgot about the incident. I
received this E-mail earlier this week, I too was approached about 10 days ago
@ a Chevron station @ Rufe Snow & 820 by a man asking if I wanted to buy
some perfume. I said no, not interested & never thought about it again until I
received this E-mail!!!)

Cindy, I was approached yesterday afternoon around 3:30 p.m. in the Wal-
Mart parking lot at Forest Drive, by two males, asking what kind of perfume I
was wearing. Then they asked if I'd like to sample some fabulous scent they were
willing to sell me at a very reasonable rate. I probably would have agreed had I
not received an E-mail some weeks ago, warning of a "wanna smell this neat
perfume?" scam.

The men continued to stand between parked cars, I guess to wait for someone else to hit on. I stopped a lady going toward them, pointed at them, and told
her about how I was sent an E-mail at work about someone walking up to you
at the malls or in parking lots, and asking you to SNIFF PERFUME that they
are selling at a cheap price.

THIS IS NOT PERFUME—IT IS ETHER! When you sniff it, you'll pass
out and they'll take your wallet, your valuables, and heaven knows what else.

If it were not for this E-mail, I probably would have sniffed the "perfume."
But thanks to the generosity of an emailing friend, I was spared whatever might
have happened to me.

I wanted to do the same for you.

PASS THIS ALONG TO ALL YOUR WOMEN FRIENDS. PLEASE BE CAREFUL this is very serious, especially for women, but men warn your loved females so this will not happen to them, God bless.

BE CAREFUL PLEASE READ AND PASS ON!

RESTROOM KIDNAPPING

Tradition Bearer: Unavailable

Source: E-mail Forward

Date: 1999

Original Source: E-mail

National Origin: Unavailable

THIS WAS FORWARDED TO ME—I'M PASSING IT ON TO YOU.
A Public notice:
Hi All,
Wanted to share something that happened today while shopping at Sam's Club. A mother was leaning over looking for meat and turned around to find her 4 yr. old daughter was missing, I was standing there right beside her, well she was calling her daughter and no luck. I asked a man who worked at Sam's to announce it over the loud speaker for Katie. Well, he did, and let me say he walked past me when I asked and went to a pole where there was a phone right there to make his announcement for all doors and gates to be locked, a code something ... so they locked all the doors at once. This took all of 3 min after I asked the guy to do this. They found the little girl 5 min later crunched in a bathroom stall, her head was half shaved, and she was dressed in her underwear with a bag of clothes, a razor, and wig sitting on the floor besides her. Whoever this person was, took the little girl, brought her into the bathroom, shaved half her head, undressed her in a matter of less than 10 min. Makes me shake to no end.

Please keep an eye out for your kids when in shopping places. It only took a few minutes to do all of this, another 5 min and she would have been out the door ... I am still in shock some sick person could do this, let alone in a matter of minutes ... The little girl is fine ... thank God for fast workers who didn't take any chances. Thanks for reading. Please keep praying for our children.

HANDSHAKE ASSAULT

Tradition Bearer: Unavailable

Source: E-mail Forward

Date: 2000

Original Source: E-mail

National Origin: Unavailable

Please read this ... it is not a forward, it is coming directly from me. THIS IS SERIOUS!

Today, my friend was walking through the sliding doors in the commons, when a guy reached out to shake her hand ... she didn't think anything of it and shook his ... as she did, she felt something sharp, but didn't think anything about it... as she walked away, she saw that blood was dripping down her hand ... she turned to look at the guy and he was gone ... she immediately rushed to Buetel ... they told her she was cut with a metal object (rust was in her skin) ... the scary thing is that she was the third person to report this happening to them ... they are testing everyone for HIV, but it is of course too soon to know.

Please be very cautious in your surroundings, if you got this E-mail from me, it means I care about you and want to you to be safe!

Send this to all of your Aggie friends because this man needs to be caught!

* * *

I just got off the phone with Stacy who works in the emergency area of Beutel and says that they have been flooded with phone calls questioning the validity of the story. She says it is just a fluke, there have been no such reports to Beutel in regard to anything of that nature. Just thought you all should know that, because I have gotten that E-mail more than once today. So respond to the people who it came from and let them know to spread the word that it is not true.

DATE RAPE DRUG

Tradition Bearer: Unavailable

Source: E-mail Forward

Date: 2000

Original Source: E-mail

National Origin: Unavailable

lease send this off to all the girls you know!!
    Please be very aware of this. It's just awful. Please forward on to any
female friends or your girlfriends etc. Ladies, be more alert and cautious
when getting a drink offer from a guy. Good guys out there, please forward this
message to your lady friends. And boyfriends, take heed.

There is a new drug that has been out for less than a year. Progesterex, that
is essentially a small sterilization pill. The drug is now being used by rapists at
parties to rape AND sterilize their victims.

Progesterex is available to vets to sterilize large animals. Rumor has it that
the Progesterex is being used together with Rohypnol, the date rape drug. As
with Rohypnol, all they have to do is drop it into the girl's drink. The girl can't
remember a thing the next morning, of all that had taken place the night before.
Progesterex, which dissolves in drinks just as easily, is such that the victim does-
n't conceive from the rape and the rapist needn't worry about having a paternity
test identifying him months later. The drug's effects AREN'T TEMPORARY.

Progesterex was designed to sterilize horses. Any female that takes it WILL
NEVER BE ABLE TO CONCEIVE. The crooks can get this drug from anyone
who is in the vet school of any university. It's that easy, and Progesterex is about
to breakout big on campuses everywhere. Believe it or not, there is even a site
on the Internet telling people how to use it.

Please forward this to everyone you know, especially the gals.

THE CHLOROFORMED ROOMMATE

Tradition Bearer: Unavailable

Source: E-mail Forward

Date: 1999

Original Source: E-mail

National Origin: Unavailable

ecently I had a conversation with my resident advisor who told me about a
guy a friend of his knew here at aTm [Texas A&M]. Apparently this guy had
gotten a potluck roommate who was nice but more or less kept to himself.
    The guy would awake morning after morning to find his rectum sore and red.
    This problem persisted so he saw a doctor about it. Well the doctor said he
had a torn sphincter, which is typical of anal intercourse. The man remarked
that he was not gay, and therefore this could not be the cause.

He returned home and went to bed puzzled, thinking about what the doctor told him the entire time. As the hours rolled by he was still awake, though laying as asleep, when he noticed his roommate get up and fool with something in his desk drawer.

His roommate then casually approached him and attempted to cover his nose and mouth with something. Apparently his roommate had been putting chloroform on a handkerchief and incapacitating him, and then having anal intercourse with him. This story was told to me not as a joke, but as true ... really.

HIV NEEDLES

Tradition Bearer: Unavailable

Source: E-mail Forward

Date: 1999

Original Source: E-mail

National Origin: Unavailable

At the police station, Dan has roll call every morning before his shift. The Sergeant addressed them of any things to be aware of. Anyway ... some sick people are going into the movie theaters and leaving HIV tainted needles on the toilet seats, to poke the people. Also this is so for change returns on the coke machines too. The needles have come back positive for the virus.

This is probably not affecting your area but just watch the media put it on the news and then here come all the "copy cats."

Well I just wanted to give you something else to worry about, when you go to a public restroom.

POISON PAYPHONE

Tradition Bearer: Unavailable

Source: E-mail Forward

Date: 1999

Original Source: E-mail

National Origin: Unavailable

Kinda makes you think about what you touch. We got a flyer about this at work ... It also stated that this has happened in a theatre seat where a hypodermic needle was stuck in the cushion ... You might want to be aware of that as well....

Please ... Read this and Pass it along and get the word out ... Thanks all.

——Original Message Follows——

Hello, this is to warn everyone of a new thing happening in communities as a gang initiation and such. If you care about anyone, please forward this to them immediately so they can learn of the possible harm. Even if you don't read this, at least forward it to people.

Hello, my name is Tina Strongman and I work at a police station, as a phone operator for 911. Lately, we've received many phone calls pertaining to a new sort of problem that has arisen in the inner cities, and is now working it's way to smaller towns. It seems that a new form of gang initiation is to go find as many pay phones as possible and put a mixture of LSD and Strychnine onto the buttons. This mixture is deadly to the human touch, and apparently, this has killed some people on the East Coast. Strychnine is a chemical used in rat poison and is easily separated from the rest of the chemicals. When mixed with LSD, it creates a substance that is easily absorbed into the human flesh, and highly fatal.

Please be careful if you are using a pay phone anywhere. You may want to wipe it off, or just not use one at all.

Please be very careful.

Let your friends and family know about this potential hazard.

Thank you.

Sgt. ———

—— Air Force Pentagon

Washington DC

CAR JACKING SCHEME

Tradition Bearer: Unavailable

Source: E-mail Forward

Date: 2004

Original Source: E-mail

National Origin: Unavailable

Be aware of new car-jacking scheme. Imagine: You walk across the parking lot, unlock your car and get inside. Then you lock all your doors, start the engine and shift into REVERSE, and you look into the rearview mirror to back out of your parking space and you notice a piece of paper stuck to the middle of the rear window. So, you shift into PARK, unlock your doors and jump out of your car to remove that paper (or whatever it is) that is obstructing your view....

When you reach the back of your car, that is when the carjackers appear out of nowhere, jump into your car and take off!!

Your engine was running, (ladies would have their purse in the car) and they practically mow you down as they speed off in your car.

BE AWARE OF THIS NEW SCHEME THAT IS NOW BEING USED.

Just drive away and remove the paper that is stuck to your window later, and be thankful that you read this E-mail. I hope you will forward this to friends and family ... especially to women! A purse contains all identification, and you certainly do NOT want someone getting your home address. They already HAVE your keys!

WORLD TRADE CENTER SURVIVOR'S SON JOINS THE TERRORISTS

Tradition Bearer: Unavailable

Source: E-mail Forward

Date: 2001

Original Source: E-mail

National Origin: Unavailable

Didn't see this in the American news, but at this point I can believe anything!!! Mohammed Junaid's mother was led to safety from the blazing World Trade Center by New York's brave firefighters and policemen. But 26-year-old Junaid's thank you has shocked New York.

In return for saving his mum's life, the Islamic-American has turned traitor and bought a one-way ticket to Pakistan to sign up for the Taliban and kill Americans.

Junaid left on what could be a suicide mission one week after his mother—an office worker on the ninth floor of the north tower—was among the survivors. About 4,500 others were not so lucky, and lost their lives in the terror strikes on September 11.

"My mother was in the north tower of the World Trade Centre but I still feel absolutely no remorse about what happened on September 11," Junaid said. "I saw the towers collapse but felt nothing for the Americans inside. I may hold an American passport, but I am not an American—I am a Muslim."

Junaid offered his own personal jihad against his own country when in Islamabad, Pakistan, as he waited to cross the border into Afghanistan to join the Taliban. "I did not feel any remorse for the Americans who died," Junaid told Britain's ITN television network.

"I'm willing to kill the Americans. I will kill every American that I see in Afghanistan. And I'll kill every American soldier that I see in Pakistan."

Junaid's parents migrated from Pakistan.

KATRINA WORKER REPORT

Tradition Bearer: Unavailable

Source: E-mail Forward

Date: 2005

Original Source: E-mail

National Origin: Unavailable

I got this from a friend in Houston who got it as an E-mail. If this is all true, it kinda makes you think.

I thought I might inform the few friends I have on my recent traumatic experience. I am going to tell it straight, blunt, raw, and I don't give a damn. Long read, I know but please do read!

I went to volunteer on Saturday at the George R. Brown convention for two reasons.

A: I wanted to help people to get a warm fuzzy.

B: Curiosity.

I've been watching the news lately and have seen scenes that have made me want to vomit. And no it wasn't dead bodies, the city under water, or the sludge everywhere. It was PEOPLE'S BEHAVIOR. The people on TV (99% being black) were DEMANDING help. They were not asking nicely but demanding as if society owed these people something. Well the honest truth is WE DON'T.

Help should be asked for in a kind manner and then appreciated. This is not what the press (FOX in particular) was showing, what I was seeing was a group of people who are yelling, demanding, looting, killing, raping, and SHOOTING back at the demanded help! So I'm thinking this can't possibly be true can it? So I decide to submit to the DEMAND for help out of SHOCK. I couldn't believe this to be true of the majority of the people who are the weakest of society. So I went to volunteer and help folks out and see the truth. So I will tell the following story and you decide:

I arrived at the astrodome only to find out that there are too many volunteers and that volunteers were needed at the George R. Brown Convention Center. As I was walking up to the Convention Center I noticed a line of cars that wrapped around blocks filled with donations. These were ordinary Houstonians coming with truckloads and trunks full of water, diapers, clothes, blankets, food, all types of good stuff. And lots of it was NEW. I felt that warm fuzzy while helping unload these vehicles of these wonderful human beings. I then went inside the building and noticed approximately 100,000 sq. ft. of clothes, shoes, jackets, toys and all types of goodies all organized and ready for the people in need. I signed up, received a name badge and was on my merry way excited to be useful.

I toured the place to get familiar with my surrounding; the entire place is probably around 2 million sq. ft. I noticed rows as far as the eye can see of mattresses, not cots, BLOW UP MATTRESSES! All of which had nice pillows and plenty of blankets. 2 to 3 bottles of water lay on every bed. These full size to queen size beds by the way were comfortable, I laid on one to see for myself. I went to look at the medical area. I couldn't believe what my eyes were seeing! A makeshift hospital created in 24 hours! It was unbelievable, they even had a pharmacy. I also noticed that they created showers, which would also have hot water. I went upstairs to the third floor to find a HUGE cafeteria created in under 24 hours! Rows of tables, chairs and food everywhere—enough to feed an army! I'm not talking about crap food either. They had Jason's Deli food, apples, oranges, Coke, Diet Coke, lemonade, orange juice, cookies, all types of chips and sandwiches. All the beverages by the way was put on ice and chilled! In a matter of about 24 hours or less an entire mini-city was erected by volunteers for the poor evacuees. This was not your rundown crap shelter, it was BUM HEAVEN.

So that was the layout: great food, comfy beds, clean showers, free medical help, by the way there was a library, and a theatre room I forgot to mention. Great stuff right?

Well here is what happened on my journey—

I started by handing out COLD water bottles to evacuees as they got off the bus. Many would take them and only 20% or less said thank you. Lots of them would shake their heads and ask for sodas! So this went on for about 20–30 minutes until I was sick of being an unappreciated servant. I figured certainly these folks would appreciate some food! So I went upstairs to serve these beloved evacuees some GOOD food that I wish I could have at the moment!

The following statements are graphic, truthful, and discuss UNRATIONAL behavior. Evacuees come slowly to receive this mountain of food that is worth serving to a king! I tell them that we have 2 types of great deli sandwiches to choose from—ham and turkey. Many look at the food in disgust and DEMAND burgers, pizza, and even McDonalds! Jason's deli is better than McDonalds! Only 1 out of ten people who took something would say "thank you," the rest took items as if it was their God-given right to be served without a shred of appreciation! They would ask for beer and liquor.

They complained that we didn't have good enough food. They refused food and laughed at us. They treated us volunteers as if we where SLAVES. No not all of them of course ... but 70% did! 20% where appreciative, 10% took the food without any comment and the other 70% had some disgusting comment to say. Some had the nerve to laugh at us. And when I snapped back at them for being mean, they would curse at me! Needless to say I was in utter shock.

They would eat their food and leave their mess on the table ... some would pick up their stuff, many would leave it for the volunteers to pick up. I left that real quick to go down and help set up some more beds. I saw many young ladies carrying mattresses and I helped for a while. Then I realized something ... there were hundreds of able-bodied young men who could help! I asked a group of young evacuees in their teens and early twenties to help.

I got cursed at for asking them to help! One said "We just lost our ****ing homes and you want us to work!" The next said, "Ya Cracker, you got a home, we don't." I looked at them in disbelief. Here are women walking by carrying THEIR ****ING BEDS and they can't lift a finger and help themselves!

WHY THE **** SHOULD I HELP PEOPLE WHO DON'T WANT TO HELP THEMESELVES!

I waved them off and turned away and was laughed at and more "white boy jokes" were made at me. I felt no need to waste my breath on a bunch of pitiful losers. I went to a nearby restroom where I noticed a man shaving.

I used the restroom, washed my hands and saw this man throw his razor towards the trash can ... he missed ... he walked out leaving his disgusting razor on the floor for some other "cracker" to pick up. Even the little kids were demanding. I saw only ONE white family and only TWO Hispanic families.

The rest were blacks ... sorry 20% to 30% decent blacks ... and 70% LOSERS! I would call them ******S, but the actual definition of a ****** is one who is ignorant, these people were not ignorant ... they were ARROGANT. The majority of which are thugs and lifetime lazy-ass welfare recipients. We are inviting the lowest of the low to Houston. And like idiots we are serving the people who will soon steal our cars, rape, murder, and destroy our city while stealing from our pockets on a daily basis through the welfare checks they take. We will fund our own destruction.

By "US" I don't mean a specific race, I mean the people who work hard, work smart, have values and morals. Only people who want to help themselves should be helped, the others should be allowed to destroy themselves. I do not want to work hard, give the government close to half the money I earn so they can in turn give it to a bunch of losers.

I don't believe in being poor for life. My family immigrated here, we came here poor, and now thank God, and due to HARD WORK we are doing fine. If immigrants, who come here, don't know the language can work and become successful ... WHY THE **** CAN'T THE MAJORITY OF THE HOMEGROWN DO IT!

If we continue to reward these losers then we will soon destroy our great country. I just witnessed selfish, arrogant, unappreciative behavior by the very people who need help the most. Now these same people who cursed me, refused my cities generosity, who refuse to help themselves are DEMANDING handouts on their own terms! They prance around as if they are owed something, and when they do receive a handout, they say it's not good enough! Well you know what ... these types of people can go to hell for all I care!

809 SCAM

Variant A

Tradition Bearer: Unavailable

Source: E-mail Forward

Date: 1999

Original Source: E-mail
National Origin: European American

SPECIAL ALERT—DO NOT EVER DIAL AREA CODE 809.
Don't respond to E-mails, phone calls, or pages that tell you to call an "809" phone number. This is a very important issue of Internet ScamBusters! because it alerts you to a scam that is spreading *extremely* quickly can easily cost you $100 or more, and is difficult to avoid unless you are aware of it.

We'd like to thank ———— and ———— (USPS) for bringing this scam to our attention. This scam has also been identified by the National Fraud Information Center and is costing victims a lot of money.

There are lots of different permutations of this scam, but here is how it works:

Permutation #1: Internet-based phone scam via E-mail. You receive an email, typically with a subject line of "*ALERT*" or "Unpaid account."

The message, which is being spammed across the Net, says: I am writing to give you a final 24 hrs. to settle your outstanding account. If I have not received the settlement in full, I will commence legal proceedings without further delay.

If you would like to discuss this matter to avoid court action, call Mike Murray at Global Communications.

Permutation #2: Phone or pager scam. You receive a message on your answering machine or our pager that asks you to call a number beginning with area code 809. The reason you're asked to call varies: it can be to receive information about a family member who has been ill, to tell you someone has been arrested, died, to let you know you have won a wonderful prize, etc.

In each case, you're told to call the 809 number right away. Since there are so many new area codes these days, people unknowingly return these calls.

If you call from the U.S., you will apparently be charged $25 per minute! Sometimes the person who answers the phone will speak broken English and pretend not to understand you. Other times, you'll just get a long recorded message. The point is, they will try to keep you on the phone as long as possible to increase the charges. Unfortunately, when you get your phone bill, you'll often be charged more than $100. Here's why it works:

The 809 area code is located in the British Virgin Islands (the Bahamas). The 809 area code can be used as a "pay-per-call" number, similar to 900 numbers in the U.S. Since 809 is not in the U.S., it is not covered by U.S. regulations of 900 numbers, which require that you be notified and warned of charges and rates involved when you call a "pay-per-call" number.

There is also no requirement that the company provide a time period during which you may terminate the call without being charged. Further, whereas many U.S. phones have 900 number blocking to avoid these kinds of charges, 900 number blocking will not prevent calls to the 809 area code. We recommend that no matter how you get the message, if you are asked to call a number with an 809 area code that you don't recognize, further investigate and/or disregard the message. Be *very* wary of E-mail or calls asking you to call an 809 area code number. It's important to prevent becoming a victim of this scam, since trying to fight the charges afterwards can become a real nightmare. That's because you did actually make the call. If you complain, both our local phone company and your long distance carrier will not want to get involved and will most likely tell you that they are simply providing the billing for the foreign company. You'll end up dealing with a foreign company that argues they have done nothing wrong.

Please forward this entire issue of Internet ScamBusters! to your friends, family and colleagues to help them become aware of this scam so they don't get ripped off.

Variant B

Tradition Bearer: Unavailable

Source: E-mail Forward

Date: 2000

Original Source: E-mail

National Origin: Unavailable

Subject: area code 809
    Might take heed of the following....
    DON'T EVER DIAL AREA CODE 809.
This one is being distributed all over the U.S. This is pretty scary—especially given the way they try to get you to call. Be sure you read this & pass it on to all your friends & family so they don't get scammed!
MAJOR SCAM:
Don't respond to E-mails, phone calls, or web pages that tell you to call an "809" phone number. This is a very important issue of ScamBusters because it alerts you to a scam that is spreading extremely quickly, can easily cost you $24,100 or more, and is difficult to avoid unless you are aware of it. We'd like

to thank ———— and ———— for bringing this scam to our attention. This scam has also been identified by the National Fraud Information Center and is costing victims a lot of money. There are lots of different permutations of this scam, but HERE'S HOW IT WORKS:

You will receive a message on your answering machine or your pager, that asks you to call a number beginning with area code 809. The reason you're asked to call varies. It can be to receive information about a family member who has been ill, to tell you someone has been arrested, died, to let you know you have won a wonderful prize, etc. In each case, you are told to call the 809 number right away. Since there are so many new area codes these days, people unknowingly return these calls. If you call from the U.S., you will apparently be charged $2,425 per minute. Or, you'll get a long recorded message. The point is, they will try to keep you on the phone as long as possible to increase the charges. Unfortunately, when you get your phone bill, you'll often be charged more than $24,100.

WHY IT WORKS:

The 809 area code is located in the British Virgin Islands (the Bahamas). The 809 area code can be used as a "pay-per-call" number, similar to 900 numbers in the U.S. Since 809 is not in the U.S., it is not covered by U.S. regulations of 900 numbers, which require that you be notified and warned of charges and rates involved when you call a "pay-per-call" number. There is also no requirement that the company provide a time period during which you may terminate the call without being charged. Further, whereas many U.S. phones have 900 number blocking to avoid these kinds of charges, 900 number blocking will not prevent calls to the 809 area code. We recommend that no matter how you get the message, if you are asked to call a number with an 809 area code that you don't recognize, investigate further and/or disregard the message. Be wary of E-mails or calls asking you to call an 809 area code number. It's important to prevent becoming a victim of this scam, since trying to fight the charges afterwards can become a real nightmare. That's because you did actually make the call. If you complain, both our local phone company and your long distance carrier will not want to get involved and will most likely tell you that they are simply providing the billing for the foreign company. You'll end up dealing with a foreign company that argues they have done nothing wrong. Please forward this entire message to your friends, family, and colleagues to help them become aware of this scam so they don't get ripped off.

Variant C

Tradition Bearer: Unavailable

Source: E-mail Forward

Date: 2000

Original Source: E-mail

National Origin: Unavailable

I think that I have received this one before but 6 of my friends sent this to me. I thought that you might be interested.

DON'T EVER DIAL AREA CODE 809.

This one is being distributed all over the U.S. This is pretty scary—especially given the way they try to get you to call. Be sure you read this & pass it on to all your friends & family so they don't get scammed!

MAJOR SCAM:

Don't respond to E-mails, phone calls, or web pages that tell you to call an "809" phone number. This is a very important issue of ScamBusters because it alerts you to a scam that is spreading *extremely* quickly—can easily cost you $24,100 or more, and is difficult to avoid unless you are aware of it. We'd like to thank ———— and ———— for bringing this scam to our attention.

This scam has also been identified by the National Fraud Information Center and is costing victims a lot of money. There are lots of different permutations of this scam, but

HERE'S HOW IT WORKS:

You will receive a message on your answering machine or your pager, which asks you to call a number beginning with area code 809. The reason you're asked to call varies. It can be to receive information about a family member who has been ill, to tell you someone has been arrested, died, to let you know you have won a wonderful prize, etc.

In each case, you are told to call the 809 number right away. Since there are so many new area codes these days, people unknowingly return these calls. If you call from the U.S., you will apparently be charged $2,425 per minute. Or, you'll get a long recorded message. The point is, they will try to keep you on the phone as long as possible to increase the charges. Unfortunately, when you get your phone bill, you'll often be charged more than $24,100.

WHY IT WORKS:

The 809 area code is located in the British Virgin Islands (the Bahamas). The 809 area code can be used as a "pay-per-call" number, similar to 900 numbers in the U.S. Since 809 is not in the U.S., it is not covered by U.S. regulations of 900 numbers, which require that you be notified and warned of charges and rates involved when you call a "pay-per-call" number. There is also no requirement that the company provide a time period during which you may terminate the call without being charged.

Further, whereas many U.S. phones have 900 number blocking to avoid these kinds of charges, 900 number blocking will not prevent calls to the 809 area code.

We recommend that no matter how you get the message, if you are asked to call a number with an 809 area code that you don't recognize and/or investigate further and just disregard the message.

Be wary of E-mails or calls asking you to call an 809 area code number. It's important to prevent becoming a victim of this scam, since trying to fight the charges afterwards can become a real nightmare. That's because you did actually make the call. If you complain, both your local phone company and your long distance carrier will not want to get involved and will most likely tell you that they are simply providing the billing for the foreign company. You'll end up dealing with a foreign company that argues they have done nothing wrong. Please forward this entire message to your friends, family, and colleagues to help them become aware of this scam so they don't get ripped off.

90# SCAM

Variant A

Tradition Bearer: Unavailable

Source: E-mail Forward

Date: 2000

Original Source: E-mail

National Origin: Unavailable

Suspicious phone call:
Got a call last night from an individual identifying himself as an AT&T service technician who was conducting a test on our telephone lines. He

stated that to complete the test I should touch nine (9), zero (0), the pound sign (#) and then hang up.

Luckily, I was suspicious and refused. Upon contacting the telephone company, I was informed that by pushing 90#, you give the requesting individual full access to your telephone line, which allows them to place long distance telephone calls billed to your home phone number. I was further informed that this scam has been originating from many of the local jails/prisons. I have also verified this information with CUB telecom, Pacific Bell, MCI, Bell Atlantic, GTE and NYNEX.

Please beware. DO NOT press 90# for ANYONE. The GTE Security Department requested that I share this information with EVERYONE I KNOW.

PLEASE pass this on to everyone YOU know. If you have mailing lists and/or newsletters from organizations you are connected with, I encourage you to pass on this information to them, too.

Variant B

Tradition Bearer: Unavailable

Source: E-mail Forward

Date: 2000

Original Source: E-mail

National Origin: Unavailable

This is an age-old scam, but beware. In moments of stupidity, we sometimes assume that everyone on the other end of the phone line is legitimate.

I received a telephone call last evening from an individual identifying himself as an AT&T service technician who was conducting a test on the telephone lines. He stated that to complete the test I should touch nine (9), zero (0) the pound sign (#), and then hang up.

Luckily, I was suspicious and refused. Upon contacting the telephone company, I was informed that by pushing 90# you give the requesting individual full access to your telephone line, which enables them to place long distance calls billed to your home phone number. I was further informed that this scam has been originating from many local jails/prisons. I have also verified this information with UCB Telecom, Pacific Bell, MCI, Bell Atlantic, and GTE.

Please beware. DO NOT press 90# for anyone. The GTE Security Department requested that I share this information with everyone I Know. Please pass this on to everyone you know. If you have mailing lists and/or newsletters from organizations you are connected with, I encourage you to pass on this information to them, too.

Please let your friends know.

Sales Rep.

AT&T

SLAVEMASTER

Tradition Bearer: Unavailable

Source: E-mail Forward

Date: 2001

Original Source: E-mail

National Origin: Unavailable

Warning from State Police—Please be careful!!!! State Police Warning!!!!!! Serious. This is something from the State Police. Please read this "very carefully" ... then send it out to all the people online that you know.

Something like this is nothing to take casually; this is something you DO want to pay attention to. Think of it as a bit of advice too. If a person with the screen-name of SweetCaliGuy4evr contacts you, do not reply. DO not talk to this person; do not answer any of his/her instant messages or E-mail. Whoever this person may be, he/she is a suspect for murder in the death of 56 women (so far) contacted through the Internet.

Please send this to all the women on your buddy list and ask them to pass this on, as well. This screen-name was seen on Yahoo, AOL, and Excite, so far. This is not a joke! Please send this to men too ... just in case!

ANGER MANAGEMENT

Tradition Bearer: Unavailable

Source: E-mail Forward

Date: 2006

Original Source: E-mail

National Origin: Unavailable

When you occasionally have a really bad day, and you just need to take it out on someone, don't take it out on someone you know—take it out on someone you don't know.

I was sitting at my desk when I remembered a phone call I had forgotten to make. I found the number and dialed it. A man answered, saying, "Hello."

I politely said, "Could I please speak with Robin Carter?"

Suddenly, the phone was slammed down on me. I couldn't believe that anyone could be so rude. I realized I had called the wrong number. I tracked down Robin's correct number and called her. I had accidentally transposed the last two digits of her phone number.

After hanging up with her, I decided to call the "wrong" number again. When the same guy answered the phone, I yelled, "You're an asshole!" and hung up.

I wrote his number down with the word "asshole" next to it, and put it in my desk drawer.

Every couple of weeks, when I was paying bills or had a really bad day, I'd call him up and yell, "You're an asshole!" It always cheered me up.

When Caller ID came to our area, I thought my therapeutic "asshole" calling would have to stop. So, I called his number and said, "Hi, this is John Smith from the Telephone Company. I'm just calling to see if you're familiar with the Caller ID program?"

He yelled, "NO!" and slammed the phone down.

I quickly called him back and said, "That's because you're an asshole!"

One day I was at the store, getting ready to pull into a parking spot. Some guy in a black BMW cut me off and pulled into the spot I had patiently waited for. I hit the horn and yelled that I had been waiting for that spot. The idiot ignored me. I noticed a "For Sale" sign in his car window so, I wrote down his number.

A couple of days later, right after calling the first asshole (I had his number on speed dial), I thought I had better call the BMW asshole, too.

I said, "Is this the man with the black BMW for sale?"

"Yes, it is."

"Can you tell me where I can see it?"

"Yes, I live at 1802 West 34th Street. It's a yellow house, and the car's parked right out in front."

"What's your name?" I asked.

"My name is Don Hansen," he said.

"When's a good time to catch you, Don?"

"I'm home every evening after five."

"Listen, Don, can I tell you something?"

"Yes?"

"Don, you're an asshole."

Then I hung up, and added his number to my speed dial, too. Now, when I had a problem, I had two assholes to call.

But after several months of calling them, it wasn't as enjoyable as it used to be. So, I came up with an idea. I called Asshole #1.

"Hello."

"You're an asshole!" (But I didn't hang up.)

"Are you still there?" he asked.

"Yeah," I said.

"Stop calling me," he screamed.

"Make me," I said.

"Who are you?" he asked.

"My name is Don Hansen."

"Yeah? Where do you live?"

"Asshole, I live at 1802 West 34th Street, a yellow house, with my black Beamer parked in front."

He said, "I'm coming over right now, Don. And you had better start saying your prayers."

I said, "Yeah, like I'm really scared, asshole."

Then I called Asshole #2.

"Hello?" he said.

"Hello, asshole," I said.

He yelled, "If I ever find out who you are...!"

"You'll what?" I said.

"I'll kick your ass," he exclaimed.

I answered, "Well, asshole, here's your chance. I'm coming over right now."

Then I hung up and immediately called the police, saying that I lived at 1802 West 34th Street, and that I was on my way over there to kill my gay lover. Then I called Channel 13 News about the gang war going down on West 34th Street. I quickly got into my car and headed over to 34th street.

When I got there, I saw two assholes beating the crap out of each other in front of six squad cars, a police helicopter, and the channel 13 News crew.

NOW, I feel better.... This is Anger Management at its very best!!

GULLIBILITY VIRUS

Tradition Bearer: Unavailable

Source: E-mail Forward

Date: 2000

Original Source: E-mail

National Origin: Unavailable

WARNING, CAUTION, DANGER, AND BEWARE!
Gullibility Virus spreading over the Internet!

* * *

Midsomer Norton, Somerset, England—Christmas Day 1998

The Institute for the Investigation of Irregular Internet Phenomena announced today that many Internet users are becoming infected by a new virus that causes them to believe without question every groundless story, legend, and dire warning that shows up in their inbox or on their browser.

The Gullibility Virus, as it is called, apparently makes people believe and forward copies of silly hoaxes relating to cookie recipes, E-mail viruses, taxes on modems, and get-rich-quick schemes.

"These are not just readers of tabloids or people who buy lottery tickets based on fortune cookie numbers," a spokesman said, "most are otherwise normal people, who would laugh at the same stories if told to them by a stranger in a bar. However, once these same people become infected with the Gullibility Virus, they believe anything they read on the Internet."

"My immunity to tall tales and bizarre claims is all gone," reported one weeping victim. "I believe every warning message and sick child story that my friends forward to me, even though most of the messages are anonymous."

Another victim, now in remission, said, "When I first heard about Good Times, I just accepted it without question. After all, there were dozens of other recipients on the mail header, so I thought that the virus must be real."

It was a long time, the victim added, before she could stand up at a Hoaxees Anonymous meeting and state, "My name is Jane, and I've been hoaxed."

Now, however, she is spreading the word. "Challenge and check whatever you read," she advises.

Internet users are urged to examine themselves for symptoms of the virus, which include the following:

* The willingness to believe improbable stories without thinking
* The urge to forward multiple copies of such stories to others
* Lack of desire to take three minutes to check if a story is true

Tony is an example of someone recently infected. He told one reporter, "I read on the Net that the major ingredient in almost all shampoos makes your hair fall out, so I stopped using shampoo." When told about the Gullibility Virus, Tony said he would stop reading email, so that he would not become reinfected.

Anyone with symptoms like these is urged to seek help. Experts recommend that at the first feelings of gullibility, Internet users should rush to their favorite search engine and look up the item tempting them to thoughtless credence. Most hoaxes, legends, and tall tales have been widely discussed and exposed by the Internet community.

Courses in critical thinking are also widely available, and there is online help from many sources, including:

Department of Energy Computer Incident Advisory Capability at
http://ciac.llnl.gov/ciac/CIACHoaxes.html
Computer Virus Myths page at
http://www.kumite.com/myths
IBM's Hype Alert web site at
http://www.av.ibm.com/BreakingNews/HypeAlert
Symantec Anti Virus Research Center Hoax Page at
http://www.symantec.com/avcenter/hoax.html
Network Associates Virus Hoax Listing at
http://www.nai.com/services/support/hoax/hoax.asp
Dr. Solomon's Hoax Page at
http://www.drsolomon.com/vircen/vanalyse/va005.html
The Urban Legends Web Site at
http://www.urbanlegends.com
Urban Legends Reference Pages at
http://www.snopes.com
Mining Company Urban Legends Page at
http://urbanlegends.miningco.com
Datafellows Hoax Warnings at
http://www.Europe.Datafellows.com/news/hoax.htm

Those people who are still symptom free can help inoculate themselves against the Gullibility Virus by reading some good material on evaluating sources, such as:

Evaluating Internet Research Sources at
http://www.sccu.edu/faculty/R_Harris/evalu8it.htm

Evaluation of Information Sources at
http://www.vuw.ac.nz/~agsmith/evaln/evaln.htm
Bibliography on Evaluating Internet Resources at
http://refserver.lib.vt.edu/libinst/critTHINK.HTM
Lastly, as a public service, Internet users can help stamp out the Gullibility Virus by sending copies of this message to anyone who forwards them a hoax.

* * *

This message is so important, we're sending it anonymously!
Forward it to all your friends right away!
Don't think about it!
This is not a chain letter! This story is true!
This story is so important, we're using lots of exclamation points!
If you are worried that you or your loved ones may be affected you should send a dollar bill (or its equivalent in your local currency), and a list of their names and email addresses, to:
The Home for the Hopelessly Gullible, 12, Redfield Road, Midsomer Norton, BA3 2JN, Bath, England, and we will, ABSOLUTELY FREE, determine if any of you are affected with the Gullibility Virus and advise our findings in the strictest confidence.

* * *

ACT NOW BEFORE THE MILLENNIUM! DON'T DELAY! LIMITED TIME! THIS SERVICE IS CHOLESTEROL-FREE AND CONTAINS NO SODIUM, ANIMAL PRODUCTS, MSG, GLUTEN, OR TROPICAL OILS.

THE MOTHER OF ALL URBAN LEGENDS

Tradition Bearer: Unavailable

Source: E-mail Forward

Date: 2003

Original Source: E-mail

National Origin: Unavailable

I was on my way to the post office to pick up my case of free M&M's (sent to me because I forwarded an E-mail to five other people, celebrating the fact that the year 2000 is "MM" in Roman numerals), when I ran into a friend whose neighbor, a young man, was home recovering from having been served a rat in his bucket of Kentucky Fried Chicken (which is predictable, since as everyone knows, there's no actual chicken in Kentucky Fried Chicken, which is why the government made them change their name to KFC).

Anyway, one day this guy went to sleep and when he awoke he was in his bathtub and it was full of ice and he was sore all over and when he got out of the tub he realized that HIS KIDNEY HAD BEEN STOLEN. He saw a note on his mirror that said "Call 911!" but he was afraid to use his phone because it was connected to his computer, and there was a virus on his computer that would destroy his hard drive if he opened an E-mail entitled "Join the crew!"

He knew it wasn't a hoax because he himself was a computer programmer who was working on software to prevent a global disaster in which all the computers get together and distribute the $250 Neiman Marcus cookie recipe under the leadership of Bill Gates. (It's true—I read it all last week in a mass E-mail from BILL GATES HIMSELF, who was also promising me a free Disney World vacation and $5,000 if I would forward the E-mail to everyone I know.)

The poor man then tried to call 911 from a pay phone to report his missing kidneys, but a voice on the line first asked him to press #90, which unwittingly gave the bandit full access to the phone line at the guy's expense. Then reaching into the coin-return slot he got jabbed with an HIV-infected needle around which was wrapped a note that said, "Welcome to the world of AIDS."

Luckily he was only a few blocks from the hospital—the one where that little boy who is dying of cancer is, the one whose last wish is for everyone in the world to send him an E-mail and the American Cancer Society has agreed to pay him a nickel for every E-mail he receives. I sent him two E-mails and one of them was a bunch of X's and O's in the shape of an angel (if you get it and forward it to more than 10 people, you will have good luck but for only 10 people you will only have OK luck and if you send it to fewer than 10 people you will have BAD LUCK FOR SEVEN YEARS).

So anyway the poor guy tried to drive himself to the hospital, but on the way he noticed another car driving without its lights on. To be helpful, he flashed his lights at him and was promptly shot as part of a gang initiation.

Send THIS to all the friends who send you their mail and you will receive 4 green M&Ms—if you don't, the owner of Proctor and Gamble will report you to his Satanist friends and you will have more bad luck: you will get sick from the Sodium Laureth Sulfate in your shampoo, your spouse will develop a skin rash from using the antiperspirant which clogs the pores under your arms, and the U.S. government will put a tax on your E-mails forever.

I know this is all true 'cause I read it on the Internet.

ORGAN THEFT PARODY

Tradition Bearer: Unavailable

Source: E-mail Forward

Date: 2005

Original Source: E-mail

National Origin: Unavailable

WARNING!!!
I know you have read the scare-mail about the person whose kidneys were stolen while he was passed out. While that was an "urban legend" this one is not. It's happening every day. I'm sending this warning to all of my closest friends. You, too, may have been a victim. Read on....

My thighs were stolen from me during the night of September 30th a few years ago. It was just that quick. I went to sleep in my body and woke up with someone else's thighs. The new ones had the texture of cooked oatmeal. Whose thighs were these? What happened to mine?

I spent the entire summer looking for them. I searched—in vain—at pools and beaches, anyplace where female limbs might be exposed. I became obsessed. I had nightmares filled with cellulite and flesh that turned to bumps in the night. Finally, hurt and angry, I resigned myself to living out my life in jeans and Sheer Energy pantyhose.

Then, just when my guard was down, the thieves struck again. My butt was next!!! I knew it was the same gang, because they took pains to match my new butt, although it was badly attached. It was three inches lower than the original to the thighs they had stuck me with earlier.

A year later, it was my breasts. Once full, yet perky, they now lay like bags of water on my chest, no longer proudly pointing forward to greet the world, but looking down at my feet, as though hanging in shame.

Two years ago, I realized my arms had been switched. One morning while fixing my hair, I watched, horrified but fascinated, as the flesh of my upper arms swung to and fro with the motion of the hairbrush. Bat wings!!! And I didn't even see the Bat Signal!! This was really getting scary!!!

My body was being replaced, cleverly and fiendishly, one section at a time. In the end, in deepening despair, I gave up my t-shirts. What could they do to me next? Age? Age had nothing to do with it. Age is supposed to creep up, unnoticed and intangible, something like maturity. NO, I was being attacked, repeatedly and without warning!

That's why I've decided to share my story ... I can't take on the medical profession all by myself. Women of the world, wake up and smell the coffee! That isn't really "plastic" those surgeons are using. You know where they're getting those replacement parts, don't you? The next time you suspect someone has had a face "lifted," look again! Was it lifted from you? Check out those tummy tucks and butt raisings. Look familiar? Are those your eyelids on that movie star? I think I finally have found my thighs, and I hope Cindy Crawford paid a really good price for them.

This is NOT a hoax!!! This is happening every night to women in every town all across the world. Warn your friends !!!!

FINALLY PUTTING TO REST E-MAIL MYTHS

Tradition Bearer: Unavailable

Source: E-mail Forward

Date: 1999

Original Source: E-mail

National Origin: Unavailable

Whoever decided to create this note and forward it on should receive some type of humanitarian award. It says it all!

1. Big companies don't do business via chain letters. Bill Gates is not giving you $1,000, and Disney is not giving you a free vacation. There is no baby food company issuing class action checks. Procter and Gamble is not part of a satanic cult or scheme, and its logo is not satanic. MTV will not give you backstage passes if you forward something to the most people. You can relax; there is no need to pass it on "just in case it's true." Furthermore, just because someone said in a message, four generations back, that "we checked it out and it's legit," does not actually make it true.

2. There is no kidney theft ring in New Orleans. No one is waking up in a bathtub full of ice, even if a friend of a friend swears it happened to their cousin. If you are hell-bent on believing the kidney theft ring stories, please see: *http://urbanlegends.tqn.com/library/weekly/aa062997.htm.*

And I quote: "The National Kidney Foundation has repeatedly issued requests for actual victims of organ thieves to come forward and tell their stories. None have." That's "none" as in "zero." Not even your friend's cousin.

3. Neiman Marcus doesn't really sell a $200 cookie recipe. And even if they do, we all have it. And even if you don't, you can get a copy at: *http://www.bl.net/forwards/cookie.html*. Then, if you make the recipe, decide the cookies are that awesome, feel free to pass the recipe on.

4. If the latest NASA rocket disaster(s) DID contain plutonium that went to particulate over the eastern seaboard, do you REALLY think this information would reach the public via an AOL chain letter?

5. There is no "Good Times" virus. In fact, you should never, ever, ever forward any mail containing any virus warning unless you first confirm that an actual site of an actual company that actually deals with viruses. Try: *http://www.norton.com*. And even then, don't forward it. We don't care. And you cannot get a virus from a flashing IM or email, you have to download ... ya know, like, a FILE!

6. There is no gang initiation plot to murder any motorist who flashes headlights at other car driving at night without lights.

7. If you're using Outlook, Internet Explorer, or Netscape to write E-mail, turn off the "HTML encoding." Those of us on Unix shells can't read it, and don't care enough to save the attachment and then view it with a web browser, since you're probably forwarding us a copy of the Neiman Marcus Cookie Recipe anyway.

8. If you still absolutely MUST forward that 10th-generation message from a friend, at least have the decency to trim the eight miles of headers showing everyone else who's received it over the last 6 months. It sure wouldn't hurt to get rid of all the ">" that begin each line either. Besides, if it has gone around that many times we've probably already seen it.

9. Craig Shergold (or Sherwood, or Sherman, etc.) in England is not dying of cancer or anything else at this time and would like everyone to stop sending him their business cards. He apparently is no longer a "little boy" either.

10. The "Make a Wish" foundation is a real organization doing fine work, but they have had to establish a special toll free hot line in response to the large number of Internet hoaxes using their good name and reputation. It is distracting them from the important work they do.

11. If you are one of those insufferable idiots who forwards anything that "promises" something bad will happen if you "don't," then something bad will happen to you if I ever meet you in a dark alley.

12. Women really are suffering in Afghanistan, and PBS and NEA funding are still vulnerable to attack (although not at the present time) but forwarding an E-mail won't help either cause in the least. If you want to help, contact your local legislative representative, or get in touch with Amnesty International or the Red Cross. As a general rule, E-mail "signatures" are easily faked and mean nothing to anyone with any power to do anything about whatever the competition is complaining about.

(P.S.: There is no bill pending before Congress that will allow long-distance companies to charge you for using the Internet.)

Bottom Line ... composing E-mail or posting something on the Net is as easy as writing on the walls of a public restroom. Don't automatically believe it until it's proven false ...ASSUME it's false, unless there is proof that it's true.

Now, forward this message to ten friends, and you will win the Publishers Clearing House sweepstakes. ;-)

GEORGE AND SADDAM

Tradition Bearer: Unavailable

Source: E-mail Forward

Date: 2001

Original Source: E-mail

National Origin: Unavailable

Saddam Hussein and George W. Bush agree to meet up in Baghdad for the first round of talks in a new peace process. When George sits down, he notices three buttons on the arm of Saddam's chair.

They begin talking and after about five minutes Saddam presses the first button. A boxing glove springs out of a box on the desk and punches Bush in the face. Annoyed, Bush carries on talking as Saddam laughs. A few minutes later the second button is pressed. This time a big boot comes out and kicks Bush in the shin. Again Saddam laughs, and again George carries on talking, not wanting to put off the bigger issue of peace between the two countries. But when the third button is pressed and another boot comes out and kicks Bush square in the privates, he's finally had enough.

"I'm headin' back home!" he calmly tells the Iraqi." We'll finish these talks in Washington in two weeks!"

Two weeks pass and Saddam flies to the United States. Saddam notices three buttons on Bush's chair arm and prepares himself for the Texan's retaliation. They begin talking and George presses the first button. Saddam ducks, but nothing happens. George snickers but they continue talking. A few minutes later he presses the second button. Saddam jumps up, but again nothing happens. Bush roars with laughter. They continue the talks but when the third button is pressed, Saddam jumps up again, but again nothing happens. Bush falls on the floor in a fit of hysterics.

"Forget this," says Saddam. "I'm going back to Baghdad!"

George W. says, through tears of laughter, "WHAT Baghdad???"

DEATH OF WILLIAM HUNG

Tradition Bearer: Unavailable

Source: E-mail Forward

Date: 2004

Original Source: E-mail

National Origin: Unavailable

Weird!!!! Anybody know if this is for real?

Las Vegas, NV—Kitschy American Idol Star William Hung, famous for his botching of Ricky Martin's "She Bangs," was found dead yesterday, apparently of an intentional heroin overdose. The announcement of his death sent shockwaves to the tens of people who still found him funny.

Ironically, Mr. Hung was found by a VH1 camera crew sent to begin filing "William Hung: Behind the 'Music.'" Viacom immediately decided to rename the special: "William Hung: fifteen minutes till death."

Friends of Mr. Hung say he had become despondent in recent days. "I don't know, it's just so sad," said Ming Tse, one of Hung's former classmates at Stanford, "I heard him the other day on Snotbubble's Morning Madhouse; he kept trying to make William say things like 'me so horny' and 'hey sailor' while playing the sound of a bomb falling. I just know William was hurting inside when Snotbubble got him to say, 'you wanna some-e egg foo young-e.' It was so sad. I just think he was tired of the commercialization of it all."

Other friends, who had lost contact with him in recent weeks, feared he was becoming too "Hollywood." "I'm not surprised he was on heroin," said Hung's engineering cohort Melvin Samples, "I mean just two months ago we were out at our usual corner table at Smitty's, and William actually went and talked to some girls. The next thing I know he's doing shots with some hipster guys; they were calling him 'Long Duck Dong' and making him say 'au-to-mo-bile.' From what I hear, it's not a long leap from that to heroin addiction."

Stanford's hippie population immediately misconstrued the situation and adopted Hung's death as a pet cause. "He was a victim of the corporate greed-machine, just like Kurt [Cobain] and Eddie [Vedder, who is actually still alive]," said one dreadlocked mourner outside the engineering department at Stanford University, where a makeshift memorial had been set up, "he just wanted to sing, and Fox decided to turn him into this joke, man, this fucking joke. They just ate him up and spit him out. Fucking Bill O'Reilly. I think it's because he was against the war." The last comment is apparently in reference to the fact that Hung once answered "no, thank you" when asked whether he was "for or against the war in Iraq."

The Las Vegas police released part of his suicide note. It read, "I have no reason of living ... my art which is my importance to the best everybody laugh to ... I make end here ... goodbye world of cruel."

Although Hung's immediate family disowned him seconds after his appearance on American Idol, it is believed he has an aunt in Toledo, Ohio who will take care of funeral arrangements.

WHITE SUBSTANCE DELAYS AGGIE FOOTBALL PRACTICE

Tradition Bearer: Unavailable

Source: E-mail Forward

Date: 2001

Original Source: E-mail

National Origin: Unavailable

The Texas A&M Aggie afternoon football practice was delayed on Tuesday for nearly two hours. One of the players, while on his way to practice happened to look down and notice a suspicious looking, unknown white powdery substance on the practice field. Head coach R. C.

Slocum immediately suspended practice while the CSPD and FBI were called in to investigate. After a complete field analysis, the FBI determined that the white, powdery substance unknown to the players was the goal line chalk. Practice was resumed when FBI Special Agents decided that the team was not likely to encounter that substance again.

TALES FROM NORTHERN MICHIGAN

Tradition Bearer: Unavailable

Source: E-mail Forward

Date: 2003

Original Source: E-mail

National Origin: Unavailable

Lena called the airlines information desk and inquired, "How long does it take to fly from Minneapolis to Fargo?"

"Just a minute," said the busy clerk.

"Vell," said Lena, "if it has to go dat fast, I tink I'll just take da bus."

* * *

The judge had just awarded a divorce to Lena, who had charged non-support.

He said to Ole, "I have decided to give your wife $400 a month for support."

"Vell, dat's fine, Judge," said Ole. "And vunce in a while I'll try to chip in a few bucks myself."

* * *

Ole's neighbor Sven had a boy, Sven Junior, who came home one day and asked, "Papa, I have da biggest feet in da third grade. Is dat becoss I'm Norvegian?"

"No," said Sven, "It's because you're NINETEEN."

* * *

Lars asked Ole, "Do ya know da difference between a Norvegian and a canoe?"

"No, I don't," said Ole.

"A canoe will sometimes tip," explained Lars.

* * *

Ole is so cheap that after his airplane landed safely, he grumbled: "Vell, dere gose five dollars down da drain for dat flight insurance!"

* * *

Ole wore both of his winter jackets when he painted his house last July. The directions on the can said "put on two coats."

* * *

Lars: "Ole, stant in front of my car and tell me if da turn signals are vorking."
Ole: "Yes, No, Yes, No, Yes, No, Yes, No...."

* * *

Lena was being interviewed for a job as maid for the very wealthy Mrs. Diamond, who asked her: "Do you have any religious views?"

"No," said Lena, "but I've got some nice pictures of Norway."

* * *

Ole died. So Lena went to the local paper to put a notice in the obituaries.

The gentleman at the counter, after offering his condolences, asked Lena what she would like to say about Ole.

Lena replied, "You yust put 'Ole died.'"

The gentleman, somewhat perplexed, said, "That's it? Just 'Ole died'? Surely, there must be something more you'd like to say about Ole. If its money you're concerned about, the first five words are free. We must say something more."

So Lena pondered for a few minutes and finally said, "O.K. You put 'Ole died. Boat for sale.'"

* * *

Ole and Sven were taking a vacation in Sven's new camper. As usual, they'd become lost and were wandering around a strange town trying to find the highway. Sven was just starting down a grade to go under a bridge when he slams on the brakes.

Ole: "Vat da heck you do dat for, Sven?"

Sven: Dat sign dere says "Low Bridge. No Vehicles Over Twelve Feet High." Dis here camper is t'irteen feet!

Ole: "Cripes almighty Sven, dere ain't no cops around. Yust hit da gas pedal and go for it!"

REDNECK VASECTOMY

Tradition Bearer: Unavailable

Source: E-mail Forward

Date: 2002

Original Source: E-mail

National Origin: Unavailable

After having their 11th child, an Alabama couple decided that was enough, as they could not afford a larger bed. So the husband went to his doctor/veterinarian and told him that he and his wife/cousin didn't want to have any more children. The doctor told him that there was a procedure called a vasectomy that could fix the problem but that it was expensive.

A less costly alternative, said the doctor, was to go home, get a cherry bomb (fireworks are legal in Alabama), light it, put it in a beer can, then hold the can up to his ear and count to 10. The Alabamian said to the doctor, "I may not be the smartest man in the world, but I don't see how putting a cherry bomb in a beer can next to my ear is going to help me." "Trust me," said the doctor.

So the man went home, lit a cherry bomb and put it in a beer can. He held the can up to his ear and began to count:

"1"

"2"

"3"

"4"

"5"

At which point he paused, placed the beer can between his legs, and resumed counting on his other hand.

This procedure also works in Tennessee, Mississippi, Georgia, & West Virginia.

TOILET PAPER MIRACLE

Tradition Bearer: Unavailable

Source: E-mail Forward

Date: 2002

Original Source: E-mail

National Origin: Unavailable

Fresh from her shower, a woman stands in front of the mirror, complaining to her husband that her breasts are too small.

Instead of characteristically telling her it's not so, the husband uncharacteristically comes up with a suggestion. "If you want your breasts to grow, then every day take a piece of toilet paper and rub it between your breasts for a few seconds."

Willing to try anything, the wife fetches a piece of toilet paper and stands in front of the mirror, rubbing it between her breasts.

"How long will this take?" she asks.

"They'll grow larger over a period of years," he replies.

The wife stops. "Why do you think rubbing a piece of toilet paper between my breasts every day will make my breasts grow over the years?"

"Worked for your butt, didn't it?"

He lived, and with a great deal of therapy, HE may even walk again.

WANTED FOR ATTEMPTED MURDER

Tradition Bearer: Unavailable

Source: E-mail Forward

Date: 2000

Original Source: E-mail

National Origin: Unavailable

WANTED FOR ATTEMPTED MURDER (The actual AP headline) Linda Burnett, 23, was visiting her in-laws, and while there went to a nearby supermarket to pick up some groceries. Several people noticed her sitting in her car with the windows rolled up and with her eyes closed, with both hands behind the back of her head.

One customer who had been at the store for a while became concerned and walked over to the car. He noticed that Linda's eyes were now open, and she looked very strange. He asked her if she was okay, and Linda replied that she'd been shot in the back of the head, and had been holding her brains in for over an hour.

The man called the paramedics, who broke into the car because the doors were locked and Linda refused to remove her hands from her head. When they finally got in, they found that Linda had a wad of bread dough on the back of her head.

A Pillsbury biscuit canister had exploded from the heat, making a loud noise that sounded like a gunshot, and the wad of dough hit her in the back of her head. When she reached back to find out what it was, she felt the dough and thought it was her brains. She initially passed out, but quickly recovered and tried to hold her brains in for over an hour until someone noticed and came to her aid.

And, yes, Linda is a blonde.

* * *

1–You lock the target.
2–You bait the line.
3–You slowly spread the net and 4–You catch the man.

FREE HONDA

Tradition Bearer: Unavailable

Source: E-mail Forward

Date: 1999

Original Source: E-mail

National Origin: Unavailable

Please forward—I can't imagine that it is true but you never know. It can't hurt! :) Have a great day. Wouldn't it be fun if it were true? :)

First off, I just want everyone to know that this is the real thing.

I forwarded this message to everyone I know about 6 months ago and last week a Honda employee showed up at my house with my brand new 1999 Civic EX!!!

It is so funny because I never believed these things worked and actually I sent this one as a joke to all my friends. But they forwarded the message too and now I have received a new car!!!

My best friend actually hasn't gotten his car just yet but he checked the balance of his Honda Account and it has reached nearly $11,000!!! If you like Hondas or you just want a new car, please forward this message it is the real thing.

—Bob ———, Denver, Colorado

* * *

Friends, Look I know this sounds too good to be true, and that's what I thought too. But I called Honda's headquarters in Japan and spoke to an American representative myself and it really is true! They assured me that this the real thing! I still wasn't convinced but I called three weeks later and my

Honda account balance has reached the unbelievable sum of $12,500!!! So even if you don't believe this forward it anyway so my account will continue to grow until I get my brand new Prelude!!!

—Steve ———, Minneapolis, Minnesota

* * *

Dear valued potential customers:

Here at Honda we have been well known for over 20 years for providing the best in reliability, comfort, and style. Over the years we have risen to be one of the top auto industries here in Japan. But that isn't enough. We want to be number one in the U.S. Now our twentieth anniversary for making cars is here!!! This is the perfect opportunity for you and us here at Honda to celebrate our 20 years of excellent service. We have been trying to think of ideas to get more people to know about our cars. And with technology and E-mail being the wave of the future, we want to jump on this opportunity. So we have set up a rewards system to repay those who help us spread the word about Honda.

Our marketing staff has designed a special program that traces this message as it travels across the U.S. Anyone who forwards this E-mail, will immediately have an account at their local Honda dealer opened in their name. This account will initially be opened with a credit of $1,000 toward any new or used vehicle at their participating dealership. For each person you forward this E-mail to, the amount of $200 will be added to your account.

If the recipients of this E-mail forward it you will be rewarded an additional $100 for each person it reaches and if they also forward it your account continues to grow in $100 increments. You can log onto our Web site at *http://www.Honda.com* to check the balance of your account. If things go well and everyone participates you should see your account grow quite quickly. Follow the on screen instructions to order the specific make and model of Honda you want to buy with your account.

We hope that this is a rewarding experience for you and us. Our goal is to reach over 1 million computers by the year 2000.

I thank you for your time and business.

Sincerely,

———

Senior Honda Marketing Advisor

THE RICH ADOLESCENT'S CHAIN LETTER

Tradition Bearer: Unavailable

Source: E-mail Forward

Date: 2000

Original Source: E-mail

National Origin: Unavailable

Parents of 15-year old find $71,000 cash hidden in his closet. Does this headline look familiar? Of course it does. You most likely have seen this story recently featured on a major nightly news program.

This 15-year-old's mother was cleaning and putting laundry away when she came across a large brown paper bag that was suspiciously buried beneath some clothes and a skateboard in the back of her 15-year-old son's closet. Nothing could have prepared her for the shock she got when she opened the bag and found it was full of cash. Five dollar bills, twenties, fifties, and hundreds—all neatly rubber-banded in labeled piles.

"My first thought was that he had robbed a bank," says the 41–year-old woman, "There was over $71,000 dollars in that bag—that's more than my husband earns in a year."

The woman immediately called her husband at the car dealership where he worked to tell him what she'd discovered. He came home right away and they drove together to the boy's school and picked him up. Little did they suspect that where the money came from was more shocking than actually finding it in the closet.

As it turns out, the boy had been sending out via E-mail on the Internet a type of "chain letter" to E-mail addresses that he obtained off of the Internet. Everyday after school for the past 2 months, he had been doing this right on his computer in his bedroom.

"I just got the E-mail one day and I figured what the heck, I put my name on it like the instructions said and I started sending it out," says the clever 15–year-old.

The E-mail letter listed 3 addresses and contained instructions to send one $5 dollar bill to the person at the top of the list, then delete that address and move the other 2 addresses up, and finally to add your name to the bottom of the list. The letter goes on to state that you would receive several thousand dollars in five dollar bills within 2 weeks if you sent out the letter with your name

237

at the bottom of the 3-address list "I get junk E-mail all the time, and I really didn't think it was gonna work," the boy continues.

Within the first few days of sending out the E-mail, the Post Office Box that his parents had gotten him for his video-game magazine subscriptions began to fill up with not magazines, but envelopes containing $5 dollar bills.

"About a week later I rode [my bike] down to the post office and my box had 1 magazine and about 300 envelopes stuffed in it. There was also a yellow slip that said I had to go up to the [post office] counter—I thought I was in trouble or something (laughs)." He goes on, "I went up to the counter and they had a whole box of more mail for me. I had to ride back home and empty out my backpack 'cause I couldn't carry it all." Over the next few weeks, the boy continued sending out the E-mail. "The money just kept coming in and I just kept sorting it and stashing it in the closet, I barely had time for my homework." He had also been riding his bike to several of the area's banks and exchanging the $5 bills for twenties, fifties and hundreds. "I didn't want the banks to get suspicious so I kept riding to different banks with like five thousand at a time in my backpack. I would usually tell the lady at the bank counter that my dad had sent me in to exchange the money and he was outside waiting for me. One time the lady gave me a really strange look and told me that she wouldn't be able to do it for me and my dad would have to come in and do it, but I just rode to the next bank down the street." Surprisingly, the boy didn't have any reason to be afraid. The reporting news team examined and investigated the so-called "chain letter" the boy was sending out and found that it wasn't a chain letter at all. In fact, it was completely legal according to U.S. Postal and Lottery Laws, Title 18, Section 1302 and 1341, or Title 18, Section 3005 in the U.S. code, also in the code of federal regulations, Volume 16, Sections 255 and 436, which state a product or service must be exchanged for money received.

Every five-dollar bill that he received contained a little note that read, "Please add me to your mailing list." This simple note made the letter legal because he was exchanging a service (adding the purchaser's name to his mailing list) for a five-dollar fee. Here is the letter that the 15-year-old was sending out by E-mail, you can do the exact same thing he was doing, simply by following the instructions in this letter:

* * *

Here are instructions on how to make $10,000 U.S. cash in the next 2 weeks:

* * *

If you don't try it you will never know.

There are 3 addresses listed below.

Send the person at the top of the list a $5 bill wrapped in 2 pieces of paper (to securely hide it), along with a note that says:

"Please add me to your mailing list."

Then delete that name, move the other 2 up and put your name at the bottom.

Now start sending this ENTIRE E-mail back out to people. When 20 people receive it, those 20 people will move your name up to the middle position and they will each send out 20. That totals 400 people that will receive this letter with your name in the middle.

Then, those 400 people will move your name up to the top and they will each send out 20 E-mails. That totals 8,000 people that will receive this E-mail with your name at the top and they will each send you a $5 bill.

8,000 people each sending you a $5 bill = $40,000 cash. That's if everyone responds to this E-mail, but not everyone will, so you can expect more realistically to receive about $10,000 cash $5 bills in your mailbox.

This will work for anyone, anywhere in the world in any country, but send only a U.S. CASH $5 bill.

The more E-mails you send out, the more cash you will receive. If each person sends out 100 E-mails, there will be 1,000,000 people that receive this letter when your name reaches the top. If only 1% of those people respond, you will still get $50,000 cash.

THE POWERS THAT BE: SACRED TALES

CHRISTIANS CHARGED FOR READING BIBLE IN PRISON

Tradition Bearer: Unavailable

Source: E-mail Forward

Date: 2005

Original Source: E-mail

National Origin: Unavailable

I wouldn't have believed this, but my friend checked this out and it really was on Fox News...
PENNSYLVANIA CHRISTIANS FACE 47 YEARS IN PRISON FOR READING THE BIBLE IN PUBLIC.

Philadelphia charges Christians with hate crimes, inciting a riot, and using a deadly weapon. Bill O'Reilly reported on the situation on Fox News Channel.

Dear Friend,

What we have been saying has now happened. You cannot quote what the Bible has to say about homosexuality in public or you will be charged with a "hate crime." Philadelphia is only the beginning. If we fail to take a stand here, this "crime" will soon be applied across America.

In the 27 years of this ministry, I have never witnessed a more outrageous miscarriage of justice than what is happening in Philadelphia. Four Christians are facing up to 47 years in prison and $90,000 in fines for preaching the Gospel on a public sidewalk, a right fully protected by the First Amendment.

On October 10, 2004, the four Christians were arrested in Philadelphia. They are part of Repent America. Along with founder Michael Marcavage, members of Repent America—with police approval—were preaching near Outfest, a homosexual event, handing out Gospel literature and carrying banners with Biblical messages.

When they tried to speak, they were surrounded by a group of radical homosexual activists dubbed the Pink Angels. A videotape of the incident shows the Pink Angels interfering with the Christians' movement on the street, holding up large pink symbols of angels to cover up the Christians' messages and blowing high pitched whistles to drown out their preaching.

Rather than arrest the homosexual activists and allow the Christians to exercise their First Amendment rights, the Philadelphia police arrested and jailed the Christians!

They were charged with eight crimes, including three felonies: possession of instruments of crime (a bullhorn), ethnic intimidation (saying that homosexuality is a sin), and inciting a riot (reading from the Bible some passages relating to homosexuality) despite the fact that no riot occurred. You may think I am exaggerating. I'm not. Our AFA Center for Law and Policy is representing these four individuals at no cost. We will take this case all the way to the Supreme Court if necessary to get justice.

There is so much more about this case I don't have room for it in this letter. We have prepared a 25-minute VHS/DVD in which two AFA-CLP attorneys discuss the case in detail.

Please help us with our expenses in representing these committed Christians. With your tax-deductible gift of $15, less than the cost of a cup of coffee once a month for the next year, we will send your choice of either the VHS or DVD. Watch the VHS/DVD, then share it with your Sunday school class and church. This VHS/DVD should be required viewing in every church in America.

PROCTER AND GAMBLE AND LIZ CLAIBORNE CONFESS TO CHURCH OF SATAN ON SALLY

Tradition Bearer: Unavailable

Source: E-mail Forward

Date: 1999

Original Source: E-mail

National Origin: Unavailable

The President of Procter & Gamble appeared on the Sally Jesse Raphael show on March 1, 1998. He announced that "due to the openness of our society," he was coming out of the closet about his association with the church of Satan. He stated that a large portion of his profits from Procter & Gamble Products goes to support this satanic church.

When asked by Sally Jesse if stating this on TV would hurt his business, he replied, "THERE ARE NOT ENOUGH CHRISTIANS IN THE UNITED STATES TO MAKE A DIFFERENCE."

Product list includes:

Cleaning supplies: Bold, Cascade, Cheers, Joy, Comet, Dash, Spic & Span, Tide, Top Job, Oxidol, Ivory Dreft, Gain, Mr. Clean, Lest Oil, Bounty Towels.

Food: Duncan Hines, Fisher Nuts, Fisher Mints, Dehydrated Fruits

Coffee: Folgers, High Point

Shortening Oils: Crisco, Puritan, Fluffo

Deodorant: Secret, Sure

Diapers: Luvs, Pampers

Hair Care: Lilt, Head & Shoulders, Prell, Pert, Vidal Sassoon, Ivory

Acne Product: Clearasil

Mouthwash/Toothpaste: Scope, Crest, Gleem

Peanut Butter: JIF

Personal Hygiene: Always, Attend Undergarments

Lotions: Oil of Olay, Wondra

Soap: Camay, Coast, Ivory, Lava, Safeguard, Zest, Oil of Olay

Fabric Softener: Downy, Bounce

Citrus Punch: Sunny Delight

Medication: Aleve, Pepto-Bismol

If you are not sure about the product, look for a Procter & Gamble written on the products, or the symbol of a ram's horn, which will appear on each product beginning on January 1, 2000. The ram's horn will form the 666, which is known as Satan's number. Christians should remember that if they purchase any of these products, they will be contributing to the church of Satan. Inform other Christians about this and STOP buying Procter & Gamble Products. Let's show Procter & Gamble that there are enough Christians to make a difference.

On a previous Jenny Jones Show, the owner of Procter &Gamble said that if Satan would prosper him, he would give his heart and soul to him. Then he gave Satan credit for his riches. Anyone interested seeing this tape, should send $3.00 to:

SALLY TRANSCRIPTS
515 WEST 57TH STREET
NEW YORK NY 10019

WE URGE YOU TO MAKE COPIES OF THIS AND PASS IT ON TO AS MANY PEOPLE AS POSSIBLE. THIS NEEDS TO STOP.

LIZ CLAIRBORNE ALSO PROFESSES TO WORSHIP SATAN AND RECENTLY OPENLY ADMITTED ON THE OPRAH WINFREY SHOW THAT HALF OF HER PROFITS GO TOWARDS THE CHURCH OF SATAN.

"TOUCHED BY AN ANGEL" CANCELLATION

Tradition Bearer: Unavailable

Source: E-mail Forward

Date: 2000

Original Source: E-mail

National Origin: Unavailable

CBS will be forced to discontinue "Touched by an Angel" for using the word God in every program. ———, an atheist, successfully managed to eliminate the use of Bible reading from public schools a few years ago. Now her organization has been granted a Federal Hearing on the same subject by the Federal Communications Commission (FCC) in Washington, DC.

Their petition, Number 2493, would ultimately pave the way to stop the reading of the gospel of our Lord and Savior, on the airwaves of America. They got 287,000 signatures to back their stand!

If this attempt is successful, all Sunday worship services being broadcast on the radio or by television will be stopped. This group is also campaigning to remove all Christmas programs and Christmas carols from public schools!! You as a Christian can help! We are praying for at least 1 million signatures. This would defeat their effort and show that there are many Christians alive, well, and concerned about our country. As Christians we must unite on this.

Please don't take this lightly. We ignored this lady once and lost prayer in our school and in offices across the nation. Please stand up for your religious freedom and let your voice be heard. Together we can make a difference in our country while creating an opportunity for the lost to know the Lord.

Please press "forward" and only delete out what is not needed, and forward this to everyone on your list. Now, please sign your name at the bottom. Don't delete anything, just go to the next number and type your name. Please do not sign jointly, such as Mr. & Mrs. Each person should sign his/her own name. Please E-mail this to everyone you know, and help us defeat this organization and keep the right of our freedom of religion.

THE DALAI LAMA'S INSTRUCTIONS FOR LIFE

Tradition Bearer: Unavailable

Source: E-mail Forward

Date: 2005

Original Source: E-mail

National Origin: Unavailable

This is what The Dalai Lama has to say for 2005. This is a nice reading, but short. All it takes is a few seconds to read and think. Do not keep this message. The mantra must leave your hands within 96 hours. You will get a very pleasant surprise. This is true even if you are not superstitious.
INSTRUCTIONSFORLIFE

Take into account that great love and great achievements involve great risk.
When you lose, don't lose the lesson.
Follow the three Rs:
Respect for self
Respect for others and
Responsibility for all your actions.
Remember that not getting what you want is sometimes a wonderful stroke of luck.
Learn the rules so you know how to break them properly.
Don't let a little dispute injure a great friendship.
When you realize you've made a mistake, take immediate steps to correct it.

Spend some time alone every day.

Open your arms to change, but don't let go of your values.

Remember that silence is sometimes the best answer.

Live a good, honorable life. Then when you get older and think back, you'll be able to enjoy it a second time.

In disagreements with loved ones, deal only with the current situation. Don't bring up the past.

Share your knowledge. It's a way to achieve immortality.

Be gentle with the earth.

Once a year, go someplace you've never been before.

Remember that the best relationship is one in which your love for each other exceeds your need for each other.

Judge your success by what you had to give up in order to get it.

Approach love and cooking with reckless abandon.

FORWARD THIS MANTRA E-MAIL TO AT LEAST 5 PEOPLE AND YOUR LIFE WILL IMPROVE.

0–4 people: Your life will improve slightly.

5–9 people: Your life will improve to your liking.

9–14 people: You will have at least 5 surprises in the next 3 weeks.

15 people and above: Your life will improve drastically and everything you ever dreamed of will begin to take shape.

LIFE LESSONS

Tradition Bearer: Unavailable

Source: E-mail Forward

Date: 2005

Original Source: E-mail

National Origin: Unavailable

Five (5) lessons to make you think about the way we treat people.

1—First Important Lesson—Cleaning Lady.

During my second month of college, our professor gave us a pop quiz.

I was a conscientious student and had breezed through the questions until I read the last one:

"What is the first name of the woman who cleans the school?"

Surely this was some kind of joke. I had seen the cleaning woman several times. She was tall, dark-haired and in her 50s, but how would I know her name?

I handed in my paper, leaving the last question blank. Just before class ended, one student asked if the last question would count toward our quiz grade.

"Absolutely," said the professor. "In your careers, you will meet many people. All are significant. They deserve your attention and care, even if all you do is smile and say "hello."

I've never forgotten that lesson. I also learned her name was Dorothy.

2—Second Important Lesson—Pickup in the Rain

One night, at 11:30 p.m., an older African American woman was standing on the side of an Alabama highway trying to endure a lashing rainstorm. Her car had broken down and she desperately needed a ride. Soaking wet, she decided to flag down the next car.

A young white man stopped to help her, generally unheard of in those conflict-filled '60s. The man took her to safety, helped her get assistance and put her into a taxicab. She seemed to be in a big hurry, but wrote down his address and thanked him. Seven days went by and a knock came on the man's door. To his surprise, a giant console color TV was delivered to his home. A special note was attached.

It read:

"Thank you so much for assisting me on the highway he other night. The rain drenched not only my clothes, but also my spirits. Then you came along. Because of you, I was able to make it to my dying husband's bedside just before he passed away ... God bless you for helping me and unselfishly serving others."

Sincerely, Mrs. Nat King Cole.

3—Third Important Lesson—Always remember those who serve.

In the days when an ice cream sundae cost much less, a 10-year-old boy entered a hotel coffee shop and sat at a table. A waitress put a glass of water in front of him.

"How much is an ice cream sundae?" he asked.

"Fifty cents," replied the waitress.

The little boy pulled is hand out of his pocket and studied the coins in it.

"Well, how much is a plain dish of ice cream?" he inquired.

By now more people were waiting for a table and the waitress was growing impatient. "Thirty-five cents," she brusquely replied.

The little boy again counted his coins. "I'll have the plain ice cream," he said.

The waitress brought the ice cream, put the bill on the table and walked away. The boy finished the ice cream, paid the cashier and left. When the waitress came back, she began to cry as she wiped down the table. There, placed neatly beside the empty dish, were two nickels and five pennies.

You see, he couldn't have the sundae, because he had to have enough left to leave her a tip.

4—Fourth Important Lesson—The obstacle in Our Path.

In ancient times, a King had a boulder placed on a roadway. Then he hid himself and watched to see if anyone would remove the huge rock.

Some of the king's wealthiest merchants and courtiers came by and simply walked around it. Many loudly blamed the King for not keeping the roads clear, but none did anything about getting the stone out of the way.

Then a peasant came along carrying a load of vegetables. Upon approaching the boulder, the peasant laid down his burden and tried to move the stone to the side of the road. After much pushing and straining, he finally succeeded.

After the peasant picked up his load of vegetables, he noticed a purse lying in the road where the boulder had been. The purse contained many gold coins and a note from the King indicating that the gold was for the person who removed the boulder from the roadway.

The peasant learned what many of us never understand! Every obstacle presents an opportunity to improve our condition.

5—Fifth Important Lesson—Giving When it Counts.

Many years ago, when I worked as a volunteer at a hospital, I got to know a little girl named Liz who was suffering from a rare & serious disease. Her only chance of recovery appeared to be a blood transfusion from her 5-year-old brother, who had miraculously survived the same disease and had developed the antibodies needed to combat the illness.

The doctor explained the situation to her little brother, and asked the little boy if he would be willing to give his blood to his sister.

I saw him hesitate for only a moment before taking a deep breath and saying, "Yes I'll do it if it will save her."

As the transfusion progressed, he lay in bed next to his sister and smiled, as we all did, seeing the color returning to her cheek. Then his face grew pale and his smile faded.

He looked up at the doctor and asked with a trembling voice, "Will I start to die right away."

Being young, the little boy had misunderstood the doctor; he thought he was going to have to give his sister all of his blood in order to save her.

Now you have 2 choices:

1. Delete this email, or
2. Forward it to people you care about.

I hope that you will choose No. 2

"Work like you don't need the money, love like you've never been hurt, and dance like you do when nobody's watching."

"We will have genuine joy and happiness only as we learn patience."—Joseph B. Wirthlin

HOTLINE TO HEAVEN

Tradition Bearer: Unavailable

Source: E-mail Forward

Date: 2000

Original Source: E-mail

National Origin: Unavailable

At their annual meeting before the beginning of the football season, all the top Big 12 Football programs decided to have Golden Phones installed in each of their respective offices.

One day a recruit named Marco walked into Frank Solich's Nebraska office and saw his Golden Phone sitting there. "Wow," Marco exclaimed, "What's that?"

Frank responded, "Well son, that's my Golden Phone; it's a direct line to Heaven."

"Wow, that's pretty neat," Marco responded. "Do you think I could make a call on that phone?"

"Well yes, but it's going to cost you about $100. You can make the check out to the University of Nebraska Foundation," replied Frank.

"That's a lot of money. I don't think I should spend that much. Thanks anyway," Marco replied as he left the office.

A few weeks later Marco took a campus visit at the University of Texas and went into Coach Brown's office where again he saw a Golden Phone.

"What exactly is that phone for?" asked Marco

Coach Brown replied, "That's my direct line to Heaven."

"Do you think I could make a call from that phone?" asked Marco.

"Well sure, but it's going to cost you about $200, and you can make the check out to the University of Texas Foundation," replied Brown.

"Oh never mind, I don't have that kind of money. Thanks though."

Marco shook his head and left Coach Brown's office.

The next weekend, Marco took his official visit to the campus of Texas A&M University and made the office of Coach R. C. Slocum his first stop.

Upon arriving, the first thing Marco noticed was the Golden Phone on Coach Slocum's desk.

Marco asked if that was a direct line to Heaven.

When Coach Slocum replied that it was, Marco again asked if he could make a call using the phone.

"Well sure you can, but it will cost you 35 cents," replied Slocum.

Upon hearing this, Marco's eyes got real big and he said, "Really? Then why did Coach Solich and Coach Brown tell me it would cost so much more?"

Coach Slocum looked up from behind his desk and smiled, saying, "Because, son, here at Texas A&M, it's a local call."

WAILING WALL

Tradition Bearer: Unavailable

Source: E-mail Forward

Date: 2002

Original Source: E-mail

National Origin: Unavailable

A reporter goes to Israel to cover the fighting. She is looking for something emotional and positive and of human interest. Something like that guy in Sarajevo who risked his life to play the cello every day in the town square.

In Jerusalem, she heard about an old Jew who's been going to the Wailing Wall to pray, twice a day, every day, for a long, long time. So she went to check it out.

She goes to the Wailing Wall and there he is! She watches him pray and after about 45 minutes, when he turns to leave, she approaches him for an interview. "Rebecca Smith, CNN News. Sir, how long have you been coming to the Wailing Wall and praying?"

"For about 50 years."

"What do you pray for?"

"For peace between the Jews and the Arabs. For all the hatred to stop. For our children to grow up in safety and friendship."

"How do you feel after doing this for 50 years?"

"Like I'm talking to a fucking wall."

THE POWERS THAT BE: SECULAR TALES

BLACK VOTE CANCELLED

Tradition Bearer: Unavailable

Source: E-mail Forward

Date: 2003

Original Source: E-mail

National Origin: Unavailable

As everyone should be aware, in 1965, President Lyndon B. Johnson signed the Voters Rights Act. This was created to allow blacks the right to vote.

In 1982, President Ronald Reagan signed an amendment to extend this right for an additional twenty-five years. You guessed it ... In 2007 (four years from now), Congress will decide whether or not blacks should retain the right to vote. In order for this to be passed, thirty-eight states will have to approve an extension. For me, as well as many others, this was the first time that we had heard this—thus, bringing concern to all of us! What many blacks before us fought and even died for as well as the milestones that we, as blacks have achieved, this can be taken away from us ... AGAIN!

If this issue has taken you by surprise as well, I encourage YOU to contact your Congressperson, alderperson, senator—anyone in government, that you put your vote behind and ask them what are they doing to—firstly, to get the extension and furthermore, make our right to vote a LAW. This has to become a law in order for our right to vote to no longer be up for discussion, review and/or evaluation. (Remember: blacks are the only group of people who require permission under the United States Constitution to vote!)

As Black people, we cannot "drop the ball" on this one! We have come too far to be forced to take such a large step back. So, please let's push on and forward to continue to build the momentum towards gaining equality.

Please pass this on to others, as I am sure that many more individuals are not aware of this.

ELEVATOR INTIMIDATION

Tradition Bearer: Unavailable

Source: E-mail Forward

Date: 1999

Original Source: E-mail

National Origin: Unavailable

On a recent weekend in Atlantic City, a woman won a bucketful of quarters at a slot machine. She took a break from the slots for dinner with her husband in the hotel dining room. But first she wanted to stash the quarters in her room. "I'll be right back and we'll go to eat," she told her husband and she carried the coin-laden bucket to the elevator. As she was about to walk into the elevator she noticed two men already aboard. Both were black. One of them was big ... very big ... an intimidating figure. The woman froze.

Her first thought was: These two are going to rob me. Her next thought was: Don't be a bigot, they look like perfectly nice gentlemen. But racial stereotypes are powerful, and fear immobilized her. She stood and stared at the two men. She felt anxious, flustered, ashamed. She hoped they didn't read her mind, but knew they surely did; her hesitation about joining them on the elevator was all too obvious.

Her face was flushed. She couldn't just stand there, so with a mighty effort of will she picked up one foot and stepped forward and followed with the other foot and was on the elevator. Avoiding eye contact, she turned around stiffly and faced the elevator doors as they closed. A second passed, and then another second, and then another. Her fear increased! The elevator didn't move.

Panic consumed her. My God, she thought, I'm trapped and about to be robbed! Her heart plummeted. Perspiration poured from every pore.

Then ... one of the men said, "Hit the floor." Instinct told her: Do what they tell you.

The bucket of quarters flew upwards as she threw out her arms and collapsed on the elevator carpet. A shower of coins rained down on her. Take my money and spare me, she prayed. More seconds passed. She heard one of the men say politely, "Ma'am, if you'll just tell us what floor you're going to, we'll push the button." The one who said it had a little trouble getting the words out. He was trying mightily to hold in a belly laugh. She lifted her head and looked up at the two men. They reached down to help her up.

Confused, she struggled to her feet. "When I told my man here to hit the floor," said the average sized one, "I meant that he should hit the elevator button for our floor. I didn't mean for you to hit the floor, ma'am." He spoke genially. He bit his lip. It was obvious he was having a hard time not laughing.

She thought: My God, what a spectacle I've made of myself. She was too humiliated to speak. She wanted to blurt out an apology, but words failed her. How do you apologize to two perfectly respectable gentlemen for behaving as though they were going to rob you?

She didn't know what to say. The 3 of them gathered up the strewn quarters and refilled her bucket. When the elevator arrived at her floor they insisted on walking her to her room. She seemed a little unsteady on her feet, and they were afraid she might not make it down the corridor. At her door they bid her a good evening. As she slipped into her room she could hear them roaring with laughter while they walked back to the elevator. The woman brushed herself off. She pulled herself together and went downstairs for dinner with her husband.

The next morning flowers were delivered to her room—a dozen roses. Attached to EACH rose was a crisp one-hundred-dollar bill. The card said: "Thanks for the best laugh we've had in years."

Signed, Eddie Murphy and Michael Jordan.

PRESIDENT BUSH'S IQ

Tradition Bearer: Unavailable

Source: E-mail Forward

Date: 2003

Original Source: E-mail
National Origin: Unavailable

W hy doesn't this come as any surprise?!?
President Bush Has Lowest IQ of all Presidents of past 50 Years
In a report published Monday, the Lovenstein Institute of Scranton,
Pennsylvania, detailed its findings of a four-month study of the intelligence quotient of President George W. Bush.

Since 1973, the Lovenstein Institute has published its research to the education community on each new president, which includes the famous "IQ" report among others.

According to statements in the report, there have been twelve presidents over the past 50 years, from F. D. Roosevelt to G. W. Bush who were all rated based on scholarly achievements, writings that they alone produced without aid of staff, their ability to speak with clarity, and several other psychological factors which were then scored in the Swanson/Crain system of intelligence ranking.

The study determined the following IQs of each president as accurate to within five percentage points:

147, Franklin D. Roosevelt (D)
132, Harry Truman (D)
122, Dwight D. Eisenhower (R)
174, John F. Kennedy (D)
126, Lyndon B. Johnson (D)
155, Richard M. Nixon (R)
121, Gerald Ford (R)
175, James E. Carter (D)
105, Ronald Reagan (R)
098, George H. W. Bush (R)
182, William J. Clinton (D)
091, George W. Bush (R)

or, in IQ order:

182, William J. Clinton (D)
175, James E. Carter (D)
174, John F. Kennedy (D)
155, Richard M. Nixon (R)
147, Franklin D. Roosevelt (D)

132, Harry Truman (D)
126, Lyndon B. Johnson (D)
122, Dwight D. Eisenhower (R)
121, Gerald Ford (R)
105, Ronald Reagan (R)
098, George H. W. Bush (R)
091, George W. Bush (R)

The six Republican presidents of the past 50 years had an average IQ of 115.5, with President Nixon having the highest IQ, at 155. President G. W. Bush was rated the lowest of all the Republicans with an IQ of 91. The six Democrat presidents had IQs with an average of 156, with President Clinton having the highest IQ, at 182. President Lyndon B. Johnson was rated the lowest of all the Democrats with an IQ of 126. No president other than Carter (D) has released his actual IQ, 176.

Among comments made concerning the specific testing of President G. W. Bush, his low ratings were due to his apparent difficulty to command the English language in public statements, his limited use of vocabulary (6,500 words for Bush versus an average of 11,000 words for other presidents), his lack of scholarly achievements other than a basic MBA, and an absence of any body of work which could be studied on an intellectual basis. The complete report documents the methods and procedures used to arrive at these ratings, including depth of sentence structure and voice stress confidence analysis.

"All the Presidents prior to George W. Bush had a least one book under their belt, and most had written several white papers during their education or early careers. Not so with President Bush," Dr. Lovenstein said. "He has no published works or writings, so in many ways that made it more difficult to arrive at an assessment. We had to rely more heavily on transcripts of his unscripted public speaking."

The Lovenstein Institute of Scranton Pennsylvania think tank includes high caliber historians, psychiatrists, sociologists, scientists in human behavior, and psychologists. Among their ranks are Dr. Werner R. Lovenstein, world-renowned sociologist, and Professor Patricia F. Dilliams, a world-respected psychiatrist.

This study was commissioned on February 13, 2001, and released on July 9, 2001, to subscribing member universities and organizations within the education community.

TICKET RIP-OFF

Tradition Bearer: Unavailable

Source: E-mail Forward

Date: 1999

Original Source: E-mail

National Origin: Unavailable

A friend told me told me a coworker of his went to the Mets game the other night. He was selling an extra ticket for face value. Some asshole cop arrested him for scalping.

This makes me sick. They took him to a holding cell at Shea, and took his extra tickets from him. They did give him a court date and let him keep one ticket to get back in the game.

Here's the kicker. That mother-fucking cop who arrested him sat in his seat! He had to sit next to the Giuliani Nazi Stormtrooper that busted him. I gotta get more details ... this is sickening.

The cop obviously abused his power to get a free ticket to the game. I hope the judge tosses this out in court. NYC judges do indeed toss shit like this out sometimes....

What bullshit....

THE LITTLE ALLIGATOR'S PROBLEM

Tradition Bearer: Unavailable

Source: E-mail Forward

Date: 2002

Original Source: E-mail

National Origin: Unavailable

Two alligators are sitting on the edge of a swamp. The small one turns to the big one and says; "I don't understand how you can be so much bigger than me. We're the same age, we were the same size as kids ... I just don't get it."

"Well," says the big alligator, "what have you been eating?"

"Lawyers, same as you," replies the small alligator.

"Hm. Well, where do you catch 'em?"

"Down at that law firm on the edge of the swamp."

"Same here. Hm. How do you catch 'em?"

"Well, I crawl under a BMW and wait for someone to unlock the door. Then I jump out, bite 'em, shake the shit out of 'em, and eat 'em!"

"Ah!" says the big alligator, "I think I see your problem. See, by the time you get done shakin' the shit out of a lawyer, there's nothing left but lips and a briefcase..."

GO TO SCHOOL

Tradition Bearer: Unavailable

Source: E-mail Forward

Date: 2003

Original Source: E-mail

National Origin: Unavailable

Last year on Spanish television I heard a story about this gentleman who knocks on his son's door. "Jaime," he says, "wake up!"

Jaime answers, "I don't want to get up, Papa."

The father shouts, "Get up, you have to go to school."

Jaime says, "I don't want to go to school."

"Why not?" asks the father.

"Three reasons," says Jaime. "First, because it's so dull; second, the kids tease me; and third, I hate school."

And the father says, "Well, I am going to give you three reasons why you *must* go to school. First, because it is your duty; second, because you are forty-five years old, and third, because you are the headmaster."

GASOLINE COMPANY BOYCOTT

Variant A

Tradition Bearer: Unavailable

Source: E-mail Forward

Date: 2002

Original Source: E-mail
National Origin: Unavailable

Gasoline prices are projected to reach $3 a gallon by the summer. Do you want prices to come down? If some united, intelligent action is taken, consumers can have a significant impact.

Last year, the "don't buy gas on a certain day" campaign was laughed at by the oil companies who knew consumers were only going to hurt themselves by refusing to buy gas, because of the personal inconvenience. Let's not repeat history.

BUYERS control the marketplace ... not sellers. With the price of gasoline going up (currently between $1.50 and $1.95) and rising daily, consumers need to act. The only way we will see the price of gas come down is if impact the bottom line of the oil sellers and not purchasing THEIR gas!! We can do that WITHOUT inconveniencing ourselves.

Since we all rely on gas for our cars, we can't just stop buying it. We CAN, however, force a price war.

Here's the idea:

For the rest of the year (beginning now—just after April 1st), DON'T purchase gasoline from the two biggest companies—EXXON and MOBIL. If they aren't selling gas, they will be lower the sale price. If they lower the price, other companies will have to follow suit.

To have an impact, we need to reach literally millions of Exxon and Mobil gas buyers. It's simple. The person who started this email message sent this to about thirty people. If each of them send it to 10 more (30 x 10 = 300) and those 300 send it to at 10 more (300 x 10= 3,000) ... and so on, by the time this message reaches the sixth generation of people, we will have reached over 3 MILLION consumers! If those three million get excited and pass this on to ten friends each, then 30 million people will have been contacted! If it goes only one level further, you guessed it ... and THREE HUNDRED MILLION PEOPLE!

So, please send this to ten people.

How long would it take to reach 300 million? If each of us sends this email out to ten more people within one day of receipt, all 300 MILLION people could conceivably be contacted within 8 days of origin. I'll bet you didn't think you and I had that much potential, did you? Acting together we can make a difference. If this makes sense to you, please pass this message on.

GIVE IT A TRY. If the oil companies lower prices, we all win.

Start now by sending this to 10 people and filling up at a non-Exxon, non-Mobil station.

Variant B

Date: 2004

G AS WAR!
  Join the resistance!!!!
  I hear we are going to hit close to $3 a gallon by the summer. Want gasoline prices to come down? We need to take some intelligent, united action. Phillip Hollsworth, offered this good idea: This makes MUCH MORE SENSE than the "don't buy gas on a certain day" campaign that was going around last April or May! The oil companies just laughed at that because they knew we wouldn't continue to "hurt" ourselves by refusing to buy gas. It was more of an inconvenience to us than it was a problem for them. BUT, whoever thought of this idea, has come up with a plan that can really work.

Please read it and join with us!

By now you're probably thinking gasoline priced at about $1.50 is super cheap. Me too! It is currently $1.97 for regular unleaded in my town. Now that the oil companies and the OPEC nations have conditioned us to think that the cost of a gallon of gas is CHEAP at $1.50 to $1.75, we need to take aggressive action to teach them that BUYERS control the marketplace ... not sellers. With the price of gasoline going up more each day, we consumers need to take action. The only way we are going to see the price of gas come down is if we hit someone in the pocketbook by not purchasing their gas!

And, we can do that WITHOUT hurting ourselves. How? Since we all rely on our cars, we can't just stop buying gas. But we CAN have an impact on gas prices if we all act together to force a price war.

Here's the idea: For the rest of this year, DON'T purchase ANY gasoline from the two biggest companies (which now are one), EXXON and MOBIL. If they are not selling any gas, they will be inclined to reduce their prices. If they reduce their prices, the other companies will have to follow suit. But to have an impact, we need to reach literally millions of Exxon and Mobil gas buyers.

It's really simple to do!! Now, don't wimp out on me at this point ... keep reading and I'll explain how simple it is to reach millions of people!!

I am sending this note to about thirty people. If each of you send it to at least ten more (30 x 10 = 300) ... and those 300 send it to at least ten more (300 x 10 = 3,000) ... and so on, by the time the message reaches the sixth generation of people, we will have reached over THREE MILLION consumers! If those three million get excited and pass this on to ten friends each, then 30 million people will have been contacted!

If it goes one level further, you guessed it ... THREE HUNDRED MILLION PEOPLE!!!

Again, all you have to do is send this to 10 people. That's all. (If you don't understand how we can reach 300 million and all you have to do is send this to 10 people ... Well, let's face it, you just aren't a mathematician. But I am ... so trust me on this one.)

How long would all that take? If each of us sends this email out to ten more people within one day of receipt, all 300 MILLION people could conceivably be contacted within the next 8 days!!! I'll bet you I didn't think you and I had that much potential, did you! Acting together we can make a difference.

If this makes sense to you, please pass this message on. PLEASE HOLD OUT UNTIL THEY LOWER THEIR PRICES TO THE $1.30 RANGE AND KEEP THEM DOWN.

THIS CAN REALLY WORK.

E-MAIL CHARGE

Variant A

Tradition Bearer: Unavailable

Source: E-mail Forward

Date: 1999

Original Source: E-mail

National Origin: Unavailable

IMPORTANT READ!!!!! ... PLEASE FORWARD ASAP!!!
Guess the warnings were true !!!!!!
Federal Bill 602P 5-cents per E-mail sent.
It figures! No more free E-mail!
We knew this was coming!!

Please read the following carefully if you intend to stay online and continue using E-mail: The last few months have revealed an alarming trend in the government of the United States attempting to quietly push through legislation that will affect your use of the Internet. Under proposed legislation the U.S. Postal Service will be attempting to bilk E-mail users out of "alternate postage fees."

Bill 602P will permit the Federal Govt. to charge a 5-cent surcharge on every E-mail delivered, by billing Internet Service Providers at source. The consumer would then be billed in turn by the ISP. Washington DC lawyer Richard Stepp is working without pay to prevent this legislation from becoming law.

The U.S. Postal Service is claiming that lost revenue due to the proliferation of E-mail is costing nearly $230,000,000 in revenue per year. You may have noticed their recent ad campaign "There is nothing like a letter." Since the average citizen received about 10 pieces of email per day in 1998, the cost to the typical individual would be an additional 50 cents per day, or over $180 dollars per year, above and beyond their regular Internet costs. Note that this would be money paid directly to the U.S. Postal Service for a service they do not even provide. The whole point of the Internet is democracy and noninterference. If the federal government is permitted to tamper with our liberties by adding a surcharge to E-mail, who knows where it will end. You are already paying an exorbitant price for snail mail because of bureaucratic efficiency. It currently takes up to 6 days for a letter to be delivered from New York to Buffalo. If the U.S. Postal Service is allowed to tinker with email, it will mark the end of the "free" Internet in the United States. One congressman, Tony Schnell (R) has even suggested a "twenty to forty dollar per month surcharge on all Internet service" above and beyond the government's proposed E-mail charges. Note that most of the major newspapers have ignored the story, the only exception being *The Washingtonian* which called the idea of E-mail surcharge "a useful concept who's time has come" (March 6th, 1999, Editorial) Don't sit by and watch your freedoms erode away!

Send this email to all Americans on your list and tell your friends and relatives to write to their congressman and say "No!" to Bill 602P.

———

Assistant to ———
Attorneys at Law

Variant B

Date: 2000

Subject: another way the government is trying to take our money...
        VOTE NO ON Bill 602P!!!!
        I guess the warnings were true. Federal Bill 602P 5 cents per E-mail sent. It figures! No more free E-mail! We knew this was coming!! Bill 602P

will permit the Federal Government to charge a 5-cent charge on every delivered E-mail.

Please read the following carefully if you intend to stay online, and continue using E-mail. The last few months have revealed an alarming trend in the Government of the United States attempting to quietly push through legislation that will affect our use of the Internet. Under proposed legislation, the U.S. Postal Service will be attempting to bill E-mail users out of "alternative postage fees." Bill 602P will permit the Federal Government to charge a 5-cent surcharge on every E-mail delivered, by billing Internet Service Providers at source. The consumer would then be billed in turn by the ISP.

Washington DC lawyer Richard Stepp is working without pay to prevent this legislation from becoming law. The U.S. Postal Service is claiming lost revenue, due to the proliferation of E-mail, is costing nearly $230,000,000 in revenue per year. You may have noticed their recent ad campaign: "There is nothing like a letter." Since the average person received about 10 pieces of E-mail per day in 1998, the cost of the typical individual would be an additional 50 cents a day—or over $180 per year—above and beyond their regular Internet costs. Note that this would be money paid directly to the U.S. Postal Service for a service they do not even provide.

The whole point of the Internet is democracy and noninterference. You are already paying an exorbitant price for snail mail because of bureaucratic efficiency. It currently takes up to 6 days for a letter to be delivered from coast to coast. If the U.S. Postal Service is allowed to tinker with E-mail, it will mark the end of the "free" Internet in the United States.

Our congressional representative, Tony Schnell (R) has even suggested a "$20–$40 per-month surcharge on all Internet service" above and beyond the governments proposed E-mail charges.

Note that most of the major newspapers have ignored the story—the only exception being *The Washingtonian* —which called the idea of E-mail surcharge "a useful concept who's time has come" (March 6th, 1999, Editorial).

Do not sit by and watch your freedom erode away! Send this to E-mail to EVERYONE on your list, and tell all your friends and relatives write their congressional representative and say "NO" to Bill 602P. It will only take a few moments of your time and could very well be instrumental in killing a bill we do not want.

Please forward!

NEIMAN MARCUS COOKIES

Tradition Bearer: Unavailable

Source: E-mail Forward

Date: 1999

Original Source: E-mail

National Origin: Unavailable

This a not a joke—this is a true story. My daughter and I had just finished a salad at Neiman Marcus Cafe in Dallas and decided to have a small dessert. Because both of us are cookie lovers, we decided to try the "Neiman Marcus cookie." It was so excellent that I asked if they would give me the recipe and the waitress said with a small frown, "I'm afraid not but you can buy the recipe.

"Well," I asked, "how much?"

She responded, "Only two-fifty, it's a great deal!" I agreed, just add it to my tab I told her.

Thirty days later, I received my VISA statement from Neiman-Marcus and was $285.00. I looked again and I remembered I had only spent $9.95 for two salads and about $20.00 for a scarf. As I glanced at the bottom of the statement, it said "Cookie Recipe—$250.00." That's outrageous!

I called Neiman's Accounting Dept. and told them the waitress said "two-fifty," which clearly does not mean "two hundred and fifty dollars" by any *POSSIBLE* interpretation of the phrase.

Neiman Marcus refused to budge. They would not refund my money, because according to them, "What the waitress told you is not our problem. You have already seen the recipe. We absolutely will not refund your money at this point."

I explained to her the criminal statues that govern fraud in Texas. I threatened to refer them to the Better Business Bureau and the State's Attorney General for engaging in fraud.

I was basically told, "Do what you want, it doesn't matter, and we're not refunding your money."

I waited, thinking of how could get even, or even try and get any of my money back. I just said, "Okay, you folks got my $250.00 and now I'm going to have $250.00 worth of fun." I told her I was going to see to it that every cookie lover in the United States with an E-mail account has a $250.00 cookie recipe from Neiman –Marcus ... for free.

She replied, "I wish you wouldn't do this."

I said, "Well, you should have thought of that before you ripped me off," and slammed down the phone on her.

So here it is!!! Please, Please, Please pass it on to everyone you can possibly think of. I paid $250.00 for this ... I don't want Neiman-Marcus to *ever* get another penny off of this recipe.

Neiman Marcus Cookies (recipe may be halved):

2 CUPS BUTTER
4 CUPS FLOUR
2 TSP. SODA
2 CUPS SUGAR
5 CUPS BLENDED OATMEAL (measure oatmeal and blend in a blender to a fine powder).
24 OZ. CHOCOLATE CHIPS
2 CUPS BROWN SUGAR
TSP. SALT
1 8 OZ. HERSHEY BAR (grated)
4 EGGS
2 TSP. BAKING POWDER
2 TSP. VANILLA
3 CUPS CHOPPED NUTS (your choice, but we like pecans best)

Cream the butter and both sugars. Add eggs and vanilla; mix together with flour, oatmeal, salt, baking powder, and soda. Add chocolate chips, Hershey Bar, and nuts. Roll into balls and place two inches apart on a cookie sheet.

Bake for 10 minutes at 375 degrees. Makes 112 cookies.

Have fun!!! This is not a joke—this is a true story. Ride free, citizens!!
PLEASE PASS THIS TO EVERYONE YOU KNOW!!!!!!

DEADLY BALL PITS

Tradition Bearer: Unavailable

Source: E-mail Forward

Date: 2003

Original Source: E-mail

National Origin: Unavailable

My kids will never play in another ball pit. Now read this:

Hi. My name is Lauren Archer. My son Kevin and I lived in Sugarland, Texas.

On October 2, 1994, I took my only son to McDonald's for his 3rd birthday. After he finished lunch, I allowed him to play in the ball pit. When he started crying later, I asked him what was wrong.

He pointed to his back and said, "Mommy, it hurts." I looked, but couldn't find anything wrong with him at the time.

I bathed him when we got home, and it was at that point that I found a welt on his left buttock. Upon investigation, it seemed as if there was a splinter under the welt. I made a doctor appointment for the next day to have it removed. In the meantime, he started vomiting and shaking. Then, his eyes rolled back in his head.

We immediately went to the emergency room! My only son died later that night.

It turned out that the welt on his buttock was the tip of a hypodermic needle that had broken off in his skin. The autopsy revealed that Kevin had died from a heroin overdose.

The next day, the police removed the balls from the ball pit and found rotten food, half-eaten candy, diapers, feces, the stench of urine, and several hypodermic needles."

If you question the validity of this story, you can find the article on Kevin Archer in the October 10, 1994, issue of the *Houston Chronicle*.

Please forward this to all loving mothers, fathers, aunts, uncles, and grandparents.

Note: Some children have also gotten lice from ball pits. Life is not measured by the number of breaths we take, but by the moments that take our breath away."

SEND THIS TO ANYONE YOU KNOW WHO HAS SMALL CHILDREN, NIECES, NEPHEWS, OR GRANDCHILDREN!

In addition to the following true story, I will also add that my own sons were playing in the ball pit at Discovery Zone one day. One son lost his watch, and was very upset. We dug and dug in those balls, trying to find the watch. Instead, we found vomit, food, feces, and other stuff I do not want to discuss.

I went to the manager and raised heck. Come to find out, the ball pit is only cleaned out once a month. I have doubts that it is even done that often.

MONEY TALKS

Tradition Bearer: Unavailable

Source: E-mail Forward

Date: 2000

Original Source: E-mail

National Origin: Unavailable

A crusty old man walks into a bank and says to the teller at the window, "I want to open a damn checking account."

To which the astonished woman replies, "I beg your pardon, sir; I must have misunderstood you. What did you say?"

"Listen up, damn it. I said I want to open a damn checking account right now!"

"I'm very sorry sir, but we do not tolerate that kind of language in this bank."

So saying, the teller leaves the window and goes over to the bank manager to tell him about her situation.

They both return and the manager asks the old geezer, "What seems to be the problem here?"

"There's no friggin problem, dammit!" the man says, "I just won $50 million bucks in the damn lottery and I want to open a damn checking account in this damn bank!"

"I see," says the manager, "and this bitch is giving you a hard time?"

TERRORIST HALLOWEEN ATTACKS ON MALLS

Tradition Bearer: Unavailable

Source: E-mail Forward

Date: 2001

Original Source: E-mail

National Origin: Unavailable

FYI—I was very skeptical of this E-mail so I called the telephone number and it really was Laura Katsis at work. She said that she did write and send the E-mail in reaction to what her girlfriend told her. This could still be a hoax, but I am taking it a little more seriously knowing that Laura is a real person who admits writing the E-mail and who stands behind what she wrote.

—Elizabeth

Hi All—

I think you all know that I don't send out hoaxes and don't do the reactionary thing and send out anything that crosses my path. This one, however, is a friend of a friend and I've given it enough credibility in my mind that I'm writing it up and sending it out to all of you.

My friend's friend was dating a guy from Afghanistan up until a month ago. She had a date with him around 9/6 and was stood up. She was understandably upset and went to his home to find it completely emptied. On 9/10, she received a letter from her boyfriend explaining that he wished he could tell her why he had left and that he was sorry it had to be like that. The part worth mentioning is that he BEGGED her not to get on any commercial airlines on 9/11 and to not to go any malls on Halloween. As soon as everything happened on the 11th, she called the FBI and has since turned over the letter.

This is not an E-mail that I've received and decided to pass on. This came from a phone conversation with a long-time friend of mine last night.

I may be wrong, and I hope I am. However, with one of his warnings being correct and devastating, I'm not willing to take the chance on the second and wanted to make sure that people I cared about had the same information that I did.

POISONED COCA-COLA

Tradition Bearer: Unavailable

Source: E-mail Forward

Date: 2005

Original Source: E-mail
National Origin: Unavailable

THIS IS A CATEGORY-ONE ALERT FROM CNN.

CNN has learned from government sources that the Coca-Cola factories that supply the United States of America and our friends in the United Kingdom have been infiltrated by Al Qaeda terrorists.

Traces of arsenic and anthrax have been found in one out of every five cans of Coke tested. Reports have been sent out to all major networks and newspapers to put out a "Red Alert Category One," warning all drinkers of Coke to make their way to the nearest hospital for a check-up.

If you have drunk or bought Coca-Cola on or after the 25th of March 2005 then do not panic, just inform your nearest medical center and make your way there as soon as possible.

In the best interests of the U.S.A. and our friends in the UK could you forward this mail to all Coke drinkers you know, we will be posting more updates as they come in.

Regards,

———

http://www.CNN.com/

BOYCOTT DUNKIN' DONUTS

Tradition Bearer: Unavailable

Source: E-mail Forward

Date: 2001

Original Source: E-mail

National Origin: Unavailable

Attention all Americans: Boycott Dunkin' Donuts!!

In Cedar Grove, NJ, a customer saw the owner of a Dunkin' Donuts store burn the U.S. flag. In another Dunkin' Donuts store in Little Falls, a customer saw a U.S. flag on the floor with Arabic writing all over it. In Wayne, NJ, the employees of Arabic background were cheering behind the counter when the heard about the attacks. A customer threw his coffee at them and phoned the police.

We are starting a nationwide boycott of all Dunkin' Donuts. Please make sure this gets passed on to all fellow Americans during this time of tragedy. We Americans need to stick together and make these horrible people understand what country they are living in and how good they used to have it when we supported them. Numerous fast-food companies are at Ground Zero, giving away free food to volunteers.

Where is Dunkin' Donuts in all of this?

Boycott Dunkin' Donuts! Pass it on.

7–ELEVEN TERRORISM

Tradition Bearer: Unavailable

Source: E-mail Forward

Date: 2002

Original Source: E-mail

National Origin: Unavailable

Everyone knows the terrorists are around and planning something big. What the FBI and CIA won't tell us is that there is a MAJOR conspiracy afoot which could affect us all here in the USA, THIS WEEK!

Everyone knows the 7–Eleven convenience store chain. They are EVERY-WHERE, in every city and small town in the USA. In large metropolitan areas, they are sometimes only a few blocks apart. Anyone who has shopped in a 7–Eleven knows that they are owned predominantly by people of Middle-Eastern origin; in fact, the parent company of the franchise (7–Eleven Limited Partnership) is owned by a group with ties to Osama bin Laden.

On July 11th (7/11), every single 7–Eleven store has been instructed to unleash attacks on their surrounding neighborhoods. This includes blowing up the stores themselves, possibly using "dirty" nuclear bombs as well as conventional explosives, as well as outright assaults on the American people. This will cause a major disruption in ALL major American cities. If you live near a 7–Eleven, please be aware of this danger.

You are urged to boycott all 7–Eleven stores on 7/11 to keep yourself and your families safe from the terrorists. You WILL read about this on 7/12 so please be forewarned.

CITIBANK BOYCOTT

Tradition Bearer: Unavailable

Source: E-mail Forward

Date: 2001

Original Source: E-mail

National Origin: Unavailable

This came as a forward, so I don't have the number of the lady who sent this out first. The 800 number is there though.

My mother in law received a letter from a credit card company that stated Osama Bin Laden was a principal owner of Citibank. My husband called the credit card company to check the validity of the letter. Then he called Citibank (1-800-——·——). They confirmed that Osama Bin Laden is a principal owner, not a stockholder, but a principal owner. Then they said they couldn't discuss anything else.

For any of you that have a Citibank credit card ... DON'T USE IT! Osama is counting on our money. I have a Citibank Choice Card and I used it primarily for my household purchases. But I won't any more. I never would have thought that my purchases would put money into a terrorists pockets....

Call the 800 number above and verify this for yourself ... Those of you who know me, call me and I will relay this same story to you!!!!!!

Pass this on so we can freeze the flow of money to this terrorist.

AMERICAN WOMEN VS. THE TALIBAN

Tradition Bearer: Unavailable

Source: E-mail Forward

Date: 2001

Original Source: E-mail
National Origin: Unavailable

Take all American women who are within five years of menopause—train us for a few weeks, outfit us with automatic weapons, grenades, gas masks, moisturizer with SPF15, Prozac, hormones, chocolate, and canned tuna—drop us (parachuted, preferably) across the landscape of Afghanistan, and let us do what comes naturally.

Think about it. Our anger quotient alone, even when doing standard stuff like grocery shopping and paying bills, is formidable enough to make even armed men in turbans tremble. We've had our children, we would gladly suffer or die to protect them and their future. We'd like to get away from our husbands, if they haven't left already. And for those of us who are single, the prospect of finding a good man with whom to share life is about as likely as being struck by lightning.

We have nothing to lose. We've survived the water diet, the protein diet, the carbohydrate diet, and the grapefruit diet in gyms and saunas across America and never lost a pound. We can easily survive months in the hostile terrain of Afghanistan with no food at all! We've spent years tracking down our husbands or lovers in bars, hardware stores, or sporting events … finding bin Laden in some cave will be no problem.

Uniting all the warring tribes of Afghanistan in a new government? Oh, please … we've planned the seating arrangements for in-laws and extended families at Thanksgiving dinners for years … we understand tribal warfare. Between us, we've divorced enough husbands to know every trick there is for how they hide, launder, or cover up bank accounts and money sources. We know how to find that money and we know how to seize it … with or without the government's help!

Let us go and fight. The Taliban hates women. Imagine their terror as we crawl like ants with hot-flashes over their godforsaken terrain.

GUANTANAMO BAY DETAINEES

Tradition Bearer: Unavailable

Source: E-mail Forward

Date: 2005

Original Source: E-mail

National Origin: Unavailable

A person wrote a letter to the White House complaining about the treatment of a captive taken during the Afghanistan war. Here is a copy of a letter they received back:
The White House
1600 Pennsylvania Avenue
Washington, DC 20016
Dear Concerned Citizen:
Thank you for your recent letter roundly criticizing our treatment of the Taliban and Al Qaeda detainees currently being held at Guantanamo Bay, Cuba.

Our administration takes these matters seriously, and your opinion was heard loud and clear here in Washington. You'll be pleased to learn that, thanks to the concerns of citizens like you, we are creating a new division of the Terrorist

Retraining Program, to be called the "Liberals Accept Responsibility for Killers" program, or LARK for short. In accordance with the guidelines of this new program, we have decided to place one terrorist under your personal care.

Your personal detainee has been selected and scheduled for transportation under heavily armed guard to your residence next Monday. Ali Mohammed Ahmed bin Mahmud (you can just call him Ahmed) is to be cared for pursuant to the standards you personally demanded in your letter of admonishment. It will likely be necessary for you to hire some assistant caretakers. We will conduct weekly inspections to ensure that your standards of care for Ahmed are commensurate with those you so strongly recommended in your letter.

Although Ahmed is sociopathic and extremely violent, we hope that your sensitivity to what you described as his "attitudinal problem" will help him overcome these character flaws.

Perhaps you are correct in describing these problems as mere cultural differences. He will bite you, given the chance. We understand that you plan to offer counseling and home schooling. Your adopted terrorist is extremely proficient in hand-to-hand combat and can extinguish human life with such simple items as a pencil or nail clippers. We do not suggest that you ask him to demonstrate these skills at your next yoga group. He is also expert at making a wide variety of explosive devices from common household products, so you may wish to keep those items locked up, unless (in your opinion) this might offend him.

Ahmed will not wish to interact with your wife or daughters (except sexually) since he views females as a subhuman form of property. This is a particularly sensitive subject for him, and he has been known to show violent tendencies around women who fail to comply with the new dress code that Ahmed will recommend as more appropriate attire. I'm sure they will come to enjoy the anonymity offered by the burka—over time. Just remind them that it is all part of "respecting his culture and his religious beliefs"—wasn't that how you put it?

Thanks again for your letter. We truly appreciate it when folks like you, who know so much, keep us informed of the proper way to do our job. You take good care of Ahmed—and remember ... we'll be watching. Good luck!

Cordially ... Your Buddy,

Don Rumsfeld

ALLIGATORS IN THE TOILET

Tradition Bearer: Unavailable

Source: E-mail Forward

Date: 2001

Original Source: E-mail

National Origin: Unavailable

Don't go to the bathroom on October 28th! CIA intelligence reports that a major plot is planned for that day. Anyone who sits on a toilet on the 28th will be bitten on the butt by an alligator. Reports indicate that organized groups of alligators are planning to rise up into unsuspecting Americans' toilet bowls and bite them when they are doing their business.

I usually don't send E-mails like this, but I got this information from a reliable source. It came from a friend of a friend whose cousin is dating this girl whose brother knows this guy whose wife knows this lady whose husband buys hotdogs from this guy who knows a shoeshine guy who shines the shoes of a mailroom worker who has a friend who's drug dealer sells drugs to another mailroom worker who works in the CIA building. He apparently overheard two guys talking in the bathroom about alligators and came to the conclusion that we're going to be attacked.

So it must be true.

KATRINA BLUNDERS

Tradition Bearer: Unavailable

Source: E-mail Forward

Date: 2005

Original Source: E-mail

National Origin: Unavailable

The politicians are trying to pass the buck again. Check this out.

On Friday night before the storm hit Max Mayfield of the National Hurricane Center took the unprecedented action of calling Nagin and Blanco personally to plead with them to begin MANDATORY evacuation of NO and they said they'd take it under consideration. This was after the NOAA buoy 240 miles south had recorded 68-foot waves before it was destroyed.

President Bush spent Friday afternoon and evening in meetings with his advisors and administrators drafting all of the paperwork required for a state to request federal assistance (and not be in violation of the Posse Comitatus Act or having to enact the Insurgency Act). Just before midnight Friday evening the President called Governor Blanco and pleaded with her to sign the request papers so the federal government and the military could legally begin mobilization and call up. He was told that they didn't think it necessary for the federal government to be involved yet. After the President's final call to the governor she held meetings with her staff to discuss the political ramifications of bringing federal forces. It was decided that if they allowed federal assistance it would make it look as if they had failed so it was agreed upon that the feds would not be invited in.

Saturday before the storm hit the President again called Blanco and Nagin requesting they please sign the papers requesting federal assistance, that they declare the state an emergency area, and begin mandatory evacuation. After a personal plea from the President Nagin agreed to order an evacuation, but it would not be a full mandatory evacuation, and the governor still refused to sign the papers requesting and authorizing federal action. In frustration the President declared the area a national disaster area before the state of Louisiana did so he could legally begin some advanced preparations. Rumor has it that the President's legal advisers were looking into the ramifications of using the insurgency act to bypass the constitutional requirement that a state request federal aid before the federal government can move into state with troops—but that had not been done since 1906 and the constitutionality of it was called into question to use before the disaster.

Throw in that over half the federal aid of the past decade to NO for levee construction, maintenance, and repair was diverted to fund a marina and support the gambling ships. Toss in the investigation that will look into why the emergency preparedness plan submitted to the federal government for funding and published on the city's web site was never implemented and in fact may have been bogus for the purpose of gaining additional federal funding as we now learn that the organizations identified in the plan were never contacted or coordinating into any planning—though the document implies that they were.

The suffering people of NO need to be asking some hard questions as do we all, but they better start with why Blanco refused to even sign the multistate mutual aid pack activation documents until Wednesday, which further delayed the legal deployment of National Guard from adjoining states. Or maybe ask why Nagin keeps harping that the President should have commandeered 500 Greyhound busses to help him when according to his own emergency plan and documents he claimed to have over 500 busses at his disposal to use between the local school busses and the city transportation busses—but he never raised a finger to prepare them or activate them.

This is a sad time for all of us to see that a major city has all but been destroyed and thousands of people have died with hundreds of thousands more suffering, but it's certainly not a time for people to be pointing fingers and trying to find a bigger dog to blame for local corruption and incompetence. Pray to God for the survivors that they can start their lives anew as fast as possible and we learn from all the mistakes to avoid them in the future.

DEBIT CARD ABUSE BY KATRINA VICTIMS

Tradition Bearer: Unavailable

Source: E-mail Forward

Date: 2005

Original Source: E-mail

National Origin: Unavailable

KATRINA VICTIMS?
Yesterday, I was shopping for my mother in Dillard's at Lakeline Mall in Austin, TX. I admired a suit, but it was too expensive for me to purchase. You can imagine my shock when I witness the suit being purchased by a Katrina "refugee" using the government-issued debit card!!!!!!!!!!!!!!! I thought certainly there must be controls on these debit cards that would preclude recipients from using the money to purchase items other taxpayers cannot afford, but I was mistaken. I heard the sales clerk call the Dillard's business office and confirm that the "American Red Cross Debit Card" could be used for the woman's purchase. After the transaction was completed, I asked the sales clerk to confirm this and she did.

Now, when these debit cards that we the taxpayers provided are used up, what will happen? Will you give them even more of our money to purchase items the taxpayers cannot afford? I already know the answer. Based on the social welfare system that exists in our country, you will just give them more money. This system does not pass the "is this right?" test. You have hard-working, tax-paying citizens who worry every month whether they'll make it financially. And, you take their earnings and " redistribute" it to others who do not work but wear better clothes, drive newer cars and have manicures, cell phones, and designer handbags. Yeah, if you'd just send me one of those debit cards, I could buy my mother that nice suit.

I have copied everyone in my address book. I am asking them to send this to everyone in their address books. This is the reality of our social welfare system. It must stop.

Glossary

anecdote: Single episode narrative, regarded as true and commonly concentrating on an individual

animal tale: Narratives told as conscious fictions in which the characters, though they speak and behave like human beings, are animals. These animal characters are commonly stock types. For example, in many Native American traditions, Coyote is regarded as an exploitive, impulsive manipulator. In African American tales, Rabbit is typecast in the same role. The tales are most often moralistic ("don't be greedy") or etiological (why the frog has no tail) in intent.

belief tales: Legends or personal experience narratives that are told with the purpose of validating a particular folk belief.

culture hero: Character in **myth** who finishes the work that brings technology (usually symbolized as fire), laws, religion, and other elements of culture to humans. Culture heroes may take over the business of creating order out of chaos where a Supreme Creator left off. Therefore, the culture hero serves as a secondary creator or transformer of the universe. The culture hero transforms the universe by means of gifts into a universe in which humans can live. In some myths, the culture hero cleanses the universe of those things which threaten human existence: monsters, cannibals, or meteorological phenomena.

fable: Fictional narrative ending with a didactic message that is often couched in the form of a "moral" or proverb.

family saga: Chronologically and often thematically linked collection of legends constituting the folk history of a particular family, usually over several generations. The term was coined by folklorist Mody Coggin Boatright.

formulaic: Refers to conventional elements that recur in folk narrative. Examples include clichés, structural patterns, and stock characters or situations.

framing: The act of setting apart a traditional performance from other types of activity by words, occasions of performance, or other distinguishing features.

genre: Type or category

legend: Narrative told as truth and set in the historical past, which does not depart from the present reality of the members of the group

local legend: Legends derived from and closely associated with specific places and events believed to have occurred in those locales

motif: Small element of traditional narrative content; an event, object, concept, or pattern

myth: Narratives that explain the will (or intent) and the workings (or orderly principles) of a group's major supernatural figures. Myth is set in a world which predates the present reality.

natural context: Setting, in all its elements, in which a performance would ordinarily take place.

numskull: Character who behaves in an absurdly ignorant fashion, also called "noodle."

ordinary folktale: Highly formulaic and structured fictional narrative that is popularly referred to as "fairytale" and designated by folklorists as *märchen* or "wonder tale." Term coined by folklorist Stith Thompson

personal experience narrative: First-person narrative intended as truth

personal legend: Narrative intended as truth told about a specific (usually well-known) individual

stock character: Recurrent narrative character who invariably plays a stereotyped role such as trickster or fool

tale type: Standard, recurrent folk narrative plot

tall tale: Fictional narrative often told as a first-hand experience, which gradually introduces hyperbole until it becomes so great that the audience realizes the tale is a lie

trickster: Characters who defy the limits of propriety and often gender and species. Tricksters live on the margins of their worlds by their wits and are often regarded as possessing supernatural powers. Often a mythic figure such as Coyote or Hare will function as both culture hero and trickster.

validating device: Any element occurring within a traditional narrative that is intended to convince listeners that the tale is true.

variant: Version of a standard tale type

Bibliography to Volume IV

Alaska Judicial Council. "Resolving Disputes Locally: A Statewide Report and Directory." Alaska Judicial Council. 9 December 2005. http://www.ajc.state.ak.us/index.htm.

Balilci, Asen. *The Netsilik Eskimo*. Garden City, NY: Natural History Press, 1970.

Banister, Manly Andrew C. "Interview of James E. Twadell." American Life Histories: Manuscripts from the Federal Writers' Project, 1936–1940. Manuscript Division, Library of Congress. 12 October 2005. http://memory.loc.gov/ammem/wpaintro/wpahome.html.

Boas, Franz. *Chinook Texts*. Smithsonian Institution Bureau of American Ethnology Bulletin 20. Washington, DC: U.S. Government Printing Office, 1894.

———. "Notes on the Eskimo of Port Clarence, Alaska." *Journal of American Folklore* 7 (1894): 205–8.

———. "Traditions of the Ts'ets'ā´ut I." *Journal of American Folklore* 9 (1896): 257–68.

———. "Traditions of the Ts'ets'ā´ut II." *Journal of American Folklore* 10 (1897): 35–48.

Burrows, Elizabeth. "Eskimo Tales." *Journal of American Folklore* 39 (1926): 79–81.

Chance, Norman A. *The Eskimo of North Alaska*. New York: Holt, Rinehart and Winston, 1966.

Deans, James. "The Doom of the Katt-a-quins: From the Aboriginal Folk-lore of Southern Alaska." *Journal of American Folklore* 5 (1892): 232–35.

Farrand, Livingston, and Leo J. Frachtenberg. "Shasta and Athapascan Myths from Oregon." *Journal of American Folklore* 28 (1915): 207–42.

Frachtenberg, Leo J. *Coos Texts.* Columbia University Contributions to Anthropology 1. New York: Columbia University Press, 1913.

———. "Myths of the Alsea Indians of Northwestern Oregon." *International Journal of American Linguistics* 1 (1917): 64–75.

Gatschet, Albert S. "Oregonian Folklore." *Journal of American Folklore* 4 (1891): 139–43.

Golder, F. A. "Aleutian Stories." *Journal of American Folklore* 18 (1905): 215–22.

Haight, Willliam C. "Interview of Charles Imus." American Life Histories: Manuscripts from the Federal Writers' Project, 1936–1940. Manuscript Division, Library of Congress. 14 October 2005. http://memory.loc.gov/ammem/wpaintro/wpahome.html.

Kamenskii, Annatolii. *Tlingit Indians of Alaska.* Translated and with an introduction and supplementary material by Sergei Kan. Fairbanks: University of Alaska Press, 1985.

Kroeber, A. L. "Tales of the Smith Sound Eskimo." *Journal of American Folklore* 12 (1899): 166–82.

Oswalt, Wendell H. *Bashful No Longer: An Alaskan Eskimo Ethnohistory 1778–1988.* Norman, OK: University of Oklahoma Press, 1990.

Powers, Stephen. "North American Indian Legends and Fables." *Folk-Lore Record* 5 (1882): 93–143. Reprinted from *Contributions to North American Ethnology. Vol. 3, Tribes of California.* Edited by Stephen Powers. Washington, D.C.: U.S. Geographical and Geological Survey Rocky Mountain Region, 1877.

Rink, H., and Franz Boas. "Eskimo Tales and Songs." *Journal of American Folklore* 2 (1889): 123–31.

Sherbert, Andrew C. "Interview of George Estes." American Life Histories: Manuscripts from the Federal Writers' Project, 1936–1940. Manuscript Division, Library of Congress. 12 October 2005. http://memory.loc.gov/ammem/wpaintro/wpahome.html.

———. "Interview of William Harry Hembree." American Life Histories: Manuscripts from the Federal Writers' Project, 1936–1940. Manuscript Division, Library of Congress. 12 October 2005. http://memory.loc.gov/ammem/wpaintro/wpahome.html.

Suttles, Wayne, ed. *Handbook of the North American Indians.* Vol. 7, *Northwest Coast.* Washington, DC: Smithsonian Institution, 1990.

Walden, Wayne. "Interview of Fred Roys." *American Life Histories: Manuscripts from the Federal Writers' Project, 1936–1940.* Manuscript Division, Library of Congress. 12 October 2005. http://memory.loc.gov/ammem/wpaintro/wpahome.html.

Wrenn, Sarah B. "Interview of Jane Lee Smith." *American Life Histories: Manuscripts from the Federal Writers' Project, 1936–1940.* Manuscript Division, Library of Congress. 12 October 2005. http://memory.loc.gov/ammem/wpaintro/wpahome.html.

General Bibliography

Aarne, Antti, and Stith Thompson. *The Types of the Folktale: A Classification and Bibliography.* 2nd rev. ed. Folklore Fellows Communications 184. Helsinki: Academia Scientiarum Fennica, 1964.

Aaron, Abe. "Interview of Cab Drivers." American Life Histories: Manuscripts from the Federal Writers' Project, 1936–1940. Manuscript Division, Library of Congress. 12 October 2005. http://memory.loc.gov/ammem/wpaintro/wpahome.html.

Abrahams, Roger D., ed. *African American Folktales: Stories from Black Traditions in the New World.* New York: Pantheon, 1985.

———. *The Man-of-Words in the West Indies.* Baltimore: Johns Hopkins University Press, 1983.

Alaska Judicial Council. "Resolving Disputes Locally: A Statewide Report and Directory." Alaska Judicial Council. 9 December 2005. http://www.ajc.state.ak.us/index.htm.

Algren, Nelson. "Interview of Davey Day." American Life Histories: Manuscripts from the Federal Writers' Project, 1936–1940. Manuscript Division, Library of Congress. 11 November 2005. http://memory.loc.gov/ammem/wpaintro/wpahome.html.

Allen, Barbara, and Thomas Schlereth. *A Sense of Place: American Regional Cultures.* Lexington: University Press of Kentucky, 1990.

Ancelet, Barry Jean. "The Cajun Who Went to Harvard: Identity in the Oral Tradition of South Louisiana." *The Journal of Popular Culture* 23 (1989): 101–15.

Angermiller, Florence. "Interview of Jack Robert Grigsby." *American Life Histories: Manuscripts from the Federal Writers' Project, 1936–1940*. Manuscript Division, Library of Congress. 12 October 2005. http://memory.loc.gov/ammem/wpaintro/wpahome.html.

Bacon, A. M., and E. C. Parsons. "Folk-Lore from Elizabeth City County, Virginia." *Journal of American Folklore* 35 (1922): 250–327.

Backus, Emma M. "Animal Tales from North Carolina." *Journal of American Folklore* 11 (1898): 284–92.

———. "Folk-Tales from Georgia." *Journal of American Folklore* 13 (1900): 19–32.

———. "Tales of the Rabbit from Georgia Negroes." *Journal of American Folklore* 12 (1899): 108–15.

Backus, Emma M., and Ethel Hatton Leitner. "Negro Tales from Georgia." *Journal of American Folklore* 25 (1912): 125–36.

Baker, Ronald L. *Hoosier Folk Legends*. Bloomington: Indiana University Press, 1982.

Balilci, Asen. *The Netsilik Eskimo*. Garden City, NY: Natural History Press, 1970.

Banister, Manly Andrew C. "Interview of James E. Twadell." *American Life Histories: Manuscripts from the Federal Writers' Project, 1936–1940*. Manuscript Division, Library of Congress. 12 October 2005. http://memory.loc.gov/ammem/wpaintro/wpahome.html.

Barden, Thomas E., ed. *Virginia Folk Legends*. Charlottesville: University Press of Virginia, 1991.

Bates, William C. "Creole Folk-Lore from Jamaica II: Nancy Stories." *Journal of American Folklore* 9 (1896): 121–28.

Baughman, Ernest W. *Type- and Motif-Index of the Folk Tales of England and North America*. The Hague: Mouton, 1966.

Beauchamp, W. M. "Onondaga Tales." *Journal of American Folklore* 6 (1893): 173–89.

Beck, Horace. *Gluskap the Liar and Other Indian Tales*. Freeport, ME: Bond Wheelright, 1966.

Beckwith, Martha Warren. *Hawaiian Mythology*. New Haven: Yale University Press, 1940.

———. *Jamaica Anansi Stories*. New York: American Folklore Society, 1924.

"Beliefs of Southern Negroes Concerning Hags." *Journal of American Folklore* 7 (1894): 66–67.

Bergen, Fanny D. "Borrowing Trouble." *Journal of American Folklore* 11 (1898): 55–59.

———. "On the Eastern Shore." *Journal of American Folklore* 2 (1889): 295–300.

———. "Two Witch Stories." *Journal of American Folklore* 12 (1899): 68–69.

Bierhorst, John, ed. *White Deer and Other Stories Told by the Lenape.* New York: W. Morrow, 1995.

Boas, Franz. *Chinook Texts.* Smithsonian Institution Bureau of American Ethnology Bulletin 20. Washington, DC: U.S. Government Printing Office, 1894.

———. "Notes on the Eskimo of Port Clarence, Alaska." *Journal of American Folklore* 7 (1894): 205–8.

———. "Traditions of the Ts'ets'ā´ut I." *Journal of American Folklore* 9 (1896): 257–68.

———. "Traditions of the Ts'ets'ā´ut II." *Journal of American Folklore* 10 (1897): 35–48.

Boatright, Mody Coggin. *Mody Boatright, Folklorist: A Collection of Essays.* Edited by Ernest B. Speck. Austin: University of Texas Press, 1973.

Botkin, Benjamin A. *A Treasury of American Folklore: The Stories, Legends, Tall Tales, Traditions, Ballads and Songs of the American People.* New York: Crown, 1944.

———. *A Treasury of New England Folklore.* New York: Crown, 1944.

Bourke, John G. "Notes on Apache Mythology." *Journal of American Folklore* 3 (1890): 209–12.

———. "Popular Medicines, Customs and Superstitions of the Rio Grande." *Journal of American Folklore* 7 (1894): 119–46.

Bowman, Earl. "Interview of Harry Reece." American Life Histories: Manuscripts from the Federal Writers' Project, 1936–1940. Manuscript Division, Library of Congress. 12 October 2005. http://memory.loc.gov/ammem/wpaintro/wpahome.html.

———. "Interview of William D. Naylor." American Life Histories: Manuscripts from the Federal Writers' Project, 1936–1940. Manuscript Division, Library of Congress. 12 October 2005. http://memory.loc.gov/ammem/wpaintro/wpahome.html.

Brendle, Thomas R., and William S. Troxell. *Pennsylvania German Folk Tales, Legends, Once-upon-a-time Stories, Maxims, and Sayings.* Norristown: Pennsylvania German Society, 1944.

Bullock, Mrs. Walter R. "The Collection of Maryland Folklore." *Journal of American Folklore* 11 (1898): 7–16.

Bunter, Rosa. "Ghosts as Guardians of Hidden Treasure." *Journal of American Folklore* 12 (1899): 64–65.

Burrows, Elizabeth. "Eskimo Tales." *Journal of American Folklore* 39 (1926): 79–81.

Bushotter, George, and J. Owen Dorsey. "A Teton Dakota Ghost Story." *Journal of American Folklore* 1 (1888): 68–72.

Byrd, Frank. "Interview of Leroy Spriggs." American Life Histories: Manuscripts from the Federal Writers' Project, 1936–1940. Manuscript Division, Library of Congress. 12 October 2005. http://memory.loc.gov/ammem/wpaintro/wpahome.html.

Carey, George. *Maryland Folklore.* Centreville, MD: Tidewater Publishers, 1989.

Carter, Isabel Gordon. "Mountain White Folk-Lore: Tales from the Southern Blue Ridge." *Journal of American Folklore* 38 (1925): 340–74.

Chance, Norman A. *The Eskimo of North Alaska.* New York: Holt, Rinehart and Winston, 1966.

Chase, Richard. "Jack and the Fire Dragaman." *The Southern Folklore Quarterly* 5 (1941): 151–55.

———. "The Lion and the Unicorn." *The Southern Folklore Quarterly* 1 (1937): 15–19.

Claudel, Calvin. "Louisiana Tales of Jean Sot and Boqui and Lapin." *Southern Folklore Quarterly* 8 (1944): 287–99.

Claudel, Calvin, and J.-M. Carrier. "Three Tales from the French Folklore of Louisiana." *Journal of American Folklore* 56 (1943): 38–44.

Clough, Ben C. "Legends of Chappaquiddick." *Journal of American Folklore* 31 (1918): 553–54.

Comhaire-Sylvain, Suzanne. "Creole Tales from Haiti." *Journal of American Folklore* 50 (1937): 207–95.

Conant, L. "English Folktales in America: The Three Brothers and the Hag." *Journal of American Folklore* 8 (1895): 143–44.

Cooke, Elizabeth Johnston. "English Folk-Tales in America. The Bride of the Evil One." *Journal of American Folklore* 12 (1899): 126–30.

Cross, Tom Peete. "Folk-Lore from the Southern States." *Journal of American Folklore* 22 (1909): 251–55.

Currier, John McNab. "Contributions to the Folk-Lore of New England." *Journal of American Folklore* 2 (1889): 291–93.

Curtin, Jeremiah. "European Folklore in the United States." *Journal of American Folklore* 2 (1889): 56–59.

———. *Seneca Indian Myths.* New York: W.P. Dutton, 1922. Reprint, New York: Dover, 2001.

Cushing, Frank Hamilton. "A Zuni Folk-tale of the Underworld." *Journal of American Folklore* 5 (1892): 49–56.

Davis, Nita. "Interview of Bill Holcomb." American Life Histories: Manuscripts from the Federal Writers' Project, 1936–1940. Manuscript Division, Library of Congress. 12 October 2005. http://memory.loc.gov/ammem/wpaintro/wpahome.html.

———. "Interview of Dick McDonald." American Life Histories: Manuscripts from the Federal Writers' Project, 1936–1940. Manuscript Division, Library of Congress. 12 October 2005. http://memory.loc.gov/ammem/wpaintro/wpahome.html.

Deans, James. "The Doom of the Katt-a-quins: From the Aboriginal Folk-lore of Southern Alaska." *Journal of American Folklore* 5 (1892): 232–35.

Dixon, Roland B. "Achomawi and Atsugewi Tales."*Journal of American Folklore* 21 (1908): 159–77.

———. *Oceanic Mythology*. Boston: Marshall Jones, 1916.

———. "Some Coyote Stories from the Maidu Indians of California" *Journal of American Folklore* 13 (1900): 270.

Dorsey, George A. "Legend of the Teton Sioux Medicine Pipe." *Journal of American Folklore* 19 (1906): 326–29.

———. *The Mythology of the Wichita*. Norman: University of Oklahoma Press, 1995.

———. "The Two Boys Who Slew the Monsters and Became Stars." *Journal of American Folklore* 17 (1904): 153–60.

———. "Wichita Tales. 1. Origin." *Journal of American Folklore* 15 (1902): 215–39.

Dorsey, J. Owen. "Abstracts of Omaha and Ponka Myths, II." *Journal of American Folklore* 1 (1888): 204–8.

———. "Omaha Folklore Notes." *Journal of American Folklore* 1 (1888): 313–14.

———. "Two Biloxi Tales." *Journal of American Folklore* 6 (1893): 48–50.

Dorson, Richard M. *American Folklore. Chicago: University of Chicago Press,* 1959.

———. *Bloodstoppers and Bearwalkers*. Cambridge, MA: Harvard University Press, 1952.

———. *Buying the Wind: Regional Folklore in the United States*. Chicago: University of Chicago Press, 1964.

Douglas, Sir George. "The Witty Exploits of Mr. George Buchanan, the King's Fool." *Scottish Fairy and Folktales*. New York: A.L. Burt Company, 1901.

Doyle, Elizabeth. "Interview of Mollie Privett." American Life Histories: Manuscripts from the Federal Writers' Project, 1936–1940. Manuscript Division, Library of Congress. 12 October 2005. http://memory.loc.gov/ammem/wpaintro/wpahome.html

Dubois, Sylvie, and Barbara M. Horvath. "Creoles and Cajuns: A Portrait in Black and White." *American Speech* 78 (2003): 192–207.

Dubois, Sylvie, and Megan Melançon. "Creole Is; Creole Ain't: Diachronic and Synchronic Attitudes Toward Creole French Identity in Southern Louisiana." *Language in Society* 29 (2000): 237–58.

Edwards, Charles L. *Bahama Songs and Stories.* Memoirs of the American Folklore Society 3. New York: American Folklore Society, 1895.

———. "Some Tales from Bahama Folk-Lore." *Journal of American Folklore* 4 (1891): 47–54.

———. "Some Tales from Bahama Folk-Lore: Fairy Stories." *Journal of American Folklore* 4 (1891): 247–52.

Emery, W. M. "Interview of Jack Zurich." American Life Histories: Manuscripts from the Federal Writers' Project, 1936–1940. Manuscript Division, Library of Congress. 12 October 2005. http://memory.loc.gov/ammem/wpaintro/wpahome.html.

Espinosa, Aurelio. *The Folklore of Spain in the American Southwest: Traditional Spanish Folk Literature in Northern New Mexico and Southern Colorado.* Edited by J. Manuel Espinosa. Norman: University of Oklahoma Press, 1985.

———. "New Mexican Spanish Folklore." *Journal of American Folklore* 223 (1910): 345–418.

Farrand, Livingston, and Leo J. Frachtenberg. "Shasta and Athapascan Myths from Oregon." *Journal of American Folklore* 28 (1915): 207–42.

Farrer, Claire. *Thunder Rides a Black Horse: Mescalero Apaches and the Mythic Present.* 2nd ed. Prospect Heights, IL: Waveland Press, 1996.

Fauset, Arthur Huff. "Negro Folk Tales from the South (Alabama, Mississippi, Louisiana)." *Journal of American Folklore* 40 (1927): 213–303.

Fewkes, J. Walter. "A Contribution to Passamoquoddy Folklore." *Journal of American Folklore* 3 (1890): 257–80.

———. "The Destruction of the Tusayan Monsters." *Journal of American Folklore* 8 (1895): 132–37.

Fife, Austin E. "The Legend of the Three Nephites Among the Mormons." *Journal of American Folklore* 53 (1940): 1–49.

Fischer, David Hackett. *Albion's Seed: Four British Folkways in America.* New York: Oxford University Press, 1989.

Fletcher, Alice C. "Glimpses of Child-Life Among the Omaha Indians." *Journal of American Folklore* 1 (1888): 115–23.

Fornander, Abraham. *Fornander Collection of Hawaiian Antiquities and Folk-lore.* 3 vols. Honolulu: Bernice Pauahi Bishop Museum, 1916/1917–1919/1920.

Fortier, Alcee. "Louisianian Nursery-Tales." *Journal of American Folklore* 1 (1888): 140–45.

Frachtenberg, Leo J. *Coos Texts.* Columbia University Contributions to Anthropology 1. New York: Columbia University Press, 1913.

———. "Myths of the Alsea Indians of Northwestern Oregon." *International Journal of American Linguistics* 1 (1917): 64–75.

Gard, Robert E., and L. G. Sorden. *Wisconsin Lore: Antics and Anecdotes of Wisconsin People and Places.* New York: Duell, Sloan and Pearce, 1962.

Gardner, Emelyn E. "Folk-Lore from Schoharie County, New York." *Journal of American Folklore* 27 (1914): 304–25.

Gatschet, Albert S. "Oregonian Folklore." *Journal of American Folklore* 4 (1891): 139–43.

———. "Report of a Visit to Jack Wilson, the Payute Messiah." *Journal of American Folklore* 6 (1893): 108–11.

Gayton, A. H., and Stanley S. Newman. *Yokuts and Western Mono Myths.* Millwood, NY: Kraus, 1976.

Gibson, Robert O. *The Chumash.* New York: Chelsea House, 1991.

Gifford, Edward Winslow. "Western Mono Myths." *Journal of American Folklore* 36 (1923): 301–67.

Glimm, James York. *Flatlanders and Ridgerunners: Folk Tales from the Mountains of Northern Pennsylvania.* Pittsburgh: University of Pittsburgh Press, 1983.

Golder, F. A. "Aleutian Stories." *Journal of American Folklore* 18 (1905): 215–22.

Green, Archie. *Calf's Head and Union Tale: Labor Yarns at Work and Play.* Urbana: University of Illinois Press, 1996.

Grinell, George Bird. "Pawnee Mythology." *Journal of American Folkore* 6 (1893): 113–30.

Haight, Willliam C. "Interview of Charles Imus." American Life Histories: Manuscripts from the Federal Writers' Project, 1936–1940. Manuscript Division, Library of Congress. 14 October 2005. http://memory.loc.gov/ammem/wpaintro/wpahome.html.

Hale, Horatio. "Huron Folklore I: Cosmogonic Myth, The Good and Evil Minds." *Journal of American Folklore* 1 (1888): 177–83.

———. "Huron Folklore II: The Story of Tihaiha, the Sorceror." *Journal of American Folklore* 2 (1889): 249–54.

————. "Huron Folklore III: The Legend of the Thunderers." *Journal of American Folklore* 4 (1891): 189–94.

Hall, Julien A. "Negro Conjuring and Tricking." *Journal of American Folklore* 10 (1897): 241–43.

Halpert, Herbert. *Folktales and Legends from the New Jersey Pines: A Collection and a Study.* Bloomington: Indiana University Press, 1947.

————. "Pennsylvania Fairylore and Folktales." *Journal of American Folklore* 58 (1945): 130–34.

Harper, Francis. "Tales of the Okefinoke." *American Speech* 1 (1926): 407–20.

Hartman, George. "Interview of Ed Grantham." American Life Histories: Manuscripts from the Federal Writers' Project, 1936–1940. Manuscript Division, Library of Congress. 12 October 2005. http://memory.loc.gov/ammem/wpaintro/wpahome.html.

————. "Interview of E. O. Skeidler." American Life Histories: Manuscripts from the Federal Writers' Project, 1936–1940. Manuscript Division, Library of Congress. 18 October 2005. http://memory.loc.gov/ammem/wpaintro/wpahome.html.

Hayward, Silvanus. "English Folktales in America II." *Journal of American Folklore* 3 (1890): 291–95.

Henning, D. C. "Tales of the Blue Mountains in Pennsylvania." *Miners' Journal* (Pottsdam, PA), March 26, 1897.

Herrick, Mrs. R. F. "The Black Dog of the Blue Ridge." *Journal of American Folklore* 20 (1907): 151–52.

Hoffman, W. J. "Folklore of the Pennsylvania Germans III." *Journal of American Folklore* 2 (1889): 191–202.

Hubert, Levi. "Interview of Joseph Madden." American Life Histories: Manuscripts from the Federal Writers' Project, 1936–1940. Manuscript Division, Library of Congress. 12 October 2005. http://memory.loc.gov/ammem/wpaintro/wpahome.html.

————. "Interview of Mary Thomas." American Life Histories: Manuscripts from the Federal Writers' Project, 1936–1940. Manuscript Division, Library of Congress. 12 October 2005. http://memory.loc.gov/ammem/wpaintro/wpahome.html.

Hudson, Arthur Palmer, and Pete Kyle McCarter. "The Bell Witch of Tennessee and Mississippi: A Folk Legend." *Journal of American Folklore* 47 (1934): 46–58.

Hufford, David. *The Terror That Comes in the Night: An Experience-Centered Study of Supernatural Assault Traditions.* Philadelphia: University of Pennsylvania Press, 1982.

Hurston, Zora Neale. "Dance Songs and Tales from the Bahamas." *Journal of American Folklore* 43 (1930): 294–312.

"Interview of Bones Hooks." American Life Histories: Manuscripts from the Federal Writers' Project, 1936–1940. Manuscript Division, Library of Congress. 12 October 2005. http://memory.loc.gov/ammem/wpaintro/wpa-home.html.

"Interview of E. V. Batchler." American Life Histories: Manuscripts from the Federal Writers' Project, 1936–1940. Manuscript Division, Library of Congress. 12 October 2005. http://memory.loc.gov/ammem/wpaintro/wpa-home.html.

"The Irishman and the Pumpkin." *Journal of American Folklore* 12 (1899): 226.

Jack, Edward. "Maliseet Legends." *Journal of American Folklore* 8 (1895): 193–208.

James, George Wharton. "A Saboba Origin Myth." *Journal of American Folklore* 15 (1902): 36–39.

Jarreau, Lafayette, "Creole Folklore of Pointe Coupee Parish." MA thesis, Louisiana State University, 1931.

Jenks, Albert Ernest. "The Bear Maiden: An Ojibwa Folk-Tale from Lac Courte Oreille Reservation, Wisconsin." *Journal of American Folklore* 15 (1902): 33–35.Johnson, Clifton. "The Twist-Mouth Family." *Journal of American Folklore* 18 (1905): 322–23.

Johnson, John H. "Folk-Lore from Antigua, British West Indies." *Journal of American Folklore* 34 (1921): 40–88.

Johnston, Mrs. William Preston. "Two Negro Folktales." *Journal of American Folklore* 9 (1896): 194–98.

Jones, William. "Notes on the Fox Indians." *Journal of American Folklore* 24 (1911): 209–37.

Kamenskii, Annatolii. *Tlingit Indians of Alaska.* Translated and with an introduction and supplementary material by Sergei Kan. Fairbanks: University of Alaska Press, 1985.

Kawaharada, Dennis. *Ancient Oahu: Stories from Fornander & Thrum.* Honolulu: Kalamaku Press, 2001.

Kercheval, George Truman. "An Otoe and an Omaha Tale." *Journal of American Folklore* 6 (1893): 199–204.

Kittredge, George Lyman. "English Folktales in America." *Journal of American Folklore* 3 (1890): 291–95.

Knox, Robert H. "A Blackfoot Version of the Magical Flight." *Journal of American Folklore* 36 (1923): 401–3.

Kroeber, Alfred L. "Cheyenne Tales." *Journal of American Folklore* 13 (1900): 161–90.

———. *Handbook of the Indians of California.* Smithsonian Institution Bureau of American Ethnology Bulletin 78. Washington, DC: U.S. Government Printing Office, 1925.

———. "Tales of the Smith Sound Eskimo." *Journal of American Folklore* 12 (1899): 166–82.

———. "Ute Tales." *Journal of American Folklore* 14 (1901): 252–85.

Kroeber, Henriette Rothschild. "Papago Coyote Tales." *Journal of American Folklore* 22 (1909): 339–42.

Lightfoot, William E. "Regional Folkloristics." *Handbook of American Folklore.* Edited by Richard Dorson. Bloomington: Indiana University Press, 1983.

Lowie, Robert H. "Shoshonean Tales." *Journal of American Folklore* 37 (1924): 1–242.

Lummis, Charles. *Pueblo Indian Folk-Stories.* New York: Century, 1910.

Mallery, Garrick. "The Fight with the Giant Witch." *American Anthropologist* 3 (1890): 65–70.

Matthews, Washington. "A Folk-tale of the Hidatsa Indians." *The Folklore Record* 1 (1878): 136–43.

———. *Navajo Legends.* Memoirs of the American Folklore Society 5. New York: American Folklore Society, 1897.

———. "Noqoìlpi, the Gambler: A Navajo Myth." *Journal of American Folklore* 2 (1889): 89–94.

McHenry, Lawrence. "Interview of Minnie Wycloff." American Life Histories: Manuscripts from the Federal Writers' Project, 1936–1940. Manuscript Division, Library of Congress. 12 October 2005. http://memory.loc.gov/ammem/wpaintro/wpahome.html.

McMahon, William H. *Pine Barrens Legends, Lore, and Lies.* Wilmington, DE: Middle Atlantic Press, 1980.

McNeil, W. K. *Ozark Country.* Oxford: University Press of Mississippi, 1995.

Michaelis, Kate Woodbridge. "An Irish Folktale." *Journal of American Folklore* 23 (1910): 425–28.

Miller, E. Joan Wilson. "Ozark Culture Region as Revealed by Traditional Materials." *Annals of the Association of American Geographers* 58 (1968): 51–77.

Minor, Mary Willis. "How to Keep Off Witches." *Journal of American Folklore* 11 (1898): 76.

Monroe, Grace. "Interview of Middleton Robertson." American Life Histories: Manuscripts from the Federal Writers' Project, 1936–1940. Manuscript

Division, Library of Congress. 12 October 2005.
http://memory.loc.gov/ammem/wpaintro/wpahome.html.

Mooney, James. *James Mooney's History, Myths, and Sacred Formulas of the Cherokees*. Asheville, NC: Historical Images, 1992.

———. "Myths of the Cherokees." *Journal of American Folklore* 1 (1888): 97–108.

———. "Myths of the Cherokee." *Nineteenth Annual Report of the Bureau of American Ethnology 1897–1898, Part I*. Washington, DC: U.S. Government Printing Office, 1900.

———. *"The Sacred Formulas of the Cherokees." Seventh Annual Report of the Bureau of American Ethnology*. Washington, DC: U.S. Government Printing Office, 1891.

Mosley, Ruby. "Interview of Eldora Scott Maples." American Life Histories: Manuscripts from the Federal Writers' Project, 1936–1940. Manuscript Division, Library of Congress. 12 October 2005.
http://memory.loc.gov/ammem/wpaintro/wpahome.html.

Newell, William Wells. "English Folktales in America I." *Journal of American Folklore* 1 (1888): 227–34.

———. "English Folk-Tales in America." *Journal of American Folklore* 2 (1889): 213–18.

———. "The Ghost Legends of the Blue Mountains in Pennsylvania." *Journal of American Folklore* 11 (1898):76–78.

———. The Ignus Fatuus, Its Character and Legendary Origin." *Journal of American Folklore* 17 (1904): 39–60.

Oswalt, Wendell H. *Bashful No Longer: An Alaskan Eskimo Ethnohistory 1778–1988*. Norman: University of Oklahoma Press, 1990.

Owen, Mary A. "Ol' Rabbit an' de Dawg He Stole." *Journal of American Folklore* 9 (1890): 135–38.

Paredes, Américo. *With His Pistol in His Hand: A Border Ballad and Its Hero*. Austin: University of Texas Press, 1958.

Parsons, Elsie Clews. "Accumulative Tales Told by Cape Verde Islanders in New England." *Journal of American Folklore* 33 (1920): 34–42.

———. "Barbados Folklore." *Journal of American Folklore* 38 (1925): 267–92.

———. *Folk-Lore of the Sea Islands, South Carolina*. Memoirs of the American Folklore Society 16. New York: American Folklore Society, 1923.

———. *Kiowa Tales*. Memoirs of the American Folklore Society 22. New York: American Folklore Society, 1929.

———. "Pueblo Indian Folk-tales, Probably of Spanish Provenience." *Journal of American Folklore* 31 (1918): 216–55.

———. "Tales from Maryland and Pennsylvania." *Journal of American Folklore* 30 (1917): 209–17.

———. "Ten Folktales from the Cape Verde Islands." *Journal of American Folklore* 30 (1917): 230–38.

———. *Tewa Tales*. Memoirs of the American Folklore Society 19. New York: American Folklore Society, 1926.

———. "A West Indian Tale." *Journal of American Folklore* 32 (1919): 442–43.

Phipps, Woody. "Interview of Robert Lindsey." American Life Histories: Manuscripts from the Federal Writers' Project, 1936–1940. Manuscript Division, Library of Congress. 12 October 2005. http://memory.loc.gov/ammem/wpaintro/wpahome.html.

Porter, J. Hampden. "Notes on the Folk-Lore of the Mountain Whites of the Alleghenies." *Journal of American Folklore* 7 (1894): 105–17.

Pound, Louise. *Nebraska Folklore*. Lincoln: University of Nebraska Press, 1959.

Powers, Stephen. "North American Indian Legends and Fables." *Folk-Lore Record* 5 (1882): 93–143. Reprinted from *Contributions to North American Ethnology. Vol. 3, Tribes of California*. Edited by Stephen Powers. Washington, D.C.: U.S. Geographical and Geological Survey Rocky Mountain Region, 1877.

Radin, Paul. "Literary Aspects of Winebago Mythology." *Journal of American Folklore* 39 (1926): 18–52.

Radin, Paul, and A. B. Reagan. "Ojibwa Myths and Tales: The Manabozho Cycle." *Journal of American Folklore* 41 (1928): 61–146

Randolph, Vance. *Hot Springs and Hell; and other Folk Jests and Anecdotes from the Ozarks*. Hatboro, PA: Folklore Associates, 1965.

Rath, Richard Cullen. "Drums and Power: Ways of Creolizing Music in Coastal South Carolina and Georgia, 1730–1790." In *Creolization in the Americas*, edited by David Buisseret and Steven G. Rheinhardt. College Station: University of Texas at Arlington Press, 2000.

Ray, Marie. "Jean Sotte Stories." *Journal of American Folklore* 21 (1908): 364–65.

Rink, H., and Franz Boas. "Eskimo Tales and Songs." *Journal of American Folklore* 2 (1889): 123–31.

Romanofsky, Fred. "Interview of Cabbies." American Life Histories: Manuscripts from the Federal Writers' Project, 1936–1940. Manuscript Division, Library of Congress. 22 October 2005. http://memory.loc.gov/ammem/wpaintro/wpahome.html.

Roth, Terry, and Sam Schwartz. "Interview of Mr. Wollman." American Life Histories: Manuscripts from the Federal Writers' Project, 1936–1940.

Manuscript Division, Library of Congress. 16 October 2005. http://memory.loc.gov/ammem/wpaintro/wpahome.html.

Russell, Frank. "Myths of the Jicarilla Apaches." *Journal of American Folklore* 11 (1898): 253–71.

Sapir, Jean. "Yurok Tales." *Journal of American Folklore* 41 (1928): 253–61.

"The Sea Tick and the Irishman." *Journal of American Folklore* 12 (1899): 226.

Seip, Elisabeth Cloud. "Witch-Finding in Western Maryland." *Journal of American Folklore* 14 (1901): 39–44.

Sherbert, Andrew C. "Interview of George Estes." American Life Histories: Manuscripts from the Federal Writers' Project, 1936–1940. Manuscript Division, Library of Congress. 12 October 2005. http://memory.loc.gov/ammem/wpaintro/wpahome.html.

———. "Interview of William Harry Hembree." American Life Histories: Manuscripts from the Federal Writers' Project, 1936–1940. Manuscript Division, Library of Congress. 12 October 2005. http://memory.loc.gov/ammem/wpaintro/wpahome.html.

Showers, Susan. "Two Negro Stories Concerning the Jay." *Journal of American Folklore* 11 (1898): 74.

Shuman, Amy. "Dismantling Local Culture." *Western Folklore* 52 (1993): 345–64.

Simpson, George E. "Loup Garou and Loa Tales from Northern Haiti." *Journal of American Folklore* 55 (1942): 219–27.

Simpson, George E., and J. B. Cineas. "Folk Tales of Haitian Heroes." *Journal of American Folklore* 54 (1941): 176–85.

Skinner, Alanson. "European Folk-Tales Collected Among the Menominee Indians." *Journal of American Folklore* 26 (1913): 64–80.

Smiley, Portia. "Folk-Lore from Virginia, South Carolina, Georgia, Alabama, and Florida." *Journal of American Folklore* 32 (1919): 357–83.

Smith, Janet. "Interview of Elfego Baca." American Life Histories: Manuscripts from the Federal Writers' Project, 1936–1940. Manuscript Division, Library of Congress. 12 October 2005. http://memory.loc.gov/ammem/wpaintro/wpahome.html.

Smith, Pamela Coleman. "Two Negro Stories from Jamaica." *Journal of American Folklore* 9 (1896): 278.

Sparkman, P. S. "Notes of California Folklore: A Luiseño Tale." *Journal of American Folklore* 21 (1908): 35–36.

Speck, Frank G. "European Folk-Tales among the Penobscot." *Journal of American Folklore* 26 (1913): 81–84.

———. "European Tales among the Chickasaw Indians." *Journal of American Folklore* 26 (1913): 292.

———. "Penobscot Transformer Tales." *International Journal of American Linguistics* 1 (1918): 187–244.

Spencer, J. "Shawnee Folk-Lore." *Journal of American Folklore* 22 (1909): 319–26.

Spitzer, Nicholas R. "All Things Creole: Mout de tour le monde." *Journal of American Folklore* 116 (2003):57–72.

St. Clair, H. H., and R. H. Lowie. "Shoshone and Comanche Tales." *Journal of American Folklore* 22 (1909): 265–82.

Steiner, Roland. "Braziel Robinson Possessed of Two Spirits." *Journal of American Folklore* 13 (1900): 226–28.

———. "Sol Lockheart's Call." *Journal of American Folklore* 48 (1900): 67–70.

Stewart, Omer C. *The Northern Paiute Bands.* Millwood, NY: Kraus, 1976.

Stirling, Matthew W. *Origin Myth of Acoma and Other Records.* Smithsonian Institution Bureau of American Ethnology Bulletin 135. Washington, DC: U.S. Government Printing Office, 1942.

Strong, William D. *University of California Publications in American Archaeology and Ethnology.* Vol. 26, *Aboriginal Society in Southern California.* Berkeley: University of California Press, 1929.

Suplee, Laura M. "The Legend of Money Cove." *Journal of American Folklore* 31 (1918): 272–73.

Suttles, Wayne, ed. *Handbook of the North American Indians.* Vol. 7, *Northwest Coast.* Washington, DC: Smithsonian Institution, 1990.

Swanton, John R. *Myths and Tales of the Southeastern Indians.* Smithsonian Institution Bureau of American Ethnology Bulletin 88. Washington, DC: U.S. Government Printing Office, 1929.

Swenson, May. "Interview of Anca Vrbooska." American Life Histories: Manuscripts from the Federal Writers' Project, 1936–1940. Manuscript Division, Library of Congress. 12 October 2005. http://memory.loc.gov/ammem/wpaintro/wpahome.html.

———. "Interview of John Rivers." American Life Histories: Manuscripts from the Federal Writers' Project, 1936–1940. Manuscript Division, Library of Congress. 12 October 2005. http://memory.loc.gov/ammem/wpaintro/wpahome.html.

Taylor, Archer. "An Old-World Tale from Minnesota." *Journal of American Folklore* 31 (1918): 555–56.

Taylor, Helen Louise, and Rebecca Wolcott. "Items from New Castle, Delaware." *Journal of American Folklore* 51 (1938): 92–94.

Tejada, Simeon. "Interview of Manuel Jesus Vasques." *American Life Histories: Manuscripts from the Federal Writers' Project, 1936–1940.* Manuscript Division, Library of Congress. 12 October 2005. http://memory.loc.gov/ammem/wpaintro/wpahome.html.

Thomas, Howard. *Folklore from the Adirondack Foothills.* Prospect, NY: Prospect Books, 1958.

Thompson, Stith. *The Motif Index of Folk Literature.* Rev. ed. 6 vols. Bloomington: Indiana University Press, 1955–1958.

Totty, Francis. "Interview of Maurice Coates." *American Life Histories: Manuscripts from the Federal Writers' Project, 1936–1940.* Manuscript Division, Library of Congress. 12 October 2005. http://memory.loc.gov/ammem/wpaintro/wpahome.html.

Townsend, Edward. "Interview of A. Harry Williams." *American Life Histories: Manuscripts from the Federal Writers' Project, 1936–1940.* Manuscript Division, Library of Congress. 16 October 2005. http://memory.loc.gov/ammem/wpaintro/wpahome.html.

Trowbridge, Ada Wilson. "Negro Customs and Folk-Stories of Jamaica." *Journal of American Folklore* 9 (1896): 279–87.

Walden, Wayne. "Interview of Annette Hamilton." *American Life Histories: Manuscripts from the Federal Writers' Project, 1936–1940.* Manuscript Division, Library of Congress. 16 October 2005. http://memory.loc.gov/ammem/wpaintro/wpahome.html.

———. "Interview of Fred Roys." *American Life Histories: Manuscripts from the Federal Writers' Project, 1936–1940.* Manuscript Division, Library of Congress. 12 October 2005. http://memory.loc.gov/ammem/wpaintro/wpahome.html.

———. "Interview of Mrs. R. Ivanoff." *American Life Histories: Manuscripts from the Federal Writers' Project, 1936–1940.* Manuscript Division, Library of Congress. 12 October 2005. http://memory.loc.gov/ammem/wpaintro/wpahome.html.

Weigle, Martha, and Peter White. *The Lore of New Mexico.* Albuquerque: University of New Mexico Press, 1988.

Weippiert, G. W. "Legends of Iowa." *Journal of American Folklore* 2 (1889): 287–90.

Welsch, Roger. *Shingling the Fog and Other Plains Lies.* Chicago: Swallow, 1972.

West, John O. *Mexican-American Folklore.* Little Rock, AR: August House, 1988.

Westervelt, W. D. *Hawaiian Legends of Ghosts and Ghost-Gods.* Boston: Ellis Press, 1916.

———. *Hawaiian Legends of Old Honolulu*. Boston: G.H. Ellis Press, 1915.

———. *Hawaiian Legends of Volcanoes*. Boston: G.H. Ellis Press, 1916.

Will, George F. "No-Tongue, A Mandan Tale." *Journal of American Folklore* 26 (1913): 331–37.

———. "No-Tongue, A Mandan Tale." *Journal of American Folklore* 29 (1916): 402–6.

Williams, Ellis. "Interview of Zenobia Brown." American Life Histories: Manuscripts from the Federal Writers' Project, 1936–1940. Manuscript Division, Library of Congress. 20 October 2005. http://memory.loc.gov/ammem/wpaintro/wpahome.html.

Williams, Mentor L., ed. *Schoolcraft's Indian Legends*. East Lansing: Michigan State University Press, 1956.

Wilson, Howard Barrett. "Notes of Syrian Folk-Lore Collected in Boston." *Journal of American Folklore* 16 (1903): 133–47.

Wiltse, Henry M. "In the Southern Field of Folk-Lore." *Journal of American Folklore* 13 (1900): 209–12.

Wissler, Clark. "Some Dakota Myths I." *Journal of American Folklore* 20 (1907): 121–31.

———. "Some Dakota Myths II." *Journal of American Folklore* 20 (1907): 195–206.

"Witchcraft in New Mexico." *Journal of American Folklore* 1 (1888): 167–68.

Wrenn, Sarah B. "Interview of Annie Cason Lee." American Life Histories: Manuscripts from the Federal Writers' Project, 1936–1940. Manuscript Division, Library of Congress. 11 October 2005. http://memory.loc.gov/ammem/wpaintro/wpahome.html.

———. "Interview of Jane Lee Smith." American Life Histories: Manuscripts from the Federal Writers' Project, 1936–1940. Manuscript Division, Library of Congress. 12 October 2005. http://memory.loc.gov/ammem/wpaintro/wpahome.html.

Wrenshall, Letitia Humphreys. "Incantations and Popular Healing in Maryland and Pennsylvania." *Journal of American Folklore* 15 (1902): 268–74.

Zingerle, Ignaz and Joseph. *Kinder- und Hausmärchen*, gesammelt durch die Brüder Zingerle. Innsbruck: Verlag der Wagner'schen Buchhandlung, 1852.

Cumulative Index

Boldface numbers refer to volume numbers.

"A Bewitched Churning," 2:174
"A Bewitched Gun," 2:6, 2:179
"A Drunkard's Promise," 1:303
"A Giant's Rock-Throwing," 3:281
"A Loup Garou Disguises as a
  Beggar," 2:289
"A Messenger to the Indians," 3:241
"A Patriot's Answer to an Iraqi,"
  4:183
"A Pioneer Crossing the Midwest,"
  1:148, 1:243
"A Sight of Alligators," 2:124
"A Wonderful Testimony," 3:242
A`yûn'inï ("Swimmer"), 2:28
"A Zange Disguises as a Snake,"
  2:287
Abenaki, 1:4, 1:12, 1:29; tales, 1:18,
  1:64
"Above Ground and Below Ground,"
  1:281

Abrahams, Roger, 2:39, 2:205
Achomawi, 3:271; tales, 3:271
Acoma Pueblo: corn/agriculture
  influencing mythology, 3:7; kinship
  structure, 3:8; sacred number
  "four," 3:7–8; tales, 3:7
"Adam and Eve," 2:231, 2:291
"The Adams Diggings," 3:4, 3:92
"The Adventures of Haininu and
  Baumegwesu," 3:305
African American jokes: ethnic
  jokes, 1:309, 2:42, 2:73, 2:74,
  2:75, 2:223; master/slave, 1:263,
  1:358, 1:360, 2:122; preacher as
  stock character, 1:315, 2:78,
  2:167, 2:206
African American tales, 1:138; and
  Brer Rabbit, 2:5; Caribbean,
  2:231–44, 2:245–75, 2:277–90,
  2:291–300; with cowboy, 3:224;
  and dangers of nonsensical behavior motif, 2:39; and dangers of
  "putting on airs," 2:92; and dog
  ghost motif, 1:327; Jamaica, 1:292;
  Mid-Atlantic, 1:265–70, 1:272–82,
  1:283–323, 1:326–29, 1:334–44,
  1:347, 1:350, 1:353, 1:357–62;
  Northeast, 1:138; Plains and

Plateau, 3:223; and "signifying"
  (rhetorical device), 2:85, 2:104;
  South, 2:20, 2:25–28, 2:31–34,
  2:36–46, 2:56, 2:62–71, 2:73–76,
  2:77, 2:83–87, 2:91, 2:96, 2:106,
  2:121, 2:126, 2:130, 2:131, 2:149,
  2:159–71, 2:194, 2:199–209,
  2:223, 2:226; tradition in Mid-
  Atlantic, 1:261, 1:263; Trinidad,
  1:42, 1:363
African tales: Cape Verde, 1:94,
  1:141, 1:365; and influence in
  South and Caribbean, 2:4, 2:277,
  2:280, 2:286; Zomo the Hare, 2:94
Ahahe, 3:212
"Aiini," 1:148, 1:178
"Akua," 3:292
Alabama, 2:2; tales, 2:21, 2:98,
  2:100
Aleuts, 4:3, 4:5, 4:42; tales, 4:42,
  4:146, 4:148, 4:151. See also Inuit
Algonquian cultures, 1:4, 1:291:147;
  migration to Midwest, 1:148,
  1:149; push west, 3:179
"All Dressed Up and No Place to
  Go," 2:223

"Allen Chesser's Initiation: The
Bear Fight," **2**:46; original ver-
sion, **2**:305
"Alligators in the Toilet," **4**:274
Alsea, **4**:116; tales, **4**:116
Alutiiq, **4**:5
Ambers, Lou, **1**:190
American Revolution, **1**:148
"American Vampires," **1**:120
"American Women vs. the Taliban,"
4:272
"Amhuluk, the Monster of the
Mountain Pool," **4**:142
"An Act of Kindness," **4**:176
Anansi, **2**:33, **2**:236, **2**:249, **2**:250,
2:252, **2**:270; *Jamaica Anansi
Stories*, **2**:242, **2**:298
"Anansi and the Lady in the Well,"
2:270
Anasazi, **3**:36
Ancelet, Barry Jean, **2**:119
Anderson, Ella, **1**:269
Anderson, Mrs. C. A., **4**:42, **4**:146,
4:151
Anderson, W. T., **1**:357
Anecdotes, **1**:149, **4**:279
"Anger Management," **4**:218
Anglo American tales: Northeast,
1:26, **1**:50, **1**:54, **1**:72, **1**:77, **1**:87,
1:104, **1**:107, **1**:112, **1**:120,
1:123, **1**:143; Northwest, **4**:45;
South, **2**:79, **2**:115, **2**:132, **2**:137,
2:155, **2**:171, **2**:172, **2**:174,
2:178, **2**:179, **2**:193, **2**:195,
2:196; tradition in Mid-Atlantic,
1:261; tradition in Southwest,
3:5, **3**:86

Animal tales/fables, **1**:42, **1**:149,
1:168, **1**:263, **1**:268, **1**:314,
3:306, **4**:279; animal spouse,
1:337, **2**:277; animal/fish allows
itself to be taken motif, **4**:4; animals in night quarters motif, **1**:55;
bear, **1**:21, **2**:28; coyote, **3**:22,
3:109, **3**:111, **3**:228, **3**:230,
3:268, **3**:306, **3**:331, **4**:16, **4**:74;
and exploits of trickster/culture
hero, **2**:31; "The Fish Lover,"
2:298; fox, **3**:22, **3**:115; Frog and
fresh water, connection between
(Northwest), **4**:141; imitation and
acceptance themes, **3**:109; nur-
ture motif, **1**:45; Prairie Falcon,
3:268, **3**:335, **3**:367; Raven, **4**:40,
4:99; salmon, **4**:3, **4**:4; snakes,
2:35, **3**:365. *See also* Trickster
legends
"Annancy and the Yam Hills," **2**:250
"The Antelope Boy," **3**:41, **3**:47
Apaches, **3**:36; common tale with
Northern Athabascan, **4**:86; and
the horse, **3**:5; Jicarilla, **3**:4; tales,
3:17, **3**:20, **3**:22, **3**:115; Warm
Spring and Victorio's War, **3**:84
Appalachian region, **2**:5–6
"Are You Man?" **2**:107, **2**:220
Arikara, **1**:149, **3**:132; and Skidi
Pawnee, **3**:160; tales, **3**:159
"Arikara Creation," **3**:159
"The Arkansas Shakes," **2**:127
Armenian tales: Northeast, **1**:100
Armstrong, Henry, **1**:190
"Arrow Young Men: Creation of the
World," **4**:7, **4**:11
"Ash Girl," **3**:77
Athabascan people, **3**:4, **3**:5, **4**:35.
See also Apaches; Navajo;
Ts'ets'ā'ut
"Attacker in the Backseat," **4**:192
"Aunt" Sarah, **1**:347
Austin, Stephen F., **3**:5
Austin, Tom, **3**:287, **3**:342
"Avenging Ghosts," **2**:192, **2**:196

"B' Helephant and B'V'wale
(Brother Elephant and Brother
Whale)," **2**:313
Babcock, Maud May, **3**:242
Baca, Elfego, **3**:4, **3**:63
Bacon, A. M., **1**:309
Bacon, Emma, **1**:263
"Bale of Cotton or Bag of Salt,"
2:259
Barrett, Richard, **2**:231, **2**:291
Barrow, Louise Lavinia, **2**:253,
2:254
Batchler, E. V., **3**:92
"Battle with the Comanches,"
1:148, **1**:193
"Battling Witches," **1**:352
Bear, **1**:21
"Bear Maiden," **1**:148, **1**:173
Bear Songs. *See* "Origin of the Bear:
The Bear Songs"
"Beauty and the Beast," **1**:50, **1**:337
"The Beaver and the Woodrat,"
4:115
Beckwith, Martha, **1**:292, **2**:242,
2:250, **2**:298, **3**:274–75, **3**:312
Belief tales, **1**:120, **1**:342, **1**:352,
2:168, **2**:197, **3**:123, **3**:353,
4:279; validating devices for,
1:344
"The Bell Witch," **2**:181
Bella Bella, **4**:35
"The Bent Gun," **2**:130
Berdache, **2**:21
Bergen, Fanny D., **1**:57, **1**:328
"The Bewitched Mill," **1**:110
"The Bewitched Wives," **4**:143
Bible: backward reading of, **2**:194
Big Beaver, **3**:361
"The Big Cyclone," **1**:224
"Big Fred," **4**:120
Big Man-eater, **2**:98, **2**:100
Big Turtle, **1**:149, **1**:188
"The Big Worm," **2**:279; original
version, **2**:318
"Bill Foscett," **3**:133, **3**:220
Billy the Kid, **3**:86

"The Fleeing Pancake," **1**:87

Fletcher, Alice C., **1**:168

"The Flood," **1**:147, **1**:151

"Folk Bible," **2**:291

"Folk speculation": and legends,
   1:271

Folktale, ordinary, **4**:280

Foolish John character. *See* Jean Sot

"The Forgetful Boy," **1**:104

Formulaic, **4**:280

Fornander, Abraham, **3**:312

Fortier, Alcee, **2**:225

Foscett, Marshall W. S., **3**:133

"Fox and Deer," **3**:115

"Fox and Kingfisher," **3**:115, **3**:116

"Fox and Mountain Lion," **3**:115,
   3:117

"Fox and Rabbit," **3**:118

"The Fox and the Wolf," **2**:76

"Fox and Wolf," **1**:148, **1**:198, **2**:59

Fox peoples. *See* Mesquakie (Fox)

"The Fox [Wolf] Hangs by His
   Teeth to the Horse's Tail," **2**:77

Foxfire, **1**:265

Framing, **4**:280

"Free Honda," **4**:235

French influence: Cajun traditions,
   2:4; in Caribbean, **2**:3; Creole
   traditions, **2**:3–4; French
   American tales, **2**:222, **2**:224,
   2:312; French and Indian War,
   1:148, **1**:162; in Midwest, **1**:148,
   1:179, **1**:208; and Native
   Americans, **2**:55; in Northeast,
   1:5; in South, **2**:3–4

Frisco Affair, **3**:63

"Froth of Water," **1**:45

"The Further Adventures of No-
   Tongue," **3**:199

Fuseli, John Henry, **1**:112

Gabe, **1**:28

"Ga'na'a's Adventures among the
   Cherokee," **1**:4, **1**:5, **1**:32

Gardner, Emelyn, **1**:97

"Gasoline Company Boycott,"
   4:259; variant B, **4**:261

"General John H. Morgan's Raid
   Through Southern Indiana,"
   1:149, **1**:247

"General John H. Morgan's Raid
   Through Southern Indiana II:
   Ripley County," **1**:253

Genre, **4**:280. *See also* Motifs/tale
   types

Gentry, Jane, **2**:79, **2**:115, **2**:134,
   2:137, **2**:145, **2**:152, **2**:155

"George and Saddam," **4**:228

Georgie (African-American), **1**:343

German: influence in Mid-Atlantic
   tradition, **1**:262, **1**:264, **1**:330–35,
   1:346, **1**:352; influence in
   Northeast, **1**:6; Midwest tales,
   1:223; Northeast tales, **1**:52,
   1:97, **1**:107, **1**:111, **1**:115, **1**:121,
   1:126, **1**:263

"Getting Rid of the Overseer,"
   1:263, **1**:294

Ghost Dance Religion, **3**:269, **3**:361

"Ghost Legends of the Blue
   Mountains," **1**:3, **1**:121

"The Ghost of Alex," **2**:209

"The Ghost Penitente," **3**:5, **3**:127

"Ghost Wife," **3**:261

"The Ghosts of the Blue
   Mountain," **1**:6

"The Giant Woman," **4**:55, 66; variant B, **4**:58; variant C, **4**:60

Gill, Fred, **2**:271

"The Girl and the Fish," **2**:298;
   original version, **2**:319

"Girl as helper in hero's flight"
   motif, **1**:52, **2**:272

"The Girl Who Married Her
   Brother," **4**:71, **4**:82

"The Girls Who Married Stars,"
   4:61

"The Give-away," **2**:254

"The Giver Creates the World," **4**:7,
   4:12, **4**:20

Gladden, George, **3**:86

Glooscap, **1**:4, **1**:12; "Glooscap,"
   1:12, **1**:45

"Gluska'be Steals Summer for the
   People, Escapes from the Crows,
   and Overcomes Winter ," **1**:4,
   1:15, **1**:45

"Gluska'be the Deceiver," **1**:61

"Go to School," **4**:259

"Going to Heaven," **1**:263, **1**:358,
   1:359

"The Gold Brick," **4**:124

"The Gold Bug," **1**:27

"Goofer dust," **2**:168

"Grandfather's Escape to Free
   Haven," **1**:261, **1**:272

"Grandmother O-Ne-Ha-Tah,
   Mother Oo-Kwa-E, and the Lost
   Boy," **1**:5, **1**:20–21

Grandmother Spider, **3**:58

"Grandmother's Revenge," **4**:182

"Di Granni Shdil," **1**:367. *See also*
   Granny Steel

"Granny Cobb, the Witch," **1**:110,
   1:111

"Granny Steel," **1**:6, **1**:125; original
   version, **1**:367

Grantham, Ed, **1**:243

La Graisse [The Grease Girl], **2**:3,
   2:312

Graveyard dirt, power of, **2**:168

"The Grease Girl," **2**:222; original
   version, **2**:312

"The Great Snowfall," **4**:89

Greeley, Horace, **2**:227

Green, Augustine O., **1**:317

Green, Valerie, **2**:118, **4**:217

Grigsby, Jack Robert, **3**:86

Grimm, Brothers, **1**:55, **1**:97

Imus, Charles, 4:156
"In Liquor," 1:303
"In the Bee Tree," 1:300
"In the Cow's Belly," 2:257
"Incriminating the Other Fellow,"
   2:62; original version, 2:309
Indian Removal Act (1830), 2:2
Indian Territory, 2:2, 2:105, 3:132
Inuit, 4:3, 4:5
Irish American tales: Mid-Atlantic,
   1:344; Midwest, 1:194, 1:225;
   Northeast, 1:81, 1:91; Northwest,
   4:156
"The Irishman and the Pumpkin,"
   1:225, 2:73, 2:223
Iroquois Confederacy, 1:4–5, 1:128,
   1:164; contact with the French,
   1:5; legends, 1:4; and Shawnee,
   1:148
Irving, Washington, 1:122
Isleta Pueblo: moieties, 3:42; tales,
   3:41, 3:47, 3:109; Tiwa, 3:42
"It Was So Cold That…," 1:147,
   1:216
Ivanoff, Mrs. R., 3:238

"Jack and the Bean Pole," 1:262,
   1:275
"Jack and the Bean Tree," 2:5, 2:98
"Jack and the Beanstalk," 2:6,
   2:134
"Jack and the Fire Dragaman,"
   2:140
"Jack-O'-M-Lantern," 1:371
"Jack-O'-My-Lantern," 1:265,
   1:327; original version, 1:371
"Jack the Giant Killer," 2:6, 2:79
Jackson, Henry, Jr., 1:190

Jackson, "Pappy," 2:220
Jackson, Thomas, 4:116
"Jake Strauss," 1:6, 1:115; original
   version, 1:368
"James Harris," 2:199
"Jane Fonda Nomination," 4:189;
   variant B, 4:191
"Jean Sot Feeds Cows Needles," 2:4,
   2:110
Jean Sot, 2:4; stock character, 2:113
"Jean Sot Kills the Duck," 2:4,
   2:111
"Jean Sot and the Cowhide," 2:113
Jeffries, James Jackson "Jim," 3:238
Jenkins, Julius, 2:204
Jenks, Albert Ernest, 1:173
"Jim Johns and the Tiger," 2:217
John and Master tales, 1:263,
   1:360, 2:122, 2:126
"John Kerry's Medals," 4:166
"John the Fool and John the
   Smart," 2:262
Johnson, Arthur John "Jack," 3:238
Johnson, Elsie, 1:321
Johnson, Josephine, 1:306
Johnson, Robert, 1:354, 2:37, 2:162
Johnson, Sextus E., 3:241
"Joke on Jake," 3:132, 3:233
Jokes, 1:104, 1:148, 1:263, 1:357,
   1:359, 2:73, 2:120, 2:167, 2:208,
   4:100; articulating intergroup
   strife, 2:259; beleaguered wife
   stock character, 2:167; Boudreaux
   stock character, 2:119; Cajun
   jokes, 2:119; drunkard stock
   character, 2:167; ethnic, 1:225,
   1:263, 1:309, 1:310, 1:312,
   1:313, 1:317, 2:73, 2:74, 2:75,
   2:223, 2:260, 3:233; master/slave,
   1:263, 1:358, 1:360, 2:122; myth
   parody, 2:243; practical, 4:100;
   Preacher as stock character,
   1:315, 2:78, 2:167, 2:206. See also
   African American jokes; John and
   Master tales
Joseph, Termeus, 2:286

Joshua, 4:7; tales, 4:7, 4:74, 4:86
"Judgment Day," 1:357
"Jumping into the Breeches," 1:310

Kalapuya, 4:142; tales, 4:142
"Kamapuaa on Oahu and Kauai,"
   3:318
"Kampuaa Legends: Legends of the
   Hog God," 3:312
"Kanati and Selu: The Origin of
   Corn and Game," 2:11,
Karok, 4:14; tales, 4:14, 4:16, 4:25
"Katrina Blunders," 4:275
"Katrina Worker Report," 4:208
Kearny, Stephen W., 3:5
"Keeping off Witches," 1:343
"Kentucky Fried Chicken Becomes
   KFC," 4:165
Kickapoo, 1:147, 1:149, 1:162,
   1:164–65; tales, 1:188
Kidd, Captain, 1:27
"The Killing of the Dutchman,"
   4:94
"The Kind and the Unkind Girls,"
   2:224
"The King and Old George
   Buchanan," 2:132
Klamath Billie, 4:18, 4:28, 4:71,
   4:79, 4:82, 4:83, 4:84, 4:91, 4:92,
   4:96
Kroeber, A. L., 3:179, 4:37

La Foria, 3:17, 3:19, 3:22, 3:114
La Patten, 1:292
Lakota, 3:132; Ogalala (Sioux),
   3:188, 3:227, 3:254; tales, 3:188
"Lazy Jack and His Calf Skin," 1:77,
   2:115
"Lazy Maria," 1:97
" Legend of Sattik," 4:4, 4:140
"Legend of the Breadfruit Tree,"
   3:269, 3:292
"Legend of the Teton Sioux
   Medicine Pipe," 3:132, 3:251
"Legendary Origin of the
   Kickapoos," 1:149, 1:164

Mono, 3:268, 3:277; tales, 3:277, 3:306, 3:335, 3:367, 3:369
"Moon Cheese: Two Irishmen at the Well," 1:263, 1:312
Mooney, James, 2:176
Morgan, John Hunt, 1:248
Morgan, Richard, 2:242
Mormons, 3:133, 3:241
Morris, Lucy, 1:278
Moses, 1:45
Mother Corn Ceremony, 3:160
"Mother Holle," 1:97
"The Mother of All Urban Legends," 4:223
Motifs/tale types, 4:280; aimless wandering of trickster, 1:202; animal/fish allows itself to be taken, 4:4; animal motifs, 1:45, 1:55; animal spouse motif, 1:337, 2:277, 2:298; "awl elbow witches," 1:179; bargain with death, 2:161; belief tales, 1:120; brain over brawn, 2:238; cannibal figure, 2:98, 2:100, 3:173, 3:200, 4:55; Cinderella, 1:50, 3:4, 3:77; composites (examples of), 1:304; dead horse, 2:59; demon lover, 2:199; Devil's questions, 2:199; divided village (Wichita motif), 3:213; dog ghosts, 1:327; "earthdiver," 1:9, 1:151, 1:160, 3:277; Earth Mother, 1:9; evil father-in-law, 1:179; exile, 1:45; exploiting trust of romantic rival, 1:270; extraordinary birth, 1:45; "fall from grace," 2:19; "fatal deception," 1:297; girl helper in hero's flight, 1:52, 2:272; Jack tales, 2:5,

2:149; John and Master tales, 1:263; jokes, 1:148; kind and unkind, 1:73; lying, tales of, 1:91, 1:92, 3:103; magic canoe, 1:179; magic object, 1:69; magic stick beats person, 1:69; "mock plea," 1:295; numbskull stories, 1:311, 2:75, 2:121; Obstacle Flight, 2:199, 2:205, 3:255; ogres duped to fight each other, 2:79; *ordinary folktales*, 1:179; orphan and grandparents, 4:79; personal experience narratives, 1:148, 1:149; pirate legends, 1:4, 1:26; rolling skull, 1:239; rope to climb to heavens, 4:93; sacred numbers, 3:7, 3:36; shape-shifting, 1:122, 1:337, 2:86, 2:249, 2:286; "squeezing the stone," 2:79; Star Husband Type I (wish to marry a star), 4:61; stupid stories depending on a pun, 2:111; tarbaby, 2:55; task for suitors/bride as prize, 1:69; theft of butter (honey) by playing godfather, 2:64, 2:240; transformation motifs, 1:110, 3:257; trial of three brothers, 2:273; trickster greed, 1:196, 1:289, 2:106; twins, 1:9, 1:12, 2:11, 3:47, 3:52, 3:206, 3:213; two sisters, 3:8; "unfinished business," 1:324; and validating devices, 1:227; wisdom of age, 2:107, 2:221; wish to marry a star (Star Husband Type I), 1:176; witches "riding" victims, 1:110; young woman defying parent, 4:38
Mountain Chief, Walter, 3:257
"Mr. Deer's My Riding Horse," 1:290, 2:4, 2:56, 2:58; original version, 2:307
"Mr. Hard-Time," 1:310, 2:260
"Mr. Hard-times," 1:310
"Mr. Jones's Advice," 4:175

"Mr. Peacock and the Deadly Ghost," 1:328; original version, 1:376
Miss K.'s Father, 1:346
Murray, Harry, 2:243
"Muskrat's Tail," 1:149, 1:168
"My Son Ali," 1:100
"The Mysterious Deer," 2:197
Myths, 4:280; alternative look at original sin, 2:231; and legends (examples), 3:251, 3:282; memory culture vs. sacred narrative, 3:279; and primary food groups for Native Americans, 2:18; uses, 3:297; Ute, 3:173

Nakassungnaitut, 4:37
"Nancy and the Honey Tree," 2:235
Nancy, Ann, 2:33
"Nancy fools His Wife," 2:248, 2:270
Narcom, W. P., 1:301
Narrative performance, 1:41
Natchez, 2:2; tales, 2:18, 2:53
Native American cultures: in Caribbean, 2:1–2; Indian Removal Act (1830), 2:2; of Mid-Atlantic, 1:262; of Midwest, 1:147–49; of Northeast, 1:4; in Northwest, 4:3–5; in Plains and Plateau, 3:131–33; of South, 2:2; in Southwest, 3:4–5; in West, 3:268
Native American tales: Achomawi, 3:271; Acoma Pueblo, 3:7; Alabama, 2:21, 2:98, 2:100; Aleut, 4:42, 4:146, 4:148, 4:151; Alsea, 4:117; Apache, 3:17, 3:20, 3:22, 3:115; Arikara, 3:159; Biloxi, 2:54; Blackfoot, 3:257; Cherokee, 2:11, 2:29, 2:35, 2:101, 2:175, 2:213; Cheyenne, 3:178, 3:185, 3:262, 3:361; Chinook, 4:43, 4:100, 4:113, 4:127; Comanche, 3:230; Coos, 4:11, 4:55, 4:66; Creek, 2:58,

"Origin of the Bear: The Bear Songs," **2**:28

"The Origin of the Narwhal," **4**:34

"The Origin of the Sauks and Foxes," **1**:165

"The Origin of the Seasons and of the Mountains," **4**:27, **4**:30; similarities to Tlingit narrative, **4**:27

"Origin of the Universe," **3**:132, **3**:213

"The Origin of Vegetation," **1**:149, **1**:158

"The Origin of Woman," **2**:243; original version, **2**:314

Origins: tales of, **2**:25; Caribbean, **2**:231–44; Cyber Region, **4**:165–74; Mid-Atlantic, **1**:265–74; Midwest, **1**:151–71; Northeast, **1**:9–44; Northwest, **4**:7–49; Plains and Plateau, **3**:135–84; South, **2**:11–48; Southwest, **3**:7–45; West, **3**:271–96

"The Orphan and the Turkeys," **1**:196, **1**:202

Osagiwag`. *See* Sauk

Otos, **1**:148, **1**:149; tales, **1**:149, **1**:176

"Out of Her Skin," **1**:263, **1**:334, **1**:335

"Out of Their Skins," **1**:335, **1**:341

"Outwitting the King," **1**:7, **1**:89

Ozarks, **2**:5

Pa-skin, **1**:173

Paiute: "football," **3**:327; Northern (Paviotso), **3**:287; Southern

(Moapa), **3**:278; tales, **3**:278, **3**:288, **3**:326, **3**:331, **3**:342

Palmer, Francis L., **1**:54

Papa, **3**:293

Papago, **3**:111; tales, **3**:111

Parsiow, Alonzo, **1**:91

Parsons, Elsie Clews, **1**:94, **1**:262, **1**:298, **1**:309, **2**:5, **3**:77

Passamoquoddy: tales, **1**:17, **1**:64

"Paul Heym, the Wizard of Lebanon," **1**:122

Pavawut, **3**:365

Pawnee: Skidi and Arikaras, **3**:160

"Pele and Kamapuaa," **3**:322

"Pele's Long Sleep," **3**:269, **3**:353

Pennsylvania Dutch, **1**:6

Penny, Charles, **1**:42, **1**:363

Penobscot, **1**:4, **1**:12; tales, **1**:5, **1**:16, **1**:45, **1**:61, **1**:69

People of the Red Earth. *See* Mesquakie (Fox)

"Perfume Mugger," **4**:199; variant B, **4**:200; variant C, **4**:201

Personal experience narrative, **1**:148, **1**:149, **1**:243, **1**:264, **1**:330, **1**:334, **1**:343, **1**:347, **2**:6, **2**:46, **2**:123, **2**:124, **2**:162, **2**:168, **2**:217, **3**:68, **3**:80, **3**:86, **3**:224, **3**:233, **3**:362, **4**:95, **4**:121, **4**:124, **4**:157, **4**:280; "testimony," **2**:163

Personal legend, **4**:280

Personal vision quests, **3**:193

Peterson, Albert, **1**:93

Phillips, Percy, **3**:251

"Phoebe Ward, Witch," **2**:172, **2**:181

Phratries, **1**:170

Pickett, William "Bill," **3**:224

Pilgrims, **1**:5

Pimona, Molly Kinsman, **3**:277, **3**:369, **3**:377

Pirate legends, **1**:4, **1**:26

Plains and Plateau: extent of, **3**:131; heroes/heroines/tricksters/fools, **3**:185–239; Hispanic influences, **3**:132; horses, introduction of,

3:132, **3**:179, **3**:230; Mormons, **3**:133; Native American inhabitants, **3**:131–33; origins, tales of, **3**:135–84; sacred tales of the supernatural, **3**:241–63

Plains people, **3**:4

"Playing Dead Twice in the Road," **1**:263; variant A, **1**:285; variant B, **1**:286; variant C, **1**:286

"Playing Godfather," **1**:287, **2**:64, **2**:67, **2**:240

"Playing Mourner," **2**:64, **2**:240

Poe, Edgar Allan, **1**:27

"Poison Payphone," **4**:205

"Poison Perfume," **4**:198; variant B, **4**:199

"Poisoned Coca-Cola," **4**:269

Polish tales, **1**:131

Ponca, **1**:149

Poohegans, **1**:64–65

Porcupine, **1**:21; tale bearer, **3**:361

"Possessed of Two Spirits," **2**:164, **2**:167

"Possum and Weasel Have a Falling Out," **1**:288

Pow-wowing, **1**:122, **1**:264, **1**:330

Power and social stratification theme, **1**:41, **1**:86

"Prairie Falcon's Contest with Meadowlark," **3**:335, **3**:367

Pratt, **1**:359

"President Bush's IQ," **4**:255

"Priceless," **4**:188

Privett, Mollie, **3**:68

Privett, Samuel Thomas ("Booger Red"), **3**:4, **3**:68

"Proctor and Gamble and Liz Claiborne Confess to Church of Satan on Sally," **4**:242

Protest tales, **2**:227; and modeling oppression, **2**:233

"Providence Hole," **1**:148, **1**:236, **1**:238

Pueblo, **3**:4; matrilineal clans, **3**:8

"Pumpkin Sold as an Ass's Egg," **2**:73

Siouans, 1:176; and Algonquian peoples, 1:148
Siwash, 3:289
"The Six Witches," 1:350
Skeidler, E. O., 1:223
Skinner, Alanson, 1:179
"Slavemaster," 4:218
Smalley, Lisa, 2:119
Smith, Jane Lee, 4:45
Smith, Mary, 1:275, 1:314
Smith, Pedro, 2:248
"The Snake-Wife," 1:263, 1:336
"Sol Lockheart's Call," 2:163
"The Solomon Cycle," 2:291
"Some of Coyote's Adventures," 3:111
Somers, Abe, 3:361
"Sonachi," 3:25
"The Song of the Coffee Pot," 1:4, 1:134
"Soul or Sole," 1:354
South: Appalachian region, 2:5–6; Cajun traditions, 2:4; Creole traditions, 2:3; diversity of, 2:1; extent of, 2:1; heroes/heroines/tricksters/fools, 2:49–157; influence of African cultures on, 2:4–5; influence of Caribbean on, 2:5; Native American cultures, 2:2; origins, tales of, 2:11–48; sacred tales of the supernatural, 2:159–215; secular tales of the supernatural, 2:217–27; terrain, 2:1; unifying factors in tales, 2:6
Southwest: cultures influencing the region, 3:4; extent of, 3:3; heroes/heroines/tricksters/fools, 3:47–119; occupations and oral

tradition, 3:3–4; origins, tales of, 3:7–45; sacred tales of the supernatural, 3:121–28; terrain, 3:3
Spanish influence: in Caribbean, 2:3; in Plains and Plateau, 3:132; in Southwest, 3:5, 3:77; Spanish American tales, 3:123, 3:127; in West (California and Nevada), 3:268
"The Spanish Moss," 2:160
"The Sperrit House," 2:257Spider-Woman, 3:58, 3:60
"Spielberg's Crusade (Parody?)," 4:169
"The Spirit Defenders of Nïkwäsï," 2:213
Spriggs, Leroy, 1:138
St. James, 2:286–87
Star Husband Type tale, 1:176
Status elevation after exile motif, 1:45
Steiner, Roland, 2:163
Stevenson, Robert Louis, 1:27
Stewart, Gladys, 1:288
Stewart, Sam, 3:125
Stock character, 4:280
"The Stone Boy," 3:188
"The Story of Lodge Boy, After-Birth Boy, and Double-Face," 2:11
"The Story of No-Tongue," 3:192, 3:206; further adventures, 3:199–205
"The Story of Skunk," 4:116
"The Suit the Sparrow Won," 1:140; original version, 1:369
Sullivan, John L., 3:238
Supernatural legends: blacksmith, significance of, 2:20; continuity of dead with living, 2:209; envy as a motivator for attack, 1:333; haunting of violent death site, 1:124. *See also* Sacred tales of the supernatural; Secular tales of the supernatural

"Supernatural Legends of Chappaquiddick," 1:3, 1:123
Swamp "goblin," 1:265
Swanton, John R., 2:76
Sweat lodge, 3:189
Syrian American tales, 1:89, 1:134

"T-Bone Steak," 4:179
"The Table, the Ass, and the Stick," 2:273
"Tablecloth, Donkey, and Club," 1:262, 1:279, 2:273
Taboo/tabu, 3:293, 4:141; food sources, 4:127
"The Tail Fisher," 2:239
Taino, 2:1–2
Takanakapsaluk, 4:33
"Take My Place," 1:297
"Tales from Northern Michigan," 4:231. *See also* Animal tales/fables
"Tales of Fox," 3:114–19
Tales, variations in (examples), 3:369–86
"The Talking Eggs," 2:4, 2:224
Tall tales, 1:147, 1:148, 1:216, 1:220, 1:223, 2:75, 2:123, 2:125, 2:127, 2:130, 2:131, 3:238, 4:280; environmental focus, 2:132, 3:3, 3:98, 3:103, 3:346; framing devices, 3:99; Pennsylvania, 1:6; traditional motifs, 2:131
"The Tarbaby," 2:2, 2:49, 2:52, 2:233
"The Tarbaby and the Rabbit," 2:233
Tasks for suitor/bride as prize motif, 1:69
"The Tasks of Rabbit," 2:53, 2:93
Taylor, Archer, 1:225
"Teamster Boycott," 4:184
"Terrorist Halloween Attacks on Malls," 4:268
Texas Revolution (1836), 2:22
"The Theft of Fire," 3:287, 4:14, 4:18, 4:29

von Münchhausen, Baron Karl Friedrich Hieronymus, **3**:99
Vrbooska, Anca, **1**:40, **1**:85, **1**:132

"Wabasaiy," **1**:147, **1**:162, **1**:193
Waí-hu-si-wa, **3**:52
"Wailing Wall," **4**:250
"Wait Until I Get Dry," **1**:303
Wakea, **3**:293
"Wal-Mart Boycott," **4**:185
"Walking Skeleton," **3**:369; variant B, **3**:372; variant C, **3**:377
"Wanted for Attempted Murder," **4**:234
Ward, Monroe, **2**:87, **2**:140
Ward, Miles, **2**:87, **2**:140
"The Watcher Tricked," **1**:306
Waterspirits, **1**:227
Wendat (Wyandot), **1**:4, **1**:9
West (California and Nevada), **3**:267–69; gold rush, **3**:268; heroes/heroines/tricksters/fools, **3**:305, 326–46; origins, tales of, **3**:271, 277–81, 287–92; post–Civil war pressures, **3**:268; pre-European contact cultures, **3**:268; sacred tales of the supernatural, **3**:361, 364–86; Spanish influence, **3**:268; terrain, **3**:267
West (Hawaii), **3**:267, 269; extent, **3**:269; heroes/heroines/tricksters/fools, **3**:297, 312–26; nature gods ("akua"), **3**:292; origins, tales of, **3**:274, **3**:281, **3**:284, **3**:292; sacred tales of the supernatural, **3**:353; terrain, **3**:269; ti plant, **3**:284

"When Brer Deer and Brer Terrapin Runned a Race," **2**:92
"When Brer Frog Give a Big Dining," **2**:106
"When Brer 'Possum Attend Miss Fox's House-Party," **2**:64, **2**:91
"When Brer Rabbit Help Brer Terrapin," **2**:96
"When Brer Rabbit Saw Brer Dog's Mouth So Brer Dog Can Whistle," **2**:40
"When Brer Rabbit Was Presidin' Elder," **2**:77
"When Brer Wolf Have His Corn Shucking," **2**:69
"When Mr. Pine Tree and Mr. Oak Tree Fall Out," **2**:25
"When Mr. Terrapin Went Riding on the Clouds," **2**:218
"When Raven Wanted to Marry Snowbird and Fly with the Geese," **4**:98
"When the World Was Formed," **3**:17
"Where Did Adam Hide," **2**:166; original version, **2**:310
"Where's Mr. McGinnis?" **1**:313
White, Joseph (Mandarong), **1**:36, **1**:116
"White Substance Delays Aggie Football Practice," **4**:230
"Whiteberry Whittington," **1**:52, **2**:152
"Why Frog Lives in the Water," **1**:270
"Why Mr. Owl Can't Sing," **2**:38
"Why Rabbit Has a Short Tail," **2**:239
"Why the Deer has a Short Tail," **1**:149, **1**:170
"Why the People Tote Brer Rabbit Foot in their Pocket," **2**:26, **2**:40
"Why the Spider Never Got in the Ark," **2**:159
"Why We Love Children," **4**:172

Wichita, **3**:131–32, **3**:135; divided village motif, **3**:213; tales, **3**:136–59, **3**:212
"Wild Bill," **1**:148, **1**:243
Wild Bunch, **3**:221
Wiley, Betty, **1**:353
Wilkenson, Susie, **2**:132
Will, George F., **3**:193
Willoughby, Loneva, **1**:281
Wiltse, A. S., **2**:197
"The Wine, the Farm, the Princess, and the Tarbaby," **2**:4, **2**:49, **2**:53, **2**:64, **2**:233, **2**:258
Winnebago: cosmology, **1**:227; tales, **1**:188, **1**:207, **1**:227; War (1827), **1**:148
"Wisa'kä," **1**:149, **1**:159
"The Witch and the Boiler," **2**:174, **2**:178, **2**:180
"Witch Flights," **3**:5, **3**:121, **3**:124
Witchcraft: punishment for, **3**:125; vs. hoodoo, **1**:348
Witches, **1**:65; ability to slip out of their skin (cross-cultural belief), **1**:334, **4**:136; "awl-elbow," **1**:179; borrowing object of victim motif, **1**:112; cross-cultural "hag experience," **1**:112; little boy witch, **2**:204; "riding" of victims motifs, **1**:110, **2**:178; salt as antidote to evil (cross-cultural belief), **1**:334; shape-shifting, **1**:122, **2**:27; transformation motifs, **1**:110, **2**:171; with two hearts (Hopi), **3**:58. See also *Brujeria*; Pavawut
"Witches Discovered," **3**:5, **3**:122, **3**:124
"Witch's Apprentice," **1**:347, **1**:350
Wolf Clan, **1**:128
"Wolf of the Greenwood," **1**:6, **1**:52, **2**:152
"The Wolf Overeats in the Cellar," **2**:109
Wollman, Mr., **1**:131
"Woman Cat," **1**:338, **3**:123; variant A, **1**:339; variant B, **1**:340

About the Editor

Thomas A. Green is Associate Professor of Anthropology at Texas A&M University. His many books include *Martial Arts in the Modern World* (Praeger, 2003), *Martial Arts of the World: An Encyclopedia* (2001), *Folklore: An Encyclopedia of Beliefs, Customs, Tales, Music, and Art* (1997), and *The Language of Riddles: New Perspectives* (1984).